Principles of
Software
Engineering
Management

Principles of
Software
Engineering
Management

Tom Gilb
edited by Susannah Finzi

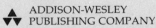
ADDISON-WESLEY
PUBLISHING COMPANY

Wokingham, England · Reading, Massachusetts · Menlo Park, California
New York · Don Mills, Ontario · Amsterdam · Bonn
Sydney · Singapore · Tokyo · Madrid · San Juan

Cover design by Crayon Design of Henley-on-Thames.
Text design by Lesley Stewart.
Typeset by Columns, Reading.
Printed and bound in Great Britain by The Bath Press, Avon.
First printed 1988. Reprinted 1988.

British Library Cataloguing in Publication Data

Gilb, Tom
  Principles of software engineering management.
  1. Computer software—Development
  2. Computer programming management
  I. Title   II. Finzi, Susannah
  005.1   QA76.76.D47

  ISBN 0–201–19246–2

Library of Congress Cataloging in Publication Data

Gilb, Tom.
  Principles of software engineering management / Tom Gilb.
    p.   cm.
  Bibliography: p.
  Includes index.
  ISBN 0–201–19246–2
  1. Computer software—Development—Management.   I. Title.
  QA76.76.D47G55   1988
  005.1—dc19   87–31927
                                                                    CIP

Author's Address

Tom Gilb, Box 102, N-1411, Kolbotn, Norway
tel. + (472) 801697

Dedicated to the software engineers of the future, with the hope that we will master our technology well, so that we can improve the quality of life on this small planet.

Foreword

Do you suffer from the 'Looking Under the Lamppost' syndrome?

This is a thought pattern best illustrated by the story of a drunk who is found searching for his lost wallet under a lamppost at a street corner. When asked where he lost the wallet, he says, 'Oh, down the street there by the alley. But I'm looking for it up here because the light is so much better!'

All of us suffer from the 'Looking Under the Lamppost' syndrome to some extent. But it can be a particular concern in software engineering management.

Our strongest lamps to date in software engineering have been in such areas as algorithms, formal specification and development methods, configuration management, and software acquisition methods based on delivering a fixed set of functional capabilities within a fixed budget and schedule. And our typical software engineering and management solutions to date have been found primarily by looking under these lampposts.

The lamps illuminating such areas as software people-management, and software maintainability, portability, robustness, and user-friendliness have been relatively faint. As a result, these areas have been frequently neglected in software project planning and management. The all-too-frequent end result has been a software project which has delivered various functional capabilities, but which also has delivered a lot of unnecessary frustration, extra work, and operational breakdowns for the people who had to develop, maintain, operate, and use it.

If you are a software engineer or manager, it is certainly important to use the strong lamps that illuminate the more well-understood parts of software development. But it's also important to use what you can of the fainter lamps providing some illumination of the less-understood, more qualitative, but equally critical aspects of software development.

Tom Gilb's book, *Principles of Software Engineering Management*, can help you a good deal with some of these poorly-illuminated aspects of software development. It can be a somewhat frustrating book, in that it goes for overall impact rather than for formality, precision or even completeness of its individual guidelines. But it is one of the few sources around which tries to deal in a practical way with the slippery concepts of managing for software quality.

The book's central theme, Design by Objectives, has a number of good things going for it. It focuses people on an explicit early concern for the qualities as well as the functional capabilities they want their software product to have. It provides techniques to express these qualities in measurable ways, so that they can be used as management objectives. And it establishes a management-by-objectives framework to keep the project focused on achieving its quality objectives.

I should note that Design by Objectives has its difficulties as well. There are not at this time any step-by-step methods for achieving even a single quality objective. There is even less methodological support for making pairwise trade-offs between quality objectives. And the problem of getting all the people on a large software project to understand fully a dozen or so quality attributes, and to reflect them consistently in their project decisions, is truly formidable.

Nevertheless, there have been projects which have achieved remarkable successes using Design by Objectives techniques. A good example is the AT&T Electronic Switching System, which managed an availability objective of 15 minutes downtime in 40 years of operation. The result has been an extremely robust system, with a number of key design decisions successfully iterated because of the project's explicit availability objective.

Besides Design by Objectives, the book also provides some valuable insights in other areas. Some particularly good sections address a Bill of Rights for company communication (Chapter 2), software inspection techniques (Chapter 12), evolutionary development (Chapter 13), and coping with deadline pressure (Chapter 17).

There are other areas in which the book provides much more fuzzy guidance than one would like to see in a management book. These include cost estimation, progress tracking, contract-related issues, project organization, documentation, test planning, and configuration management.

But these can generally be found in more conventional software management books. And *Principles of Software Engineering Management* is not a conventional software management book. It is not the kind of book you can or should deal with as a cookbook. It is best to treat it as a stimulus for your own thoughts on how to manage for software quality. It challenges you to think about some important issues, and provides some ways to get started toward addressing them.

Viewed in this light, I think you will find this book highly worth your time. It is one of the best antidotes to the software engineering 'Looking Under the Lamppost' syndrome I have seen to date.

Barry W. Boehm
Chief Scientist
TRW Defense Systems Group

Preface

Why do it? Why are the methods described in this book so important for software engineers?

Principles of Software Engineering Management addresses the critical software management problems which have not been treated elsewhere. It focuses on practical and proven ways to get higher quality software at lower cost of people and time. The approach is that of engineering and management technology – not programming technology. You won't find a single program listing in this book, but you will find plenty about real people who have really managed to get (or regain) control over complex software projects and software organizations.

This is a totally new way of thinking for most software engineers. It moves away from functional methods to attribute control methods. It moves away from the 'Waterfall Model' to the Evolutionary Delivery model. It moves away from reviews and walkthroughs to statistical process control methods using Fagan's Inspection method.

The book is strong on explicitly stated guiding principles, practical hints, practical tools for communication about complex technology, engineering measures and measuring devices for software, as well as real case studies and a broad survey of the best current practices. Software engineering management problems are exciting and challenging and the book reflects that excitement.

This book is aimed at the people who have to manage software projects of all kinds. It is primarily aimed at large environments which have considerable pressure to meet deadlines and to produce high quality software. It is for those who want the very best and latest in practical software engineering technology, because it directly addresses issues such as design specification, cost control, design engineering, project delivery, organizational improvement, people productivity and quality control.

It is also intended for teachers who want to teach advanced software engineering and management principles in a form their students can make practical use of in industry. The material has been widely taught to college students and in advanced industrial situations throughout the world, and has never failed to provoke stimulating results where students have applied the material to their practical assignments.

The dominant theme of the book dictates the basic pattern of its organization. We start by exploring how to set objectives, especially for the elusive but critical software quality area. Then we proceed to finding and evaluating solutions for reaching our quality objectives, within our resource constraints. We explore Fagan's Inspection for statistical quality and process control over design and coding work. Finally we explore a new software decomposition and structuring idea based on the untapped potential for early evolutionary delivery of software projects with feedback and control as a result.

The book's philosophy is outlined in Part One, which also provides an overview of the methods.

If you simply want to get on with a 'how to do it' description of any of the methods, then you can skip directly to those chapters of Part Two which interest you. Most chapters can be read independently of each other. A possible exception is the impact estimation chapter (11), which requires at least a general understanding of attribute specification (Chapter 9).

Part Three provides advanced supplementary material depending on your interests and needs. The chapters are designed to be read independently of each other, and the order in which you read them is not important. For example, 'deadline pressure' (Chapter 17), or 'estimation' (Chapter 16), or 'people productivity' (Chapter 14), are managerial subjects which will indicate how the individual disciplines in the book can be used to support your work as a software engineering manager. Relevant material in the first two parts of the book are referenced.

If your job as a manager involves planning the improvement of your organization, note that Part Two contains a very detailed case study of how we used the methods in the book to plan organizational improvement for a 300-person software engineering organization. Both the method and the content of this case study can serve as a template for your own efforts. The Omega Case (Chapter 21) gives an account of how one particular method (inspection) was used in a large organization, and there are numerous smaller examples throughout the book.

There is one thing that readers should keep in mind throughout the book. The major principles and methods are selected because they seem to be timeless or classical. That is, I believe that they apply to all software (and indeed systems) engineering management problems, past, present and future. I do not believe they will become invalid, regardless of the technological or economic change.

I am particularly indebted to my clients and course participants for the practical inspiration for this book. This is for all of you – who put up with the drafts of these ideas for so many years!

There were some individuals who made significant contributions to the book: Susannah Finzi, who edited the book through many metamorphoses; Alan F. Brown of ICL Bracknell, who not only contributed Chapter 21, but also was my comrade in arms in many a battle to impact his organization; Lindsey Brodie (ICL), who set the record for constructive comments; Dot Graham (freelance, National Computing Centre, UK), Felix Redmill (British Telecom), John Parcell (Reuters), Rod Homer (Midland Bank), Martin Burgess (Reuters), Marjorie Baker (freelance, ICL) all of whom took the trouble to read and provide constructive comment on the manuscript.

I am particularly indebted to Robb Wilmot who as Chief of ICL, along with Technical Director Mike Watson, encouraged me to spread my ideas within the organization (including their boardroom), as well as Peter Hall who was key to making sure these ideas received a hearing at the highest executive levels.

For professional inspiration through the years: Barry Boehm and TRW; Mike Fagan, Ron Radice, Harlan Mills at IBM FSD, Horst Remus and John L. Bennett of IBM.

Box 102, N-1411,   *Tom Gilb*
Kolbotn, Norway
tel. +(472) 801697

Acknowledgements

The publisher would like to thank all the individual authors cited in Chapter 15 who gave permission to quote from their works.

Thanks are also due to the following:

Sven Sønsteby for Figures 1.1, 2.1, 2.2 and 2.3.

Clarkson N. Potter Inc. for Figure 3.1.

Collins Publishers for quotations from *The Third Wave* by Alvin Toffler and from *A Passion for Excellence* by Tom Peters and Nancy Austin.

William Heinemann Limited for a quotation from *Management* by Peter Drucker.

The Institute of Electrical and Electronics Engineers Inc. for material from *IEEE Transactions on Software Engineering*, Dec. 1975, March 1979, Nov. 1984, Jan. 1986 and July 1986; also from *IEEE Computer*, June 1982; and from *Proceedings of 14th Annual Conference on Frontiers in Education*, Oct. 1984.

IBM Corporation for material from *IBM Systems Journal*, (1976), **15**, (3); (1977), **16** (1); (1980), **19**, (4); and from *Technical Report 21.802* (1981).

Cahners Publishing Co. for material from *Datamation*, Jan., 1980.

The Association for Computing Machinery for quotations from *Communications of the ACM*, July 1982 and from *ACM Computing Surveys*, March 1969.

Data Processing Digest for material from the eighth issue, 1984.

Nordisk Datanytt for material from the seventeenth issue, 1986.

Taylor & Francis for a quotation from *Behaviour and Information Technology*, (1983), **2**, (1).

Elsevier Science Publishing Co. Inc. for material from 'Program Evolution' by Lehman and Belady which originally appeared in the *Journal of Systems and Software*, (1980), **1**, (3).

AT&T for material from *AT&T Technical Journal*, (1986), **65**, (2).

Harper & Row Publishers Limited for a quotation from *In Search of Excellence* by Peters and Waterman.

Microsoft Press and Penguin Books for a quotation from *Programmers at Work* by Susan Lammers.

William Morrow & Co. Inc. for a quotation from *Peak Performers* by Charles Garfield.

William Morris Agency for a quotation from *High Output Management* by Andrew S. Grove.

Simon & Schuster, Inc. for a quotation from *The Changemasters* by Rosabeth Moss Kanter.

Random House Inc. for a quotation from *A Passion for Excellence* by Tom Peters and Nancy Austin.

Massachusetts Institute of Technology and Cambridge University Press for material reprinted from *Out of the Crisis* by W. Edwards Deming, by permission of MIT and W. Edwards Deming. Published by MIT, Center for Advanced Engineering Study, Cambridge, MA 02139. © 1986 W. Edwards Deming.

Oxford University Press, Inc. for a quotation from *The Oregon Experiment* by Christopher Alexander, Murray Silverstein, Sara Ishikawa *et al*. Copyright © 1975 by The Center for Environmental Structure.

Horizon Press for a quotation from Frank Lloyd Wright, *An Autobiography*.

John Wiley & Sons Inc. for a quotation from *The Master Architect – Conversations with Frank Lloyd Wright* edited by Patrick J. Meehan.

Grafton Books for a quotation from *Design for the Real World* by Victor Papanek.

Unwin Hyman Ltd. for material from *Evolution and its Modern Critics* by A. Morley Davies published by Thomas Murby & Co.

Contents

Part Three   Advanced insights and practical experiences

PART ONE

Why do it?

1

The pre-natal death of the Corporate Information System (CIS) project

■ Introduction

Invisible targets are hard to hit (except by chance); a real case study shows what happens when you try. The chapter ends with some initial – and fundamental – principles.

■ 1.1 A software project disaster

The new President of a European Corporation made a tough decision. He simply had to 'give up' on a very large scale computer project which was considered vital to the management of the Corporation in the troubled years ahead. (Japanese competition was already threatening the Corporation's very existence.)

The Corporate Information System – CIS as it was known internally – had been started by his predecessors five years earlier, with a budget which included eighty work-years of corporate computer staff for development. By the time the new President took over, it had already used twice that budget in costly internal professional resources, but was nowhere near to producing any useful results at all.

The Corporation had done all the 'right things':

- The Corporation had consulted American business management publications and had accepted the idea that a centralized corporate-wide information system was needed.
- The Corporation had hired a famous Californian 'think tank' to do a feasibility study, which took two calendar years (and fifteen work-years) to complete.
- The Corporation made use of the largest computer manufacturer's biggest and most modern computers and database software.
- The Corporation uncomplainingly paid several million dollars extra development costs, when the initial budgets were used up.
- The Corporation was using all the latest structured programming techniques recommended by the computer suppliers.

■ 1.2 Failure symptoms

The Corporation found that EDP applications will, if anything, magnify some organizational problems (Figure 1.1). There were three main problem areas:

1. The project 'functioned.' All the necessary programs were actually running, but the programmers and the project staff claimed they needed more time and more computer resources to

'tune the system' so that it would be able to operate at the necessary speed.

2. There were about 20 000 transactions to be fed into the computer daily, just to keep it up to date. One single transaction could cause the computer to use up to twenty minutes of its time to update all the consequences of that transaction within the highly integrated system. Fortunately not all updates were so time-consuming. But every effort to tune the system to better efficiency totally failed to get a day's normal updating through the large computer within one day.

3. Furthermore, they discovered that it would take an estimated two years of additional development effort for them to be able to add a new factory, or to add a single one of their wholly-owned suppliers to the integrated system. Apart from the intolerable delay involved, they were faced with the fact that these kinds of changes within the Corporation were taking place at the rate of about one every six months.

■ 1.3 The consequences

When the Corporate Information System project was thrown out, they were left with no new management control systems. They also lost five years in which their competitors might well have achieved some real results in this area.

This was the unpleasant reality that confronted the new President just one year after he took on his job. It is the sort of thing that shouldn't happen, but it does.

■ 1.4 Preventing the disaster

How could this disaster have been prevented?

The President of the Corporation had the courage not to throw good money after bad. But the system developers themselves did not apparently have the courage to admit their own failure. When I asked one of the programmers about the project, he said: 'I knew it wouldn't do the job, but *my* programs worked.' He did not feel the need to worry about whether the entire system was a failure, as long as his own component functioned.

Let us consider some of the reasons the CIS project failed. Admittedly this analysis is done with hindsight, but it may teach us something about avoiding failure.

I would describe the reasons for the project's failure as the failure

Figure 1.1 A symptom of failure.

to determine and control project attributes critical for survival, the failure to find an architecture suited to those critical attributes, and the failure to 'evolve' a useful system in smaller useful steps.

The **critical attributes** of a system are those qualities and resources which can cause the collapse of the system as a whole if they are allowed to go beyond certain limits (the **worst acceptable level**). It is necessary for project managers to determine these dangerous attribute areas, and to take steps to manage them.

In the CIS case we see an example of two critical attributes which it should have been possible to determine and control. The most critical one was the practical daily operational performance of the system. Even after all efforts have been made to improve performance, it still could not do a single day's work in a day on the largest machine available. The second was the system's ability to integrate new business units.

It should have been possible, at an early stage in the project, to estimate the order of magnitude of transactions to be handled by the system per day. The number was in fact approximately twenty thousand. There are 86 400 seconds in 24 hours, so it was necessary that an average transaction was handled in roughly one second of machine time. Some transactions were taking minutes in practice.

■ 1.5 Clearer performance requirement specifications for CIS

There should have been a specification somewhat like this:

Work capacity: practical work capacity must be sufficient to handle a normal day's work in a normal office day.

Worst case (for trial use): four seconds on average per transaction.

Planned level (initial real use): less than one second on average per transaction.

Planned level (if transactions more than 100 000 a day): 0.2 seconds per transaction.

In practice, I could not (on interviewing the project leader) find any sign of such specifications. The assumption was that sufficient computer capacity would be available. Because these initial specifications were not made a part of the formal requirements for the system, nobody felt obliged to worry about them. They concentrated their efforts on other requirements instead. But the failure to meet these levels was the immediate and direct reason for the failure of the entire project.

There was another requirement which would have caused the failure of the system, even if the work capacity requirements had been met. It was the ability to integrate new business units, such as new factories, into the corporate system. The initial efforts at such integration led to the estimate that it would take two years of effort to integrate a major business unit – and that such changes were happening on the average about every six months!

■ 1.6 An adaptability requirement specification for CIS

The specification for adaptability, with hindsight, should have looked like this:

Adaptability: the system shall be capable of integrating all new business units and requirements in such a way that the system itself is never the delaying factor.

Worst acceptable case: major new business units, such as a factory or supplier, shall be integrated within six months and no more than ten programmer/analysts, or five work-years, of total effort.

Planned level: major business units should be able to be added or removed from the system with less than six work-months of qualified effort.

Nobody was concerned with this adaptability requirement. They concentrated their efforts on getting the initial business configuration to work. Yet in the five-year period of the project, it was a constantly moving target.

I often wonder how this Corporation could have paid outside consultants for a fifteen work-year feasibility study without the consultants discovering a need for such requirements.

Note that there certainly are several other critical attribute specifications that should have been made (for example availability, usability, and portability) and were not. Adaptability and work capacity are merely the ones that we know killed the project in practice.

■ 1.7 Architecture and engineering

As there were no clearly stated attribute requirement specifications, then the most basic input to the engineering and architectural process was missing. This, in my experience, is often exactly what happens.

For example, since the work capacity requirements were not clearly stated, then designers could probably not see that the large database software system supplied by the hardware manufacturer was too slow and clumsy. The use of this database management software system is a major architectural decision. It should never have been chosen to be at the heart of such a tightly integrated system. The manufacturer was not the one to rely on for warnings of the danger. He stood to earn a lot of money if the system was used.

At the more detailed software engineering level, both of the above-mentioned critical attributes should have been the subject of a great deal of design work in the file and program module organization, in order to meet the demanding specifications. These critical attributes were not specified, and the effort was, as usual, turned towards the application functions and the programming. The critical factors were simply left to kill the entire system.

■ 1.8 Evolutionary delivery

All these above errors in the CIS project might have been discovered early enough to correct. But this could only have happened if some practical experience with using the system was gained soon enough to realize that something was wrong with the work capacity or adaptability. Instead, delivery was based on the 'big bang' approach. They planned for the entire dream system, after five years of effort, or nothing at all.

In a post-mortem discussion with CIS-company people on this issue, they agreed with me about what would have happened if they had used **evolutionary delivery** of the system, producing it in much smaller useful steps (for example once each quarter of a year).

In the very worst case, if nothing at all could be achieved using the system, they would have discovered this early, when they failed to make the first delivery-step pay off, or even work at all. They could have cut their losses at an early stage and devoted their resources to finding a better solution.

If a major problem was discovered in, say, work capacity, after a number of delivery steps were made, then it would have been easier to analyze the cause and be in a position to fix it. If it was not fixable, then it might at least have been possible to skip over this dangerous step and accomplish other vital steps instead.

As the situation was, in fact, nobody was able to separate the unworkable from the workable. It was too difficult to analyze the cause and effect relationships. And it was too difficult to pick out the offending parts of the system.

■ 1.9 The CIS errors are common to most software engineering projects

The CIS case is quite real. It happened to Volvo of Sweden. And, they were kind enough to give me background data for my use here.

Volvo's own reaction to the case was to set up sophisticated project monitoring groups ('shark rooms' they call them), and to avoid such tightly integrated and centralized systems. I don't know if this is the best thing they could have done. This book argues for a different course of action.

The CIS is still typical of a multitude of projects, from all branches of software building, which I see many times a year and all over the world. They all commit the same sins:

1. Unclear specification of critical system attributes (not made measurable).
2. Lack of real engineering of systems and software to achieve those critical attributes. Lack of a trained group of real software architects (softects) and software engineers. The 'bricklayers' (programmers) are left to do the architecture by default.
3. Lack of any systematic notion of evolutionary delivery, feedback and change-upon-learning processes. We are always going for the 'big bang' delivery. We are simply too foolish and immodest to realize that we must accomplish something real in order to learn what we have achieved, in order to build and design complex systems safely.

This book will explore all of these sins and omissions, and some related supporting topics.

■ 1.10 We don't have all the answers

We cannot be sure that the methods suggested in this book are *all* the methods needed to succeed. They are surely not! These methods for specifying problems and monitoring the solution as it develops, are designed to give the project manager early warning of the need for additional methods.

It is important that the reader who has absorbed this book will not rely on it blindly. He will be in a position to recognize the need for, and create additions to, the methods, where necessary.

■ 1.11 Some initial principles of software engineering management

Throughout this book the principles of software engineering management will be highlighted. Here are a few initial ideas.

The invisible target principle:
All critical system attributes must be specified clearly. Invisible targets are usually hard to hit (except by chance).

The all-the-holes-in-the-boat principle:
Your design solutions must satisfy all critical attributes simultaneously.

The clear-the-fog-from-the-target principle:
All critical attributes can be specified in measurable testable terms, and the worst-acceptable level can be identified.

The learn-before-your-budget-is-used-up principle:
Never attempt to deliver large and complex systems all at once; try to deliver them in many smaller increments, so that you can discover the problems and correct them early.

The keep-pinching-yourself-to-see-if-you-are-dreaming principle:
Don't believe blindly in any one method; use your methods and common sense to measure the reality against your needs.

The fail-safe minimization principle:
If you don't know what you're doing, don't do it on a large scale.

2

Overview

Introduction

Chapter 2 gives a management-eye view of the book. The focus is on communication, thinking tools, and motivation.

■ 2.1 The right stuff and the wrong problem

Do you remember the project in which you were really going to prove your worth? When studies, plans, reports, memos, meetings, deadlines (and ulcers) abounded, extra staff were brought in, and everyone worked overtime knowing that success with this one might bring the big break?

You got it working all right. But not only was it wildly over budget – and late – but it only partly solved the problem you thought they said they wanted it to solve. And you discovered (when you got it going at last) that that wasn't the real problem anyway. In fact it didn't even touch the real problem. And all this in spite of having bought the best equipment, and hired some very expensive consultants. Nobody could put their finger on what or who was responsible for the mess. . . .

For some of us, this scenario is (so far) only a figment of our worst imaginings. For others, it is already a reality. In fact, it may be what tempted you to spend some time with this book. How can it happen that all the 'right' measures produce the wrong results? How can we reliably manage to avoid this sort of disaster? How can we be sure of producing the results we really need? These are the questions that this book sets out to answer.

> **The disaster principle:**
> Disasters don't happen by accident; they are entirely creditable to our own management.
>
> **The right stuff principle:**
> The right solutions will always fail to produce the right results if you have not defined exactly what the 'right results' are, and then made sure you had the right solutions to achieve those results.

■ 2.2 Management failure

It has become both popular and acceptable to blame failures on anything and everything but the people involved. But we consider

Figure 2.1 The only person who should be blamed for EDP failure is a manager – as high up in the organization as possible.

these problems to be a failure of management (Figure 2.1).

The tasks of the manager are to define objectives, to create, evaluate, and select alternatives for reaching them, and to control the implementation of selected alternatives. It is common to find instead that objectives are not clearly specified, that alternatives are not thoroughly explored, and that the implementation of solutions is not properly controlled.

In short, managers rely too heavily on the recommendations of suppliers, technicians, sales 'experts' and consultants (Figure 2.2). They do not make a real effort to examine critically the alternatives which they are offered, or which they might be offered if they sought them more systematically.

Furthermore, the element of risk seems to be neither well understood, nor systematically handled. The probability of deviations from expected results is handled with far too much trust in 'experts',

Figure 2.2 They will fill you with tales of all the functions it will perform, but little information about its problems.

who are often accepted as experts only because they are incomprehensible to management.

There is insufficient control over the quality of solutions.

The network of communication between managers, problemsolvers, technicians, trade unions and customers about goals, plans and the selection of alternatives, is often inadequate. Above all, it seems to lack a common language.

Geneen's manager principle:
Managers must manage.

This principle was stated by Harold Geneen, ex Chief of ITT, in his book *Managing*. Geneen held that given a reasonable target (which he defined as ten per cent improvement yearly) a 'real' manager would be able to manage to achieve that target, without any 'surprises' for his management. 'No surprises' was another of his favorite attitudes.

■ 2.3 Multidimensional thinking

Most real-world decisions are multidimensional in nature, and the range of considerations they involve is confusingly wide. We tend to try to express problems in a simple form in order to make them intellectually manageable. This is not in itself a bad thing, but a necessary process in understanding the real world. However there is a danger that if carried too far, it becomes over-simplification. The consequence of over-simplification is that we often don't find an appropriate solution for what is, in reality, a very complex problem.

> **Einstein's over-simplification principle:**
> Things should be as simple as possible, but no simpler!

'Until now even the most profound thinkers have usually attempted to explain things in terms of a relative handful of causal forces. For even the best human mind finds it difficult to entertain, let alone manipulate, more than a few variables at a time. (While we may deal with many factors simultaneously on a subconscious or intuitive level, systematic, conscious thinking about a great many variables is damnably difficult, as anyone who has tried it knows.) In consequence, when faced with a truly complicated problem . . . we tend to focus on two or three factors and to ignore many others that may, singly or collectively, be far more important.'

(Alvin Toffler in *The Third Wave*)

> **The third wave principle:**
> You may forget some critical factors, but they won't forget you.

The systems we manage today are complex, and we don't understand them very well at the intuitive level. Our systems are dynamic, i.e. they keep changing rapidly, so that what we learned about them yesterday may no longer be relevant to today's problems.

Figure 2.3 It is the responsibility of project managers to make sure that long-term environments are considered when making short-term decisions.

They are subject to earlier and greater magnitude of change than we expect, as described in Alvin Toffler's book, *Future Shock*.

Failure to confront this state of affairs with adequate tools must lead to a failure of management control.

> 'The multipurpose corporation that is emerging demands, among other things, smarter executives. It implies a management capable of specifying multiple goals, weighting them, interrelating them, and finding synergic policies that accomplish more than a single goal at a time. It requires policies that optimize not for one, but for several variables simultaneously.'
>
> (Alvin Toffler in *The Third Wave*)

Toffler is prescribing a medicine for management problems outside software engineering. But we in software management are part of the complex world he describes. Indeed, we are on the leading edge of it. Few others besides Toffler have identified our problems as being those of control over multidimensional factors.

Toffler identifies the need for management capability to deal with multiple objectives, but he does not indicate any method for doing so. The tools described in this book were developed from other sources.

In my experience it can be assumed that people spend a lot of time *not* achieving what they want to achieve because they are not able to perceive their problems clearly, they are not able to express themselves clearly, they are not able to communicate reliably with other people, and they are not able to control situations effectively.

What is needed are tools which provide us with the means to see the real problem, to formulate, quantify and compare elements of the problem and its possible solutions, to communicate these elements to others, to control the implementation of solutions, and to measure our degree of success in achieving our ends (Figure 2.3).

> **The multidimensional tools principle:**
> If your tools can't operate in all critical dimensions, then your problems will.

■ 2.4 Structured common sense tools

> **The common sense principle:**
> Common sense is uncommon.

What follows in this book is not so much a system, as a set of ideas for aiding what is little more than the use of your ordinary common sense. This is a set of tools for management which can formulate problems to be solved (What is the *real* problem?); communicate the nature of problems to others (This is the *real* problem); analyze the quality of the proposed solutions (Solution X is 50% better at solving the real problem); control risks by proper estimation (We risk running over the deadline unless we take action); and note the early results of implementation for the improvement of later results (Solution A is not as effective as we planned, so let's change it).

These ideas are applicable to a wide range of management problems, from very small problems, to problems which involve hundreds of work-years or over a decade of calendar years to solve.

They can be used for highly technical engineering problems, as well as complex organizational ones. We will treat them here as software engineering management tools, but they can be used in many other areas of work. This is useful since many readers are probably building systems and organizations, and are not limited to software alone.

They are designed for today's problems, but they are general decision-making, analysis, estimation and specification tools. You will

Principles of software engineering management: resources

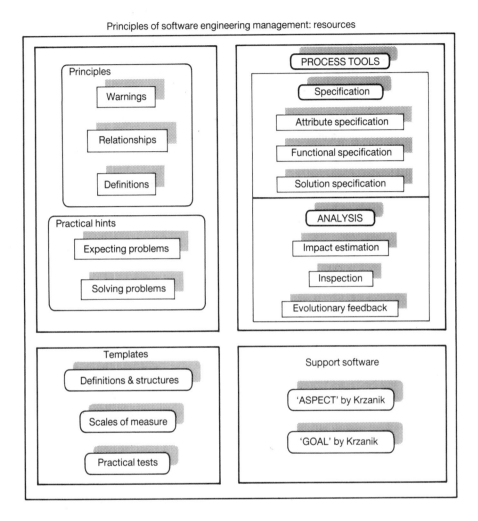

Figure 2.4 Multidimensional thinking process tools. There are principles and practical hints throughout the book. There are methods for specification, principally in Chapters 8, 9 and 10, and analysis, in Chapters 2, 5, 6, 7, 11, 13 and 16. There are a large number of practical examples of attribute definition in Chapter 19, and scattered throughout the book. There are research prototypes of related support software such as Aspect, and Goal, by Krzanik.

be able to use them for the rest of your working career, no matter what technological or economic changes emerge to shock us.

They have strong roots in the best engineering traditions. They can be regarded simply as formalized common sense, or as a more highly structured version of the ordinary thinking patterns which we apply to our problems much of the time.

The general aim is to increase the success of management efforts, to produce required results in such a way that risks are known and controlled, and to maintain control of any side-effects of the solutions we adopt.

Each tool (Figure 2.4) helps us to define, analyze and organize our ideas about what we want and how to achieve it. Between them, the tools can perform a wide range of tasks.

The thinking-tools principle:
Dynamic environments require thinking tools instead of unthinking dogmas.

The user of these tools is free to select any one of them, or a combination of them, for application to a particular problem. Users are also free to modify any tool to fit their preferences and requirements, or even to improve or extend the tool for their particular purposes.

Some of the tools are packaged as formal methods for working with problems, while others are merely principles or checklists to ensure more systematic thinking. They are all intended to stimulate readers to consider their own problems and goals in a more realistic light.

■ 2.5 Some fundamental concepts of software engineering

There are some concepts relating to software engineering which are fundamental notions in this book. We are possibly different in our use of some of these concepts from many others. So here is a statement of our viewpoint.

Software:
Software is all things which are not hardware in the system.

No man is an island:
Software has no life independent from hardware, and must consider the properties of the hardware systems on which it resides, as well as the people involved.

Engineering:
Engineering is a process of design, and trial-construction, of
something, which aims to produce a system with a specified set of
quality-and-cost attributes. We also accept the notion that
engineering is the application of heuristics to solving problems.

Software engineering:
Software engineering is primarily a design process; construction
and use confirm that the right design ideas have been found.

Software engineering specialists:
The software engineering discipline is already so complex that
specialists in sub-disciplines are required to find the best
designs.

The bricklayer principle:
Calling a programmer a software engineer does not make him an
engineer any more than calling a bricklayer a construction
engineer makes him an engineer.

The real software engineer principle:
A real software engineer can optimize any single attribute to
become ten times better than it would otherwise have been.

The software engineering process principle:
Software engineering has multiple measurable requirements as
input, and appropriate design solutions as output.

■ 2.6 The 'Bill of Rights' for company communication

The 'real problem' is communication between people. The methods
and principles set forth in this book are really devices for improving
communication between people about technological and managerial
matters.

At one point in my work there was a large multinational computer
company, which had decided to adopt the 'measurable objectives'
ideas in this book at the management level and the technical level. The
Chief Executive had decided to issue a booklet to popularize the
concept: The XYZ Co. Way to Set Objectives. I became involved in the
work of drafting the booklet, together with Personnel Division people.

One day, I got suspicious of the concept of telling all the bright professionals in the company how they should act. I thought it was about time we granted them some rights instead of giving them duties.

So I drafted the Company Communication Bill of Rights. It was a hit with the people I was working with, and with the Chief Executive. But we ran into severe political problems with the Personnel Director (later fired!) who felt that we were giving too much power to the masses! Perhaps he did not appreciate that with each right comes a corresponding set of obligations?

The Bill of Rights we wrote looked like this:

1. You have a right to *know* precisely what is expected of you.
2. You have a right to *clarify* things with colleagues, anywhere in the organization.
3. You have a right to *initiate* clearer definitions of objectives and strategies.
4. You have a right to get objectives presented in *measurable, quantified* formats.
5. You have a right to *change* your objectives and strategies, for better performance.
6. You have the right to *try out* new ideas for improving communication.
7. You have the right to *fail* when trying, but also to *kill* failures quickly.
8. You have a right to *challenge constructively* higher-level objectives and strategies.
9. You have a right to be *judged objectively* on your performance against *measurable* objectives.
10. You have a right to *offer constructive help* to colleagues to improve communication.

A challenge to the reader

The real problem is communication between people, and the real purpose of this book is to enlarge your tool-kit for constructing better communication bridges between people working in the software engineering environment.

While you are awaiting your opportunity to sell the Bill of Rights concept to your top management, maybe you could implement it in your part of the organization immediately, to see how it works. Don't be surprised if your colleagues use it to encourage you to communicate more clearly yourself. That's one of the objectives.

■ 2.7 Some job descriptions

Here are some of the professional occupation descriptions which we will presume in this text. Some of the terms are invented by the author for the purpose of this book (infotect, softect and softcrafter). The term software engineer is defined in a way which deviates from the practice of many others:

Infotect
Softect
Software engineer
Specialist software engineer
Softcrafter
Moderator
Inspector

The *infotect* is the information systems architect. The *-tect* function is responsible for a design which satisfies the overall quality and resource requirements of the user or client. The infotect is responsible for the overall design of an information system, which itself may or may not use computers. *Infotecture* is practiced by infotects.

The *softect* is a software architect. He is dealing with the design of a computer system software, remembering that software is all non-hardware components of the system, and not merely limited to computer programs. Softects synchronize the work of software engineering specialists, and are themselves a particular class of software engineer (namely a generalist synchronizer). Softects perform a process called *softecture*.

A *software engineer* is primarily responsible for translation of required software system attributes into appropriate designs capable of meeting those requirements.

A *specialist software engineer* is one who is so much better versed in his speciality that he can find solutions which are ten times better, in some selected attribute, than those of the non-specialist.

A *softcrafter* is a software craftsperson who constructs software according to the design of others. For example, program coder, test case constructor, documentation writer, software package user, data inputter, quality checker.

A *moderator* is the administrative leader of an inspection process for quality control of software.

An *inspector* is someone who participates in an inspection process for software.

■ Further reading

Peters, T., and Austin, N., 1985, *A passion for excellence*, Random House (USA), Collins (UK)

Toffler, A. 1980, *The third wave*, Collins

Toffler, A. 1970, *Future shock*, Pan (UK)

3

What is the real problem?

■ Introduction

In Chapter 3 we get to the heart of the matter, the 'ends'; unambiguous requirements specifications for quality and benefit ideas. This is the cornerstone upon which all the other methods in this book are based.

■ 3.1 Lack of management clarity in stating goals

It is very rare to find the objectives of management clearly and completely stated. Time and again we see project documentation with few or no effective cost goals, vague remarks about vital subjects like 'improved customer service' and 'better product reliability,' and with no precise specification of important matters such as adaptability or productivity.

There is usually no clear distinction made between the results or the goals we must aim for – the *problem*, and the various possible courses of action for getting those results – the *solutions*. We are constantly making the mistake of specifying the means of doing something, rather than the result we want. This can only limit our ability to find better solutions to our real problem.

■ 3.2 The 'vague goals' example

Here, for example, is a direct quotation from a letter from a client who is proposing some large-scale and critical replanning:

> 'The key business attributes of the new system – I am sorry these are a bit vague but that is one reason why we need your help – are to give an appropriate customer service in supplying products, to have an appropriate stockholding consistent with that, and to have a more flexible and efficient utilization of resources leading to increased profitability.'

What do you think the client wanted, exactly?

This statement was the departure point for what turned out, when we tried to formalize the goals, to be an attempt to save $400 million per year for a Corporation!

■ 3.3 Fuzzy targets

> **The principle of fuzzy targets:**
> Projects without clear goals will not achieve their goals clearly.
> (You can't hit the bullseye if you don't know where the target is!)

"Would you tell me please, which way I ought to go from here?"

"That depends a good deal on where you want to get to," said the cat.

"I don't much care where—," said Alice.

"Then it doesn't matter which way you go," said the cat.

Lewis Carroll

Figure 3.1 The Cheshire Cat. Source: *The Annotated Alice*. Illustration by John Tenniel. Copyright © 1960 by Martin Gardner. Used by permission of Clarkson N. Potter Inc.

Does this mean that projects, in which the goals are not clear, will not reach their goals at all? Yes, often! But this failure will not be so obvious, at first, as it would have been if we had stated clear goals to begin with.

Practical hint: *If you intend to fail, or fear that failure is inevitable, then stick to unclear goals to hide your incompetence.*

Does it mean that we won't be able to prove that we have succeeded, even when we have reached our real goals? Yes, often! And the result is that we risk wasting our time and money striving to meet goals after they have already been met.

In order to make ourselves capable of choosing the 'right' solutions, controlling the speed and cost of implementation, and knowing that our solutions have actually 'worked' as intended, we must first of all state our goals clearly.

The 'goals' of a project are the results we want. We can state them as a set of requirements. It is particularly important that we do not confuse the means with the ends by inadvertently including proposed solutions (means) in our goal statement. This is a common error when people are stating their goals.

Practical hint: *If you can think of several possible alternative specifications for getting what you want, then what you are specifying is solutions. Ask yourself, 'What do I really want?' These are your real goals. Alternatively, if you can ask, 'Would I be willing to drop this specification if I got what I really want, or if this specification were in conflict with what I really want?,' then your specification is probably just a solution, not a real requirement.*

■ 3.4 The military project example: the goal

In a military systems project, a 'goal' was stated as 'consistent commonality' of the data about ships in the North Sea.

The client said he wanted:

1. *Message handling*
       reduce signal deadtime
       increase accuracy
       improve communications flow

2. *Information system*
    consistent commonality of data (common data)
    analysis and prediction (planning)
    eliminate tedious work

This is a good example of a solution idea accidentally being stated as a requirement. 'Consistency' is a goal, but 'commonality' is a device which may be used for getting consistency. There is an additional fault with the goal statement. It implies a suggestion that the multiple observations from the different services be resolved into a single 'official' observation.

This is indeed one possible solution, but it may be the *wrong* solution for meeting *all* the goals of the system. This solution could lead to artificial consistency (no conflicting observations) at the price of the accuracy and reliability of the data. Sometimes it is more useful to know that 'the experts disagree' because, as Bertrand Russell reportedly said, 'you cannot be sure either one of them is right.'

In this instance we clarified the goals by quantifying the 'required level of consistency' in the data (see Section 3.7 for details), and also the probability that inconsistent data would be marked as inconsistent when displayed to military users. We left the solution (how to achieve these two consistency objectives) to later design stages.

■ 3.5 Never end up with the means

> **The principle of the separation of ends and means:**
> Avoid mentioning solutions in your goal statements.

Concentrate on the results you want, and leave the solution statements for later.

It is useful to make a formal distinction between two kinds of goals:

'what?' and 'how well?'

Most people have no difficulty in making a series of statements on what they want their project to result in. I call this area the functional requirements specification. It is an area well understood and practised by most professionals today, so the subject will not be discussed further at this point.

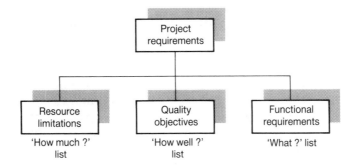

Figure 3.2 Requirements hierarchy. Project requirements can be thought of as three things: functional requirements, quality requirements, and budget requirements (or resource limitations).

■ 3.6 Attribute requirements

The difficult management problem centers around the 'how well' requirements. I call this area the **attribute specification**. Attributes are of two kinds: resources and qualities or benefits.

Resources (people, time, money) are almost always limited. Resource attributes are constraints or limits on our ability to get the qualities we want.

Qualities or benefits (performance, reliability, ease of use, ease of maintenance, security) are 'good things.' We want more quality than we can afford. We suffer when we don't have enough quality (Figure 3.2).

I find that people are pretty good at stating their resource limitations: 'I want it finished by 1 January. You can't have a larger budget than the present one.' The real difficulty seems to be in the clear, complete and unambiguous statement of our quality requirements. Note that I am using the concept of 'quality attributes' in the widest sense of 'all the good positive things' which are not *what* we want, but *how well* we want it to work. Our present management culture has not learned, or accepted as common practice, the following idea:

The principle of unambiguous quality specification:
All quality requirements can and should be stated unambiguously.

> **Kelvin's principle:**
> I often say that when you can measure what you are speaking about, and express it in numbers, you know something about it; but when you cannot measure it, when you cannot express it in numbers, your knowledge is of a meagre and unsatisfactory kind.

Here is some practical help as to how you might state ideas unambiguously.

When we do specify a goal clearly, and quantify it ('finish the project by 10 March or else!') then that goal is almost always given higher priority than other goals which are in fact more important – their importance often being obscured by the use of concepts such as 'better' or 'more effective' or 'consistent.' The only remedy is to make sure that all goals are formulated in equally clear language, at every stage of development, and in one place in the project documentation.

> **Shewhart's measurable quality principle:**
> The difficulty in defining quality is to translate future needs into measurable characteristics, so that a product can be designed and turned out to give satisfaction at a price the user will pay.

This was cited by W.E. Deming, from Walter A. Shewhart, *The Economic Control of Manufactured Product.*

Deming comments: 'This is not easy, and as soon as one feels fairly successful in the endeavor, he finds that the needs of the consumer have changed, competitors have moved in, there are new materials to work with, some better than the old ones, some worse; some cheaper than the old ones, some dearer.'

■ 3.7 The military project example: consistency

In the military system example above, consistency was a quality requirement. It was not a functional requirement. In the real world a system cannot merely be described as consistent or inconsistent. You can – and people do – but it will not get you what you want!

There are degrees of consistency. We cannot expect to get perfect consistency in a real, large and complicated system. On the other hand, we cannot tolerate 100% inconsistency either. So, the real issue becomes: how much consistency must we have, and how much consistency can we afford to pay for?

With this in mind, my client and I developed a clearer specification of the consistency requirement. We defined a scale for the consistency of the military database as 'the degree to which data was logically consistent with other data.' We specified a practical measuring device, a computer program for checking consistency of data. We estimated the present degree of consistency in our older systems (about 85%–90% consistent was the initial guesstimate). We then formulated the clear quality-attribute planned goal that: 'by two years from now, the new system will be at least 99.9% consistent in its data, using the measuring program as a basis for judgement.'

The following two examples illustrate how this was done. The exact specification we worked out in detail is shown in Example 1.

Example 1 Consistency definition

SCALE = probability of a data element being consistent with any and all other data in the system.

TEST(acceptance and at any other time) = 1000 random record sample checked by deep database correlation checker program.

NOW(system XXX, 6/85, guesstimate) 95–98% or lower (some say 85–90%).

WORST(1987) = 85–98% may increase in future due to new uses.

PLAN(1987) = 99.9 + %

AUTHORITY = user group (n.n. 4 June, 1985)

Notice how much more clear and unambiguous this is than if we had simply said 'substantially improved data consistency.' The latter statement does not answer the vital questions of 'by how much,' 'in relation to what,' and 'by when.'

This exercise in goal clarification led us to recognize that we needed to define another consistency factor in order to get full control; the probability of giving a warning signal when inconsistent data was actually used by the system. We recognized that there was a clear practical distinction between knowing the overall quality of a large base of data, and knowing whether we could trust a particular piece of data displayed on a computer screen. We set the level of this quality as: a warning signal shall be given, in at least 99% of the cases, where data is displayed which is inconsistent with any other part of the database, available at that time.

Example 2 Inconsistency detection ability

SCALE = probability that an inconsistent data element is offered to a user, without inconsistent warning being given.

TEST = 1000 simulated pollutions on test database, then count the number which get no warning.

NOW(system XXX, 6/85, guesstimate) = 100%

WORST(1987) = 1−>5%

PLAN(1987), (if not user check-request issued) = < 1%

PLAN(1987), (if user check-request issued) = < 0.1%

AUTHORITY = (none; suggestion for client consideration)

Note that this specification can be detailed for various classes of data. The most critical data classes need the highest rating.

Up to that time, consideration of this class of inconsistency had never been done because nobody had ever made it a clear requirement. There was every danger that it would be forgotten, while the project devoted its energy to 'database games.'

■ 3.8 Finding ways to measure attributes

There is a certain art to finding the necessary metrics concepts and measuring tools. Often they have no traditional written form, and it is essential that they are tailored to the case in hand. You have to exercise ordinary common sense and imagination to find workable measures. Nothing else is really required. We have only to ask ourselves what the goals really mean in practical terms.

Luckily, some attribute measures are commonly used in our systems. Chapter 19 of this book provides many 'starting kit' examples. The examples scattered throughout the book, especially those in the IBC case study (Part Two, Chapter 9) should provide enough examples for readers to create their own variations for their own projects.

■ 3.9 The 'usability' example

The Chairman of one of the world's largest multinational computer corporations had big problems. The Corporation's share prices were stagnant. The competition had become effective enough to make

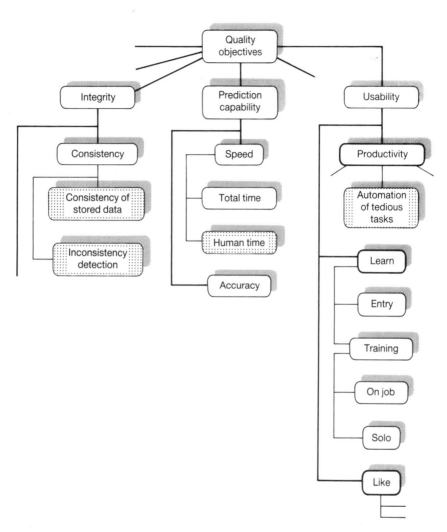

Figure 3.3 Quality requirements tree for the military project example. The purpose of the tree is to show how the detailed quality requirements are part of a larger set of quality requirements. The tree also makes it clear that some quality ideas, such as integrity, are really just high-level titles for a collection of more specific requirements. Lines not connected to any box indicate that additional quality requirements must be identified.

embarrassing inroads into their traditional market areas. The market was maturing, and customers wanted products which were easier to learn with little or no formal training. So the Chairman let it be known that 'usability' was an issue of importance.

Unfortunately, nobody who was responsible for the Corporation's many product developments knew exactly what to do with the usability issue. While acknowledging that the idea was a good one in principle, they continued development work in their old ways, unhampered by this new, though unclear, idea from the Chairman. After all, they had other priorities, like meeting deadlines set by their immediate managers.

The corporation's concern for usability finally landed on the desk of a human factors specialist in the Corporation. He knew what usability was. He knew it when he saw it, and he knew how to design it into a system. But when it came to translating the idea into something capable of being acted upon constructively by development staff, he had no precedents or adequate theory. He asked for my opinion as to how to do this.

My initial suggestion was to make usability a measurable concept for the development labs. My contact said, 'I think you understand the Corporation, but I have only one problem. I don't know how to measure usability.' Neither did I. But after thinking about the problem, he hit upon the following solution:

The complex concept of 'usability' was exploded, or broken down, into a set of sub-concepts. This led to simple ideas of how to measure each one, and thus how to measure the concept as a whole. The usability explosion was like this:

- level of personal ability required to enter training courses (if any) for the product.
- training time required to attain a pre-determined level of productivity with the product.
- the specified amount of work to be produced by a person so trained.
- the rate of errors made by a trained user, operating at the normal work rate.
- the opinion ('Gallup') of the users of the product, as to how well they liked it.

The above ideas can all be measured in one or more obvious ways. Management could then concentrate on setting usability sub-goals at the required levels for particular product areas.

Further detail on how to specify attribute requirements in quantified form is given in Chapter 9.

■ 3.10 Advantages of metrics

Another client went to the trouble of writing down the advantages found in putting quality ideas into measurable form:

Advantages of metrics for our client

1. Certainty: He is much more certain of getting what he wants.
2. Identicality: All competitors will have an identical interpretation of what they are bidding for, and thus the bids will be more surely comparable.
3. Clarification: It will stimulate a more intense and early discussion among client's personnel about what they really want.
4. Testability: It will be easier at acceptance test time to determine whether the promised specifications have really been delivered.

Advantages of metrics for our sales force

1. Fail safe bidding: The probability of a bid failing because of misunderstood requirements will be reduced.
2. Image: We will be perceived as more interested in identifying and meeting client requirements.
3. Better requirements data: We may get to know more, and earlier, than competitors, what the client really needs and wants.
4. Profitability: We can tailor our bidding and development better to meet client needs, and thus increase our possibility of making a profit on fixed price contracts.
5. Change control: If the clients have a change of needs (and they will) we can more easily show that these needs are different from earlier approved statements – and argue for a cost change.
6. Contractability: We can better transmit these specifications to third parties, in requests for proposals and in contracts, so that we do not end up being responsible for third party misunderstandings of our client needs.
7. Strength: We can present our product strengths in an impressive clear language, while competitors continue to spout vague promises.
8. Result orientation: Salesmen can speak with customers on the basis of results to be delivered, and do not have to get embroiled in a lot of talk about the deeper technology needed to arrive at those results.

Advantages of metrics for developers and contractors

1. Estimatability: We can deliver estimates based on a firmer understanding of the requirements.
2. Resource control: The customer cannot later surprise us with more demanding results requirements than we expected to have to deliver, without being willing to pay for the changes.
3. Systems engineering: We can use 'design by objectives' to engineer systematically and cost a solution to the customer's requirements. We are more likely to have a realistic understanding of the needs if we can use this process rather than the 'deliver it and see' method from which over-budgeted-cost-and-time scandals so often emerge.
4. Means control: We can ask the user and the sales force to concentrate on getting the technical result objectives, while we can be freer to select the appropriate technology for meeting the goals (including existing products).

■ 3.11 Critical attributes

When you read a typical statement of management objectives, you would be wise to work on the assumption that several of the most important attributes have not been stated. This, paradoxically, is often because these goals are so critical that management takes them for granted. Managers frequently assume that everyone else has taken these critical, but unstated, goals into account (just like they have). They assume that there is no need to state the goals explicitly.

The principle of the obvious:
'Obvious' things, which 'everybody knows' cannot be left to take care of themselves.

A critical attribute is one which, if it got out of control, would threaten the viability of the whole solution. The likelihood, or otherwise, of any single attribute actually getting out of control should not, initially, be questioned. This is what got the CIS project in trouble (Chapter 1).

Many a project has got into trouble by assuming that certain things could not go wrong. It is with good reason that a variation of Murphy's Law (if anything can happen, it will) is widely appreciated among systems designers.

> **The Achilles' heel principle:**
> Projects which fail to specify their goals clearly, and fail to exercise control over even one single critical attribute, can expect project failure to be caused by that attribute.

■ 3.12 An exercise in goal analysis for your current project

Would you like to pick out some written specification of objectives for a project you are involved in, and analyze it, using the following questions as a checklist?

1. The ambiguity test: Are all future 'benefits' (the good things you get if the project is carried out) described in such unambiguous ways that you could describe a practical test to prove that these benefits exist at the required levels in the delivered project? (Red-pencil ambiguous goals as a '?')
2. The results – not solutions – test: Are the objectives (goals or benefits required) described in terms of the ultimate end-user results, or has someone inadvertently slipped in a mention of their favorite solution? (Mark solutions with a red-pencil 'S'.)
3. The test of rewriting unambiguously: Can you rewrite the ambiguous quality (benefits) objectives in an unambiguous way?

> **Practical hint:** *You will probably need to create a scale of measure for the quality concept. If you think you don't need to, then perhaps you don't understand the problem yet. If you are not feeling too creative today, try looking at Chapter 19 or possibly Chapter 9 for some ideas. Hint: go out and get your hands dirty with the real users of the present systems. There are always comparable systems to look at, and these give clues about existing system measures and their levels.*

4. The completeness test: Have you stated all the objectives – even the obvious ones which everyone assumes?

■ 3.13 The evil circle of development

> **The evil circle principle:**
> If requirements are unclear, incomplete or wrong, then the architecture will be equally wrong.

The evil circle principle (cont.):
If the architecture is wrong, then our cost estimates will be wrong.

If the cost estimates are wrong, then people will know we are badly managed.

If the high-level requirements and architecture are wrong, then the detailed design of them will be equally wrong.

If the detailed designs are wrong, then the implementation will be wrong.

So we will end up re-doing the entire project as badly as the last time, because somebody will cover up the initial failure, and we will presume that the methods we used initially were satisfactory.

■ Further reading

Shewhart, A., 1931, *The economic control of manufactured product*, Van Nostrand Reinhold, New York

What is a solution, and what is not?

■ Introduction

Chapter 4 introduces the 'means,' which I call 'solutions'; how we find them and why we must not mix them up with our objectives – the ends.' We have shown in the previous chapters that even comparatively simple-looking problems are both complex and multidimensional. So, often, are their solutions.

■ 4.1 What is meant by a solution?

A solution is the set of ideas the implementation of which impacts at least one part of the problem positively. In other words it contributes towards at least one function or attribute requirement. It follows that a solution idea with no positive effects on our requirements is not a solution at all. Many solutions will also have negative side-effects.

Most professionals have seen one or other variant of the swing design drawing shown in Figure 4.1. As a class exercise I often ask my students (most of whom are experienced professionals) to suggest what the real point of this illustration is. Most people say things like 'communications,' 'documentation' and 'requirements specification.' All true, but not the real problem.

The central problem in this illustration is that the attribute specification is poorly done. Take another look. The functional specification is understood in all seven drawings (function = [swing on tree, for person]). The differences are in the quality provided and the resources used.

In software engineering we have been doing exactly the same thing as is illustrated here since the 1960s. We have improved the sophistication of functional specification, without a corresponding improvement in attribute specification.

The principle of a solution worth considering:
A solution worth considering is one whose positive contribution to your requirements outweighs its negative ones.

This implies that

1. We need to specify known requirements, clearly and unambiguously,
2. We need to know about all positive contributions of the solution to quality requirements,

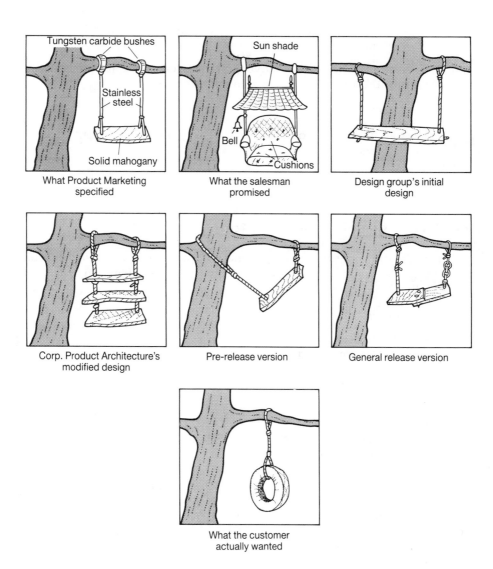

Figure 4.1 The swing solutions.

3. We need to know about negative side-effects of the solution on quality requirements.
4. We need to understand all resource consumption in relation to our budgets (our planned levels of the resources to be used).

We cannot judge the relative goodness of any solution without considering these four things systematically.

The holy cow principle of solutions:
Solutions are only valid as long as they best serve our current requirements, but no longer.

■ 4.2 How do solutions differ from goals?

Let us illustrate the basics with something non-technical first. We can express goals and solutions for most everyday problems such as the ones illustrated below.

Functional goals

- to be a father
- to be self-employed
- to reside in Paris

Attribute goals

- Health.
  (We might express it as 'at least 350 non-bed-ridden up-and-active days per year until age 70.')
- Wealth.
  (We might express it as 'debt less than property, and income greater than expenditure.')
- Wisdom.
  (We might express it as 'number of new books read per year greater than ten.')
- Happiness.
  (We might express it as 'more than 300 days per year when my inner glow makes me smile most of the day.')

Some solutions
(ways we might achieve the attribute goals)

- get a health check-up

- spend less money on alcohol and cigarettes
- get a library card and use a public library
- decide not to get unhappy and nervous about things we cannot control.

The above shows the differentiation between functions, attributes and solutions. This is intended to give simplistic reference points for the two of the three concepts which too often get mixed together in goal specification. It pays to separate them rigorously. Functional goals are a simple list of what we want in the future. Attribute goals are variable (in time) and negotiable (depends on what it costs to get it) numeric dimensions which the functions will possess. They are far more complex to deal with than the functional aspects of a problem. They can vary as our needs change and as our values and knowledge of them change – while the functional aspects might remain relatively constant.

The solutions are the answers to the questions posed by the function and attribute goals. They must be kept entirely separate from goals so that they do not accidentally become requirements. We must be free to select and change solutions whenever it seems wise to do so.

4.2.1 Definitions

Here are some definitions to match the above examples.

Functional goals are absolute requirements which have only one future state: true or untrue.

Attribute goals are requirements which can be expressed on scales of measurement.

Attribute goals refer to 'qualities' (good things of which we want as much as possible) and 'resources' (what we use to reach our goals – whether functional or attribute.) Resources are always limited.

Solutions are ideas which, if implemented, will impact the future goals.

It is useful to distinguish between them because the software engineering management process is primarily one of trying to meet the *attribute* goals using selected solutions. Software engineering management is judged primarily on how well all *attribute* requirements are met – in relation to planned levels.

4.2.2 An example

Here is a software engineering example of these three concepts:

FUNCTIONAL REQUIREMENT
TELSW: Telephone-exchange software for our project XYZ. (This can be defined further in terms of sub-requirements.)
ATTRIBUTE GOALS: (samples)
USE: The ease-of-use shall be no less, by any measure, than the best of the competition in any market. It shall be considered superior, by user survey, by at least 50% (planned 90% or more,) to all competitors.
AVAIL: The software component shall never be responsible for a single exchange being out of order for customer use for more than 10 seconds at any one time, or more than 30 seconds total per day during office hours.
DEADLINE: The software must be ready for customer delivery when the hardware is ready and the first customers are ready. Estimated as 19 Feb. and no later than 19 Oct.
SOLUTION SPECIFICATION (EXAMPLES)
TELINT: The major user interface is based on a touch-tone keyboard with 3-alphabetics on a numeric key (US Standard) and voice or tone output.
REDUND: The entire system shall be based on redundant components, including all hardware, data and tables, and distinct software. The system shall be able to function with *any* single hard or soft component out of order.
EVO: The software shall be evolved from a transport of our existing software package 'HIKE-ON' in a functionally upwards-compatible mode.

■ 4.3 The confusion of problems with solutions

Solutions are the things that problem solvers, and problem solvers only, have control over. No particular solution should ever be considered 'holy' to anyone. In other words, it should never be important whether a particular solution is used or not.

If it has been decided at the outset that we must use a particular 'solution', then that solution is a 'requirement', and it should be included from the beginning as such among the functional requirements.

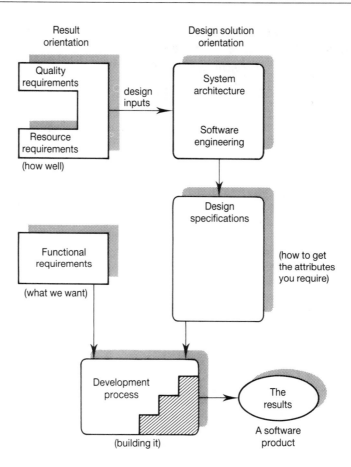

Figure 4.2 The software engineering process. Functional requirements can sometimes be directly translated by a program coder into a computer program (bottom). The software engineering function (top) is necessary when we require system attributes that the program coder cannot be expected to deliver. The software engineering function produces a design specification (like the blueprint of a house) which can be understood and used by the coder.

You should exercise caution in allowing a solution to become a requirement. It may be the best decision at the moment you take it, but later events, changes and insights may change your evaluation. You should try to keep a maximum of flexibility by keeping the solution in the solution category. This will make it easier to recognize the need for change, and to make changes without consultation with the client or user of the system.

For example, if a discussion among problem solvers revolves

around the question of using imported or domestic components, then maybe the manager should take a position on whether this is really:

- a *functional requirement* (if so, make a functional goal such as, 'the solution elements must be of domestic manufacture, wherever possible, regardless of the impact of this on attributes') or
- an *attribute requirement* (if so, make an attribute goal such as 'a maximum of domestic solution elements shall be used, consistent with the worst case level of all other attributes, and with at least 50% by value, of the solution being domestic in the worst case') or
- leave the question of domestic percentage of the solution in the 'non-holy' area of solution parts. Let the other requirements dominate the solution. It will be easier to solve the problem if you do.

■ 4.4 Specifying solutions – flexibility of viewpoint

Notice the flexibility we get in the above way of thinking. A single idea (such as domestic component value) can be treated:

- as an absolute requirement (function) (with some restrictions regarding conflict with other absolute requirements, e.g. for a politically sensitive application);
- as a variable goal (attribute) (varying somewhere between 'worst acceptable case' and somewhat over the 'planned level');
- or as a totally free idea (solution) (anything goes) which can be moulded entirely as a result of the other requirements of the system.

It is, as you can see, really a matter of priorities. Requirements have priorities over solutions. But solutions have unintended impacts on our functional requirements and attribute goals, and the relationship is complex, dynamic and challenging. It is the responsibility of the software engineering manager to ensure clear, accurate specification which has the agreement of senior management.

> **The principle of solution flexibility:**
> A solution idea can be specified as a requirement, or as an answer to a requirement, depending on your priorities.

1. A solution as a functional requirement:
    A solution can only be stated as an absolute requirement

(function) if it has a higher priority than any attribute requirement which it impacts negatively. In this case it stops being a 'solution'. For example, we might require that the software be based on UNIX†. This then becomes a functional requirement, regardless of the consequences it might have on attributes, such as cost, reliability, compatibility with other systems, or performance.

2. A solution stated as an attribute range:
A solution can be stated in terms of an attribute range, to avoid dangerous extremes. In this case it becomes an attribute requirement. For example, we may feel we require 'high performance', but choose to express this as a range between the absolute minimum we need ('worst case') and the most that would be useful ('planned level').

3. A solution stated as a non-holy solution:
A solution can be specified as a 'solution' and is subject to elimination or change in order to satisfy higher priority requirements. For example, suppose the data for a system is specified initially as a table to give flexibility for change. Later experience with the table shows that it should be dropped, in order to get the extremely high operational performance required for the most-frequently-used data elements on the table. It is therefore dropped in favor of a non-tabular design satisfying the higher-priority performance goals.

■ 4.5 The division of labor between user and developer

There is an important division of labor which needs to be both recognized, and practiced, more systematically: *managers* are responsible for formulating their problems in terms of goals; *problem solvers* are responsible for finding appropriate solutions to these problems.

These two concepts describe roles, not formal positions, and a particular manager may well wear both hats. But stating the problems and proposing solutions are two separate processes. They are linked of course, and we frequently move between them – for example in order to modify over-ambitious goals in accordance with the realities we have just learned about.

There are real dangers if we cannot, or do not, make a clear separation between goal setting and problem-solving. In simple terms, the danger is that the goal is stated in such a way that it unwittingly dictates the solutions to be used to reach it. Sometimes the solution is

† UNIX™ is a registered trademark of AT&T in the USA and other countries.

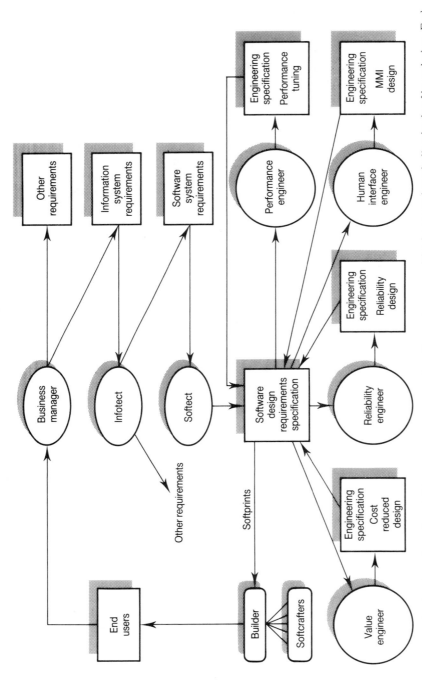

Figure 4.3 Design functions. Specialists are now necessary in software because of the large and exploding body of knowledge. End users feed requirements and problems to management which passes on information system problems to the system architect (or infotect). If the information systems involved are computerized then the design problem can be handed over to a software system architect (softect) who is responsible for synchronizing specialist design functions in their work. The softect must iterate with the specialists until a balanced package is found to satisfy the overall requirements. The softect can then hand over building specifications to the builder, who can delegate construction work to the softcrafters.

seen as a goal in itself, thus threatening the possibility that the 'real goal' will ever be achieved.

It is critical to have some formal means of keeping goals distinct from solutions. Even those of us who are aware of the need for separation usually rely on informal methods for doing so, but these are rarely adequate, and frequently lead us astray.

It is not the job of the problem-solvers to specify the function and attribute goals of a system – though they may on occasion help, clarify, suggest, show consequences, and assist in putting goals in a useful format or structure. Only the people with the real problem – the managers – can take responsibility for saying what the goals are, and what resources are going to be made available for reaching them.

On the other hand, managers can often be seen specifying a solution when in reality, what they really want are some particular attributes, which they believe (often as the result of someone's clever marketing, and often wrongly) will appear as a result of *using* a specific product or method.

Some software producer might have sold the idea that vital management information will be more rapidly accessible when their particular database management software package is used. Suddenly management seems to have a 'goal' of building a database management system. What they should have done was to specify the results they want – their goals – (for example: 'market price changes of more than 5% per day, on our desk within 10 minutes of official change'). They could then leave the technological alternatives as options to the designer. These might be, for example, a database on a computer, or a public information retrieval service which selects certain data, or simply a person who watches the movements of prices and broadcasts a message when required.

Time and again we have seen people proceeding from unclearly stated goals to the specification of solutions which get treated as though these solutions were goals in themselves.

■ 4.6 Example: renting as a goal excludes buying as a solution

For example, one chemicals Corporation client stated the goal: 'rental price not exceeding current total rental for the machines to be replaced.' This was interpreted, in practice, as meaning that the solution had to be rental of machines.

In fact it turned out that the best solution was to buy a machine which was much larger than the one envisaged in the original goal statement, and write it off economically over about twice the useful rental life of smaller computers.

Because of economies of scale, this resulted in getting a machine 30 times more powerful, for the equivalent cost per month of the old machine.

When the error in goal formulation (or at least goal interpretation!) was recognized, this solution was contracted for and used successfully for the years planned.

■ 4.7 The portability specification example

A client's Financial Director specified 'Standard COBOL' as a requirement in their contract with a software house.

What they really wanted was software portability (measured by ease and cheapness of transporting the software to other machines). They wanted to be able to move their software investment to larger machines later if need be. They did not in fact care whether COBOL itself was used at all.

We found that in this particular case, the use of COBOL would be very bad for system performance for smaller computers (which we had decided to use) which did not support the language very well at that time.

We also found that the software house had decided to interpret the requirement as 'use standard COBOL when you use COBOL at all'. But the software house had also decided to use a high-level application generator for over half of the application code, and a database management system for another good portion of the logic. Both of these would have given very low portability.

This is a good example of how a well-intentioned, but carelessly formulated software requirement can defeat the very purpose it is trying to achieve.

We changed the requirement to one which read:

Portability:

1. The software system shall be convertible to any major manufacturer's equipment which has COBOL software for less than 5% additional cost to the cost of the original development of the software.
2. The software house is required to carry out the conversion for us at this cost, or to pay the cost difference if they cannot or will not carry out the conversion.
3. This shall include all data conversion, all database management code, all supporting code or data of any nature required for a successful conversion.

4. This shall be without degradation of any critical attributes specified elsewhere in this contract for the original system (but in particular – without degrading performance, maintainability, reliability or portability [point (1) above]).

■ 4.8 Example: the State of California teacher system

The State of California specified a 'computerized system' for their teacher personnel records. What they really wanted – the real goal – was a fast, reliable and above all cheaper information processing system than the manual one they had already.

After a million dollars of investment, the ASTEC system was born.

The California State Auditors discovered, after a year of operation of the new system, that the new operational cost was $3.60 per document, as opposed to the previous manual system's cost of 50 cents. This meant over seven times more for automation, plus the initial investment.

There were no other redeeming attributes to justify this cost difference, so the new system was destroyed and replaced by the old one.

My source of this intriguing reverse-automation tale, Montgomery Phister, later provided me with a post-mortem consultant's report on the ASTEC project. This showed that by killing the automated system the State saved about one million dollars per year. The operational cost went back to the original 50 cents per document. Details were originally published in Phister's *Data Processing Technology and Economics*, Digital Press, Maynard, Mass.

The ASTEC system is a glaring example of how the specification of a solution (in this case, an 'automated system') became a goal in itself. The proof that it was regarded as a goal was that nobody reacted to the failure during the first year of operation. The misunderstood goal had been 'successfully' achieved. The real goals, among which were the control of public expenditure, were never clearly stated, never designed into the system, and never monitored for real success by the people who implemented the system.

What about your project? Would it stand up to the test of meeting the real objectives of your user?

■ 4.9 An exercise on your current project documentation

It is an instructive exercise to find a piece of project documentation, and check the following questions: Are the functional and attribute requirements clearly separated from each other? Are suggested solutions kept entirely separate from the requirements, or are they simply mixed in with the real management goals in such a way that people might get confused?

■ 4.10 Some principles for finding the right solutions

The unholy solution principle:
Solutions are never holy; they can and should be changed in the light of new requirements, conflicts with other solutions, or negative practical experience with them.

The net result principle:
Solutions should be selected and judged on their practical ability to contribute well to high-priority needs.

The hidden solution principle:
Solutions should never be specified or implied in a goal statement, unless they really are the high-priority goal itself.

The management by results principle:
Management must avoid the imposition of solution ideas, and instead concentrate on goal-priority specification.

Evaluating solutions

■ Introduction

Chapter 5 outlines some of the methods we use for evaluating the solutions we are considering; and discusses how far they take us towards our objectives.

■ 5.1 The best solution

At this point we can assume we have found one or more solutions. Solutions can be evaluated, and solutions can be compared with each other. The best solution, the one we should adopt, is the one with the best overall match with the attribute requirement specification at the planned levels. Solution can refer here to any *set* of solution ideas for any sub-system.

■ 5.2 Goal and solution mapping

Before we can find the best solution, we need to know that the components of the proposed solution will give us the attributes we want. Will the proposed solution impact the critical attributes – the ones we have decided to 'manage' – at the planned level, or at least an acceptable level (better than the 'worst case')?

We can use a simple checklist, as in Table 5.1, to see how our suggested solutions impact our goals; the examples were defined earlier (Section 4.2). At this stage, we are simply trying out various ideas for solutions.

From this example we can see that more than one solution can be used to impact a single attribute, and that some solution parts can impact more than one attribute; also the 'wisdom' attribute is not documented as being impacted by any solution part. This is a sign that 'wisdom' needs attention, if goals are to be reached.

But, this superficial analysis doesn't tell us several things we would like to know. It does not tell us the degree to which the solutions have side-effects which were *not* charted. The smoker and drinker might credit the 'don't' solutions with negative side-effects on their happiness. The solution 'be nice' could involve a temptation to offer your guests a drink, and then (in politeness) to join them.

This solution analysis does give us some idea of the expected impact of the solutions on several goals. It does show us one goal without any solution. It is a written table, and superior to sequential oral descriptions of our solution, such as 'Early to bed and early to rise, make a man healthy, happy and wise.'

Table 5.1 Goal and solution mapping.

Goals	Solutions
Health	Don't smoke. Don't drink. Early to bed.
Wealth	Don't smoke. Don't drink. Save 10% income monthly.
Wisdom	(No solution.)
Happiness	Read humorous books. Be nice to other people. Rise early.

The side-effect principle:
You must find out by how much all your critical attributes are impacted by the proposed solution.

Note that particular solution parts will often have both positive and negative side-effects on attributes other than the one to which they are initially intended to contribute.

■ 5.3 Impact estimation

There is no reason to exceed planned quality levels, and good reason not to exceed planned resource use. Most of us recognize the need for some sort of quantitative estimation technique for cost and project time, but few of us have learned any reliable method for making such estimates. For those readers who want a deeper discussion of this point, see Chapter 16.

The nearest many of us get to accurate cost and resource estimation is a form of self-delusion. On the basis of (past) experience with other projects, we make estimates for cost and completion dates. We start the project, and when about 95% of the planned resources are used up, we slam on the brakes, and skid to a halt at around 100%, or a bit more. What this really means is that we stop, rather than finish, and then congratulate ourselves on the accuracy of our estimates.

At this stage, we may have most of the essential functions of the project operating. The project is 'working' reasonably well – but it is probably not working at anywhere near the high levels of quality

What are our organizational change objectives ?					

	1	2	3	4	5	6
1	PN ST	Organizational		Objectives		
2				by 1986 end		
3	Objective	Measure	Test	Worst	Plan	Record
4						
5	Productivity	Return on investment	Finance analysis	10%	20%	30% ?
6	Flexibility	Growth/year	Pers. analysis	±20%	±30%	
7	Production cost	Relative '84	Finance analysis	−20%	−50%	
8	Competitiveness	Product sales	Budget = 100%	90%	>100%	150%
9	Predictability	Average deviation	10 key attributes	− 20%	− 8%	− 5% ?
10	Job satisfaction	% Employees + +	Pers. survey	80%	95%	98% ?

How much impact does each of the suggestions have on our goals ?

PN ST		Strategies Estimated Impact (100% = PLAN)				
		Infotect	Software Engineering	Evolution	Inspection	
Objective	Plan	PD.IN	PD. SE	PT.EVO	PT. INS	Σ Imp.
Productivity	20%	80	20	30	35	165
Flexibility	±30%	20	0	30	0	50
Production cost	− 50%	80	50	50	30	210
Competitiveness	>100%	50	50	30	30	160
Predictability	− 8%	50	50	50	20	170
Job satisfaction	95%	1	5	30	20	56
		IMPACT ESTIMATION TABLE FIRST DRAFT				

Figure 5.1 An example of impact estimation using a spreadsheet. This example was produced in an attempt to start discussion about the future organizational goals and strategies of a large corporation. The top shows suggested objectives. At the bottom is a rough estimate of the impact the suggested strategies could be expected to have. The estimates are zero for no expected impact and 100 for reaching the planned level.

which would have been insisted upon if quality levels had been more formally specified at the beginning.

However the project has been delivered. It is more or less on time, and within budget. There are a few teething troubles, but such troubles are 'natural' – in fact they seem to be unavoidable. Anyway, we have got used to them. Long-term problems arising out of these unresolved conflicts, and insufficiently planned attributes, can easily be swept under the carpet at this stage (because the solution is 'workable'). But they can cause incalculable time and expense to put right later.

Impact estimation, in which we specify how far a solution contributes to the required attributes, fills the dangerous gap between good intentions (attribute specifications) and unpleasant realities (acceptability tests for all the attributes). It gives early warning signals about possible future system failure or bad solution economy. Without such tools we are left alone with intuition in a very complex environment. The danger of making costly errors is high, when intuition is your only guide to a complex system design.

■ 5.4 Estimating

How do we quantify the contribution of a particular solution, when it is quite obvious that given the complexity of the kinds of solutions we are talking about, we cannot know the answer with any degree of precision?

> **The principle of fuzzy numbers:**
> Even if we don't know for sure, we can make a rough estimate, and improve it later.

(If we are not in a position to give any estimates, we should ask ourselves on just what grounds we are proposing the particular solution in the first place.)

As soon as we try to quantify the effects of implementing our solutions, it becomes necessary to be able to express uncertainty in a satisfactory form. Planning (predicting outcomes) on paper is simply not the same thing as implementing those plans in a real-life environment. The implementation of the simplest plan will have effects which cannot be known in advance. These effects will, in turn, have effects on other parts of the system, creating a dynamic uncertainty.

Only a fool believes in perfectly accurate predictions. Only a greater fool knows that his predictions are not 100% reliable, but fails to communicate this fact to others.

Table 5.2

Goal (Plan)	Impact estimate for solution: AUTOMATE
Double present levels	100% ± 20% (i.e. the solution will meet the plan within ±20% of planned production)
Production costs to be one half of this year's costs	50% ± 10% (i.e. about half the desired cost savings can be expected by using AUTOMATE)

The uncertain certainty principle:
Uncertainty must certainly be stated in no uncertain terms.

The contribution of a particular solution-component towards our goals, must therefore often be written in the form of uncertainty estimates or ranges of possible values. Uncertainty estimates are not required when the estimate is not controversial or significant.

Suppose that our planned level of software production is double that which we have now, and our planned level of cost is half that which we have now. We might express the partial contribution to these planned levels of, for instance, a solution to automate a particular software production process, as in Table 5.2.

This is a simplified impact estimation table. Note that the example in Figure 5.1 did not contain uncertainty estimates. They were not necessary in the context of the informal presentation described. In other situations, particularly where the estimator is not present to explain the estimate, an uncertainty estimate – and explanation of it in writing – is recommended practice.

From Table 5.2 we get a picture that the solution will contribute to solving our productivity problem, and part of our cost problems. These estimates, or 'likely results' might seem almost embarrassingly incomplete and approximate, but at least we have now managed to quantify the effect of implementing a particular solution in a clearer form than mere verbal assertions such as 'much improved' or 'more reliable.' A top-level impact estimation table is shown in Figure 5.2 and Figure 5.3 gives a graphic presentation of the table.

Incorrect estimates can be corrected later. At least we have something written down, a first estimate. This can now be subjected to

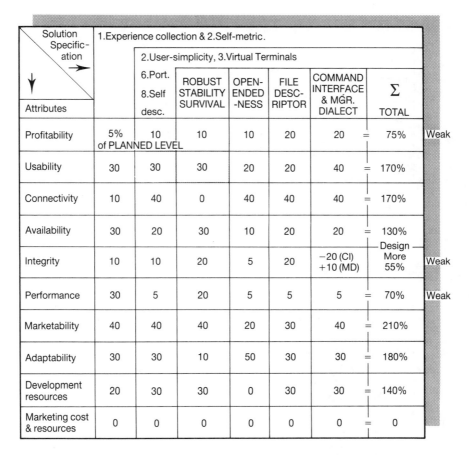

Solution Specification → / ↓ Attributes	6.Port. 8.Self desc.	ROBUST STABILITY SURVIVAL	OPEN-ENDED-NESS	FILE DESCRIPTOR	COMMAND INTERFACE & MGR. DIALECT	Σ TOTAL	
1.Experience collection & 2.Self-metric. *2.User-simplicity, 3.Virtual Terminals*							
Profitability	5% of PLANNED LEVEL 10	10	10	20	20	= 75%	Weak
Usability	30 30	30	20	20	40	= 170%	
Connectivity	10 40	0	40	40	40	= 170%	
Availability	30 20	30	10	20	20	= 130%	
Integrity	10 10	20	5	20	−20 (CI) +10 (MD)	Design More 55%	Weak
Performance	30 5	20	5	5	5	= 70%	Weak
Marketability	40 40	40	20	30	40	= 210%	
Adaptability	30 30	10	50	30	30	= 180%	
Development resources	20 30	30	0	30	30	= 140%	
Marketing cost & resources	0 0	0	0	0	0	= 0	

Figure 5.2 A top-level impact estimation table. The term top-level refers to the fact that the attribute objectives are at the highest level of specification. In addition the solutions are at the highest level of abstraction.

criticism, correction, and demands for justification. And, even if the correction is too late for the present project, we may have learned something useful about our ability to estimate.

This estimating process is very similar to what happens when we make financial budgets. Everybody knows, when we make budgets, that nobody knows if any estimate is exactly correct for future costs and incomes. Nevertheless there is wide agreement that we should try to estimate; that we should use estimates to get better control over the future; and that we should ensure better communication about future plans to all concerned. Remember that the alternative is chaotic,

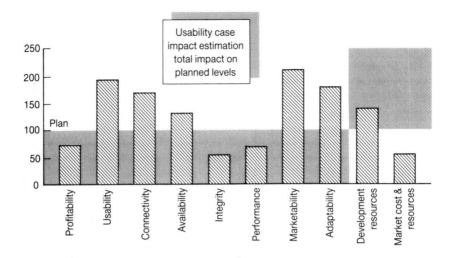

Figure 5.3 Impact estimation. Total impact chart on planned levels.

because it implies:

- no attempt to quantify most attributes of goals and of solutions, or to discuss them with the professionals responsible.
- no basis for learning about our ability, or lack of it, to make reliable estimates.
- no commitment to specific results on the part of the problem solvers. (The motivation to make predictions come true is often a powerful factor in getting results in practice.)
- no dialogue between professionals about the complex web of interactions between solutions and required attributes.

Try estimating on your own projects:

- take a proposal which you are going to make to others. Estimate the impact (as a percentage of the planned levels of critical goals) for at least three critical goals which would interest others.
- if the goals are not clear, then rewrite them so that the planned level is unambiguously stated.
- ask any colleagues, or salespeople who are proposing solutions, to estimate the impact of their suggestions on at least the five most critical objectives which you identify and define. Insist that they estimate the uncertainty of each estimate by percentage deviation from the plan.

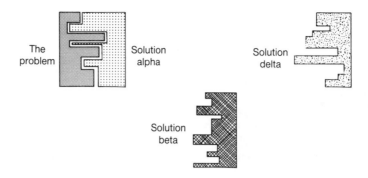

Figure 5.4 Solution comparison tries to identify the best-fit solution to the problem's multiple requirement dimension.

■ 5.5 Solution comparison

A large number of 'managerial' decisions are complex and multi-dimensional, and the problem this raises is one of which most managers are aware. In a typical management situation it is almost impossible to state a set of goals for anything without

- getting a list of many goals instead of one or two;
- finding that any and every goal is in some kind of conflict with one or more of the others;
- realizing that, quite simply, some goals are more important than others, and this makes sorting out conflicts between goals even more difficult.

The comparative analysis of complex alternatives is therefore a very common problem in management decision making. The solution comparison method is designed to help resolve this problem – to enable us to choose the 'best' option from among a number of apparently satisfactory ones. Figure 5.4 illustrates this method.

Impact estimation is a tool for deciding how well our chosen solutions match our goals. Solution comparison helps us to decide which solution alternatives to include in impact estimation, and which to leave out.

We are usually confronted with a bewildering quantity of information about each alternative solution. A typical case would be the selection from among competitive bids for hardware and software products on the commercial market.

Solution comparison uses the same mechanics as does impact estimation. The only difference is that we compare the solution

Table 5.3

	Solution 1	Solution 2	Solution 3	Impact estimation sum
Attribute 1	100	40	0	140
Attribute 2	−40	0	80	40
Attribute 3	30	5	45	80
Solution comparison	90	45	125	

(Solution 3 should be chosen on the basis of best net impact on the three attributes, planned levels.)

alternatives' total impact, as represented by the vertical sum of percentage impacts on the planned levels. The impact estimation method relies on adding up the set of chosen solutions along the horizontal axis to try to get a view of the total impact on each planned attribute level. Both methods are, of course, simplifications.

Solution comparison shares a number of features with other tools in this book. It is simply a formalization of the way in which the human mind compares complex things. The virtue of the formalization is that we are able to analyze much more complex material than the unaided mind can handle.

The fact that it is written down, numeric, and tabular, makes it easier to ensure consistency, and to communicate opinions and conclusions to others for criticism, addition and approval. The fact that it is an intentional simplification of far more complex realities is necessary for getting groups of people to use the technique in practice.

■ 5.6 The inspection method for solution evaluation purposes

The inspection method was devised by Michael E. Fagan of IBM in 1972–75. It was developed by him and colleagues in the following years for software engineering management. The method will ensure:

- that our goal and solution specifications are complete and internally consistent;
- that the figures in our goal and solution specifications are realistic;
- that our goal and solution specifications are consistent with all the higher level goals of the organization;

The objectives as seen by Project-Leader

Attributes / Objectives	Scale	Worst	Plan	Best	Now
10-year operating cost	$Value '79 +6%Exca+	85–95%	65–85%	40–60%	100%
Interactive response speed	Seconds from 'enter' to response	10–>20 seconds	3–>7 seconds	0–>1 seconds	3–>40
Data integrity	% errors	.5–>1.5%	0.3–0.8	0–0.1%	
Availability	% uptime	93–>97%	96–100	98–100	
Security	corrupt/yr	10–> 20	2–>6 yr	0–>2	
Ease of use	days training	15–>25 d	4–>6 d	0–>2	24– hour blackout
Ease of adding	% impact	2–3% hit	0 hit	0	
User report/analysis	req/yr/sy	6–18 rq	0–>4 r	0–>1	
Data completeness	req/yr/sy	5–>10 rq	0–>1 r	0	
External interface	req/day	3–>5 rq	0–>1 r	0	

High Level Insp.

GOAL INSPECTION

Benefit Analysis of Proposed Project
Objectives Approved by THE PRESIDENT

'multiplicity of information and programs
would be greatly reduced. This translates to
a reduction in the number of programmers...
and a (data storage) space reduction.'
'...It would reduce time spent in searching,
merging and reporting on information.'
'...in an emergency situation... (it) would
aid in the look-up of the required info...

p20
p21

'another advantage...would be the ability
it gives to forecasting maintenance, overhauls,
replacement and inspection of equipment...'
'It could assist the planning department with
data for their prediction of growth potential'
'generate a feeling of responsibility for getting
accurate and up-to-date (data into files)
...allow for growth in technologies...
...sophisticated & flexible tool for engineers'

Defect list
= 20 items

Space reduction
Program reduction
Maintain program reduction
Centralized ?
Forecasting
Data reliability
Accurate information
Up to date
Speed (broad)
+ 1 more
page of
defects.
All in 30 minutes

Figure 5.5 Goal inspection.

- that our specifications are expressed in a way that is clear and unambiguous to all concerned with the project.

An illustration of the high level goal inspection example follows. In 1979 the President of one of the world's largest electricity companies decided to tackle the problem of power failures, for which his company was internationally notorious. He authorized development of a new computer service to do so, by signing a 26-page document for the project (see Figure 5.5, lower left box for sample). This document was translated by the project leader into the required system attributes such as cost, security and degree of centralization (see Figure 5.5 upper left box). These were all made measurable in practice.

As an experiment, an 'inspection' was held of the correlation between what the President said he wanted, and what the project leader was intending to use as guidelines for the project for the next few years. In less than half an hour, a group of 'amateur' inspectors (my course participants) had managed to list more than 20 clear differences (see Figure 5.5, lower right box for sample) between the two documents – an experience which was somewhat of a shock to all concerned.

It wasn't that what the President had signed was hard to understand, or that there was any lack of good will to do things satisfactorily. But it was simply that the right organizational mechanisms (of clear communication) were not in place to help them.

The above is an excellent example of the corruption of communication which can take place when instructions are translated from 'managerese' into 'computerese.' The earlier we can detect such errors in specification and understanding – before solutions are implemented, or before resources have been spent in developing them in detail – the less costly the damage they will do. Inspection is a powerful partner for getting an organization to evaluate the contents of all design and code documentation at the earliest possible stages.

The inspection method is the most effective quality control method for software specification documentation we know about. While it might appear time and cost consuming to implement, the value of catching errors early has been proven to far outweigh the cost of doing inspection.

Inspection is essentially the quality control process (also called 'inspection') described in standard engineering texts. (Juran, 1974). Its general features are as follows:

- *Independent audit:* Inspection is carried out with very little help from the originators of the documentation in question.
- *Trained inspection leaders:* Inspections are led by what IBM calls 'moderators.'

- *Strict rules:* Inspections are carried out in a series of steps like 'individual preparation,' 'public meetings,' 'error-rework.'
- *Specialized roles:* In addition to the moderator role, each of the three to five inspection participants is assigned a specialized activity so that the inspection team results are maximized by a combination of deep specialization and an overlapping of responsibility.
- *Peer review:* Inspections are carried out by colleagues at all levels of seniority.
- *Management data* for work process control: *Statistics* on classes of defect found, and effort used, are kept and used for reports which are analyzed in a manner similar to financial analysis.

Fagan's inspection method can be used at all levels of software documentation, including programming languages. It has its greatest payoff when it is used to discover defects in the system objectives and strategic solutions or architecture.

Further details on the inspection method are found in Chapters 12 and 21.

■ Further reading

Juran, J.M. (ed.), 1974, *Quality control handbook*, 3rd edn., McGraw-Hill, New York

Estimating the risk

■ Introduction

Chapter 6 gives an overview of some of the ways in which we can handle uncertainty and risk.

■ 6.1 Risk

We have taken a brief look at some tools which can help us to define and analyze problems, and identify and evaluate possible solutions. However, the implementation of a solution which is based (as we have shown it is bound to be) on plans containing estimates, approximations and uncertainties, involves risk. The idea of risk is a particularly important one, and deserves more extended treatment.

> 'One of the most rigorous theorems of economics (Boehm–Bawerks Law) proves that the existing means of production will yield greater economic performance only through greater uncertainty, that is, through greater risk. While it is futile to try to eliminate risk, and questionable to try to minimize it, it is essential that the risks taken be the right risks. . . .
>
> We must be able to choose rationally among risk-taking courses of action, rather than plunge into uncertainty on the basis of hunch, hearsay, or incomplete experience, no matter how meticulously quantified.'
>
> Peter Drucker (1975), *Management*, Heinemann

6.1.1 A policy statement on risk control

Here is an example of an attempt to control risk for a software development group of 300 persons. This is the first element of the case study material which is used to illustrate Part Two of this book, the International Banking Corporation. Similar policies have been adopted by a computer manufacturer employing thousands of software engineers.

Example: IBC.Policy

1. *Basic goal*
   Our basic goal, and therefore our measure of success, is to develop systems (computerized or not) which have the *user-value-to-cost ratio* within acceptable limits. This implies that *user-value* of systems must be planned and controlled at all times, and project and operation system *cost* must be planned and controlled at all times.

2. *Future-shock-proof organization*
   The organization shall be able to succeed in spite of *future shock change* (i.e. unexpected high-impact changes) in any part of the environment – e.g. inflation, new business types, people turnover, new organizational forms, organization growth, technological changes, etc.
3. *Goal oriented people*
   Each of our professionals (managers and technicians) shall be selected, managed, and trained to be competent to help us reach planned goals.
   The goal type and planned level shall only be set by group top management, and it is our responsibility to be able to respond to these goals.
4. *Risk identification*
   All *risk elements* shall be explicitly identified and controlled by us at all stages of planning, design and management – i.e., written documentation for risk control must be present in all planning.
5. *Management by objectives*
   All activity (be it managerial, technical or system project) shall be *controlled in all critical attributes*, at all stages of development – that is what we mean by 'management by objectives'.

The risk principle:
If you don't actively attack the risks, they will actively attack you.

■ 6.2 Being responsible for risk

We can draw conclusions for action from what we see, at a fairly early stage, if we are willing to accept a certain risk that such conclusions may be incorrect, partially misleading, or have a calculable degree of error in them.

If we make the mistake of insisting on 100% safe conclusions, then we may be committed to continuing our investigations forever, and no practical change will be implemented. We should rather concentrate on knowing and controlling the degree of risk involved. We should let other people know that we are intentionally doing so. And we should take it upon ourselves to inform others of the degree of risk they run of being wrong when they accept any of our statements as a basis for action.

Knowing that there is a risk, and knowing even approximately what the level of that risk is, is a sign of professional competence.

There are too many professionals who mistakenly believe that to raise issues of risk is a sign of incompetence – because it shows that they do not have full control. This is wrong. Knowing that we must share this understanding of risk with others on our own initiative is a sign of sound professional ethics.

> **The risk sharing principle:**
> The real professional is one who knows the risks, their degree, their causes, and the action necessary to counter them, and shares this knowledge with his colleagues and clients.

■ 6.3 Expecting overruns

If we attempt to carry out large projects with unclear goal statements, inadequate planning, less than wholly competent people, and weak management methods, in areas which are so uncharted as to justify the use of research funds, we should expect overruns of resource expenditure.

We should remember that a professional engineer is expected to make a clear distinction between predictable costs (usually those based on some sort of experience data), and highly unpredictable cost factors (those based on techniques which have an inadequate or incomplete cost history). The question is, how can we, as managers, avoid the worst effects of systems full of unknowns when they 'go wrong on us'?

> **The risk prevention principle:**
> Risk prevention is more cost-effective than risk detection.
>
> **The promise principle:**
> Never make promises you cannot keep, no matter what the pressure.
>
> **The written promise principle:**
> If you do make any promises, make them yourself, and make them in writing.
>
> **The promise caveat principle:**
> When you make a promise, include your estimate of how much deviation could occur for reasons outside of your control, for reasons within your control, and for reasons others in the company can control.

The early reaction principle:
When something happens during the project that you did not foresee, which increases deviation from planned risk, immediately raise the issue, in writing, with your constructive suggestion as to how to deal with it.

The implicit promise principle:
If you suspect someone else – your boss or a client – of assuming you have made promises, then take the time to disclaim them, and repeat the promises you *have* made, if any, in writing.

The deviation principle:
When indicating possible deviation, make a list of the possible causes of deviation, as well as a list of the actions you could take to control those risks.

The written proof principle:
Hang the following sign near your desk: If you haven't got it in writing from me, I didn't promise it.

■ 6.4 Specifying the degree of uncertainty

Management involves constantly making judgements, with varied degrees of risk that these judgements lead to incorrect or inadequate decisions. We are referring here to perfectly ordinary deviations for factors such as human resources requirements, costs, implementation time, effective promised results, and capital investment.

It is common to find that when project goals, budgets and plans are drawn up for management approval, not only are the critical goals vaguely stated, as I have already indicated, but their very vagueness is not stated clearly enough!

For example, it is a poor guide for planning when we state our goals in a form such as 'must be completed as soon as possible.' It is an improvement when we say 'must be completed by 24 December at 17.00 hours G.M.T.' But it would be even more useful, if the realities dictate it, to express the goal like this: 'The project has a planned completion date of 24 December, which is also the earliest conceivable date of completion. There is a high probability of up to one week slippage due to staff sickness conditions, and a slight possibility of a delay of up to one month should the hardware supplier fail to deliver as agreed in the contract.'

In short: '24 Dec. (+7, staff sickness) and (+31, sub-contract delivery).'

When the uncertainty of the estimate is not clearly documented, management lacks information which is vital to its own proper performance.

The principle of risk exposure:
The degree of risk, and its causes, must never be hidden from decision-makers.

Present practices in this area reflect badly on the many managers who do not insist explicitly and regularly on getting clearly documented risk estimates for every significant estimate in every budget and plan. The first planning document you look at will give you examples of this failure. But it is an equally poor reflection on responsible planners and problem solvers who do not take it upon their own professional initiative to provide the 'passive' manager with the stimulant of clear written risk estimates. I have on several occasions suggested, and had accepted as planning policy, a version of the following statement:

> 'All significant, large and critical-to-success estimates are to be
> accompanied by an explicit written estimate of plus and minus
> deviations from the planned number, date or amount. This will be
> done even when no deviation is 'expected' or 'allowed.' Footnotes
> will explain the probable causes or reasons why such deviations
> could occur, so that management can evaluate the deviation
> estimates themselves, take action to limit the causes, and so
> become responsible for accepting these conditions as known risks.'

This was one of five policy statements in 'IBC. POLICY,' see Section 6.1.

You might like to consider the effect of such a policy in your own working environment. It will probably take no more than a single trial – of insisting on it being done thoroughly on one single project – to convince you that you must continue to do so for your own future protection and peace of mind.

The asking principle:
If you don't ask for risk information, you are asking for trouble.

■ 6.5 The most critical part of an estimate

The most important part of a result, a measure, an estimate, a conclusion, or a prediction is not the quantitative statement itself. It is the confidence we can place in the figures.

The cost of a project is estimated at, say, 500 work-months effort, and this has been accepted. The estimator is the first to be criticized when the actual effort turns out to be 750 work-months. If, on the other hand, the estimate was originally 500 plus or minus 300 work-months ('depending on the quality of the work-force'), then the manager who accepts the estimates is in a very different position. If he does not act to get the necessary quality of people actually working on the project, or even find out what is meant by 'quality' here, he has only himself to blame when the actual figure turns out to be 790 work-months.

I am suggesting that managers be more exposed to criticism on these grounds. But I am also suggesting that they be given more opportunity to get control of such unpleasant realities before they take effect in the real world.

One other simple way of expressing a risk element, and one which we can combine with the 'plus-or-minus deviation' idea, is the use of 'best,' 'worst,' 'planned' and 'now' levels when specifying attribute goals. (See Sections 9.7, 9.8, 9.9, 9.10 for details on these attribute levels.) Each one of these sheds light on the others, and provides a focal point for discussion as to how big the difference really is, why there is a difference, and how reliable each one of those figures actually is.

For example, if the best known performance level for a system is 99.98% availability, and the planned level is set at 99.999%, then these two pieces of information together tell a manager that a state of the art breakthrough is needed to meet the planned level. The risk of failure, or at least higher than expected costs, is very high. If, in addition, the worst acceptable level is set at only 99% while the present level is also 99%, the manager might feel better about the risk involved. After all, the level was achieved in the old system. That does not make it taken-for-granted in a new system, but at least the way to get there has been explored.

■ 6.6 A software maintenance cost example

An example follows showing software maintenance cost per line of code changed:

Present cost: $100 per line of code changed (varies between $55 and $205 depending on volume ordered).
Planned cost (by today plus two years): $45 (+ $20 due to design uncertainty).
Worst acceptable case cost: $90 (management refuse to sponsor a new system which does not result in a net saving).
Best observed case: $30 to $50 ('a corresponding company in town reported reducing their costs to the $30 level last year. Nothing better is recorded or promised.').

We should not be afraid of bringing out the truth here, because even great uncertainty, if made clear and public at an early stage, can lead directly to efforts to avoid the 'worst case' from happening, to make the planned level happen, and even to move in the direction of the best case.

■ 6.7 The 'best case delivery date' example

A project team member in New York, when we asked about the 'best case' delivery date for a software application development project, gave it as 'right now.' His colleagues tried actively to suppress his oral statement and avoid recording it. They were afraid that management would misinterpret it, and expect the entire project, with all whistles and bells, to be available immediately, instead of in the six months time which was planned.

When it was clearly explained that this early delivery date was only a valid estimate for the most critical and basic functions of the new system, things quietened down a bit. It turned out that management were both surprised and pleased by this information, and wanted to exercise the early partial delivery option.

The possibility of early delivery had never been discussed, up to that point, by anyone. Management almost missed an important competitive advantage by not asking for the 'best case.' They had also failed to create a climate where project members were unafraid to discuss such notions of deviation from 'the main plan.'

> **The 'why not the best?' principle:**
> The 'best imaginable' can be a reality, if you are willing to risk or sacrifice any other planned attributes.

■ 6.8 Try your own risk estimation

You might like to try out this on a few elements in a project of your own. Here are some simple ways in which we can specify the risk element by:

- determining various levels of an attribute (best, worst, planned, now);

- finding plus and minus deviation estimates for each figure;

- estimating the probability (which is also an uncertainty, but is still a useful way of expressing things) that a certain result will occur;

- listing the factors which can contribute to the stated variations in a particular estimate;

- simply putting a '?' after the estimate (e.g. best = 300 months ? – TG 880731). Include 'who' and 'when' information as well.

■ 6.9 Create the motivation for getting control

Common sense, openness, imagination, simple ways of expressing yourself, and the will to communicate with others effectively will all go a long way towards making predictions realistic. Realistic predictions, and the promises implied by them, are one step towards controlling the ultimate results.

Bear in mind that strong motivation (in managers and planners alike) to get and keep control over results, has an observable and decisive influence on whether or not results tend to be achieved satisfactorily, in spite of the mischievous nature of the world around us.

What have you done to create motivation to achieve results? Does everybody get paid the same no matter how badly the project runs? Do the people who keep promises, if any, get ample rewards and honors? Does your staff have a real slice of the action – like shares in your small software house, or a share of the profits via a bonus scheme? Do people who cannot keep their promises get smoked out early and corrected in their ways? Have you or your company executives created the fear that makes people make silly promises, and then make excuses. Or are people unafraid to be realistic?

6.9.1 A motivational example: Fridays free

In one case, with an application product software subsidary of a computer manufacturer, I got the Director's agreement (much to our surprise) to the following motivation idea. The development teams would plan for weekly incremental delivery of 'something working.' If they succeeded in getting it demonstrable by the end of Thursday, they could use Friday for professional purposes other than their project work. For example: attend lectures, study trips to exhibitions, research projects, write technical papers, read technical literature, or study other parts of the organization.

The group was left free to make its own plan, however small. The important thing was to be oriented towards live software results to be delivered every week, which the Director could see, and show his colleagues, as visible evidence of progress. He had been very disturbed, as was I, by a culture which allowed months to slip by with no visible progress in terms of working usable systems. We both felt that the groups would get more useful work done in those four days, than five days with no focus on results.

I stayed on for the initial planning of projects on the weekly basis. It was surprising to learn how wrong we could be about how much (or how little) we could actually get done in a week. But we kept on iterating the plans until we learned to be more realistic. This process helped us to reduce the danger of being wrong in relation to plans. It was a good thing we were doing this learning on a weekly scale rather than a yearly scale!

The uncertainty motivation principle:
Uncertainty in a technical project is half technical and half motivational, but with good enough motivation, uncertainty will not be allowed to lead to problems.

■ 6.10 Uncertainty and risk specification using impact estimation

Those who wish to get a really detailed evaluation of risk elements should refer to Chapter 11 for the description of impact estimation tables. See particularly Section 11.7 safety factors, Section 11.5 side-effect estimation, Section 11.3 limitations, Section 11.10 justification of an estimate, and other parts of this chapter.

Impact estimation is an application of the concept of 'cost estimation' to all the other attributes of a planned system. Impact estimation is limited to early planning stages. It is a modelling idea, when you need something more precise than the general risk estimation methods discussed earlier in the chapter.

However, there comes a stage when it is necessary to get 'risk feedback' from the project implemented in the real world. At this point we will use a different tool entirely, evolutionary delivery. See Chapter 7 for an initial discussion of evolutionary delivery methods.

Paper models (such as impact estimation) of complex systems can never replace the more certain knowledge of a real system working with a real user. This is where evolutionary delivery is vital, because it gives us that certain knowledge before we have committed too many of our resources to the wrong ideas. Even then there are uncertainties about the future and about scaling up.

Ng's visibility principle:
We don't trust it until we can see it and feel it.

The reality principle:
Theoretical estimation is as accurate as our oversimplified estimation models backed by obsolete historical data. The real thing is a somewhat more reliable indicator.

■ 6.11 The software import risk example

One European client, a computer manufacturer, decided to base the software for a new line of computers on the UNIX operating system and the C programming language. They found they could buy a basic package for this from a software house in California which was supplying many of my client's competitors with the same software. This decision was dictated by top management; the development team was given no say, nor was their advice asked. The marketing decision was that their market wanted (or would want) UNIX and importing the basic software for adaptation was obviously the best way to do it.

At one point I began to explore, with the quality manager, exactly what we knew about the quality requirements for the project, and for the imported component. It was quite clear that the quality requirements for our product were quite high. They included zero defects to customers in our final product, and no more than two minutes downtime per 48-hour period for the entire hardware-software delivery to our customers.

The imported component was a large part of our total delivery, much more than half, and furthermore was central to all other components. If it failed, they failed. I asked what we knew of error rates, etc. for the imported components. Nothing – what we were going to get was the 'latest,' of which there was, of course, no experience.

I asked if we had contractually committed the supplier to any particular quality levels, and appropriate acceptance tests, which were critical to our product. Apparently this had been considered unnecessary by the managers who had started all this, because, I was told, 'no matter how bad it is, our competitors will have the same bad software.'

All this was a breach of the formal company guidelines designed to improve the quality of all products, as my quality manager colleague and I knew quite well. I helped write them – and he was among the leaders in implementing them. But the decisions were apparently taken so high up (lab director level, I believe, but even this was unclear) that nobody dared challenge them.

What is the risk that the project will fail?

The final chapter of this story is not known as I write this so the reader is left with an exercise to guess what the risks are.

Here is a set of questions you can ask yourself in order to analyze a situation like the example given above.

1. What is the probability that the product will ever meet the quality specifications?
2. What is the probability that the product will be severely delayed while they try to bring it up to some minimally acceptable specifications?
3. What is the probability that at least one competitor will handle this situation in a smarter manner?
4. What is the probability that the lab director will try to lay the blame on the software development team?
5. What should the software development team do to defend themselves, and their company, against this situation?
6. What is the probability that the lab director will lose face and power – if he regularly violates company policy regarding quality, and takes quality out of the hands of the developers?

■ Further reading

Peters, T., and Waterman, R., 1982, *In search of excellence*, Harper and Row/Warner Books, New York. (Ng's Principle source)

7

An introduction to the 'evolutionary delivery' method

■ Introduction

Most textbooks and most of today's software engineering models are based on the 'waterfall model' for delivery. This can take several forms, but the principal characteristics are:

- all planning is oriented towards a single delivery date. If phased delivery is used, the phase units are substantial, and there is no formal concept of 'reworking' unsatisfactory phases.
- all analysis and design are done in detail, before coding and test.

The delivery date is normally one or more years after project start. There may be some effort to improve the design by means of prototypes. But these prototypes will usually be 'throw away.' There will be little or no real useful work by users done on them. See Figure 7.1.

The evolutionary delivery (evo) method is based on the following simple principle:

Deliver something to a real end-user.
Measure the added-value to the user in all critical dimensions.
Adjust both design and objectives based on observed realities.

The basic evo concepts are firmly rooted in engineering literature and engineering practice in other disciplines. It is time the software community recognized the potential of the method, and exploited it fully.

The 'eternal cycle' (Deming, 1986) starts early. It will usually entail modifying some existing system, rather than building a totally new one. This in itself reduces risk. It is simpler to modify a small part of an existing system and easier to get end-user testing carried out. Many projects, to permit design ideas to be tried out at all, waste considerable time and effort redeveloping sufficient parts of a system just to get small improvements tested. This is often really unnecessary – but people blindly do it.

The simplest software model of evo delivery is a personal computer user building an application for himself interactively. The personal computer programmer then becomes the user, the setter of objectives, the analyst, the designer, the coder and the tester. There is constant iteration from the earliest stages as the system is built up. The iteration cycle is typically measured in minutes, not years. The system being built is real and evolving. Users can modify design, coding detail and even their final objectives.

Evolutionary delivery consists of a collection of many concepts. The more fundamental ones are listed below. Planners can choose to

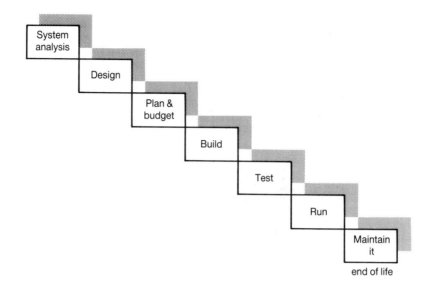

Figure 7.1 The software life cycle. This is characterized by little or no formal feedback and learning. It also requires freezing the requirements and design specification at an unrealistically early stage of knowledge and experience.

ignore some of them, but the method will lose some of its power if they do.

Planners may well find ideas additional to those mentioned here. I find that by experience and experimentation, I am constantly learning new ways to use the basic concepts better, and therefore do not pretend that the present model is complete. But it is more advanced than most models which I have found in the literature on the subject or in practice. Figure 7.2 illustrates three development models.

Here is a list of the main critical concepts. It may be taken as a superficial definition of what I mean by 'evo planning.'

1. Multi-objective driven,
2. Early, frequent iteration,
3. Complete analysis, design, build and test in each step,
4. User orientation,
5. Systems approach, not merely algorithm orientation,
6. Open-ended basic systems architecture,
7. Result orientation, not software development process orientation.

All these concepts will now be exploded into more detail with the

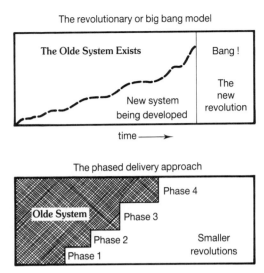

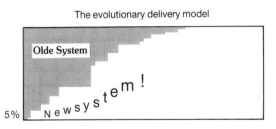

Figure 7.2 Development models. Here is a simple comparison between the non-evolutionary model, characterized by steps typically involving a year or more before delivery, and the evolutionary delivery model which typically has many more and smaller delivery steps. In addition, the evolutionary model makes substantial use of the existing system as a starting base.

following breakdown of the critical characteristics of evolutionary delivery planning.

■ 7.1 Planning for multiple objectives

Conventional software planning is overwhelmingly 'function' oriented. Planning is done in terms of the functional deliverables, i.e. *what* the software will do, rather than *'how well?'* (quality attributes) and *'at what cost?'* (the resource attributes). Present day software engineering places

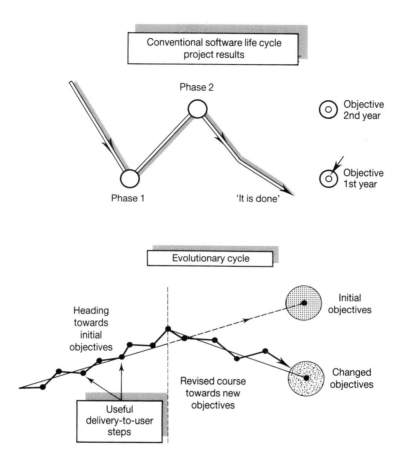

Figure 7.3 The conventional cycle versus the evolutionary one. The conventional software life cycle (top) starts with an approved but unclearly specified and communicated goal during the first year. In gigantic leaps of effort (Phase 1 and Phase 2) the project moves in roughly the right direction. Part way through the project, the objectives change ('objective second year') but this does not really matter since there is no way of matching the exact requirements to the project results. Finally, out of sheer exhaustion, the team declares that the project is completed and, again, because of unclear goal specification, who can argue? In the evolutionary alternative (bottom), the situation is the same but there is much better control over definition and measurement of objectives.

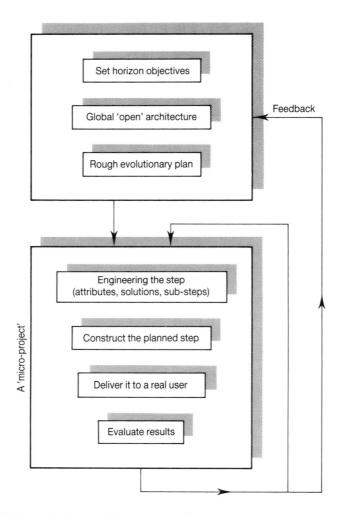

Figure 7.4 The evolutionary delivery cycle. The upper box is the long-term control mechanism and can be modified according to experience. The lower box is the 'microproject' and can fruitfully use a conventional software waterfall model's life cycle for cycles that are somewhere between one week and one quarter of a year in duration.

too little emphasis on control of the critical quality and resource attributes of the system, and thereby loses control of these attributes. A simple example is the general lack of knowledge among software engineers and teachers on such topics as how to define critical attributes like 'usability' (see Gilb (1984a) for a detailed example) or 'maintainability' (see Gilb, 1979). These subjects are so vital to the success of most present day software projects that ignorance of how to specify measures of them is roughly equivalent to an electronics engineer not knowing what volts and watts are.

Evolutionary delivery is based on iteration towards clear and measurable multidimensional objectives. The set of objectives must contain all functional, quality and resource objectives which are vital to the long-term and short-term survival of the system under development (see Gilb, 1976b).

This discipline is missing from almost every international software project I have encountered (though some are better than others). Such projects are not, in this respect, related to the real world needs of the user.

■ 7.2 Early, frequent iteration

In most software engineering projects, the planning schedule allows for delivery of the first practical and useful results one or more years ahead. There are a number of apparently plausible excuses for this lack of early confrontation with real users by developers, but in my view these excuses are invalid. I have found that the original planners of such projects are themselves the first to agree that there is, in fact, a real possibility of earlier delivery which they had not considered. Their problem in finding early and frequent software delivery cycles is one of both lack of motivation and lack of method.

The management of such projects would, of course, dearly love to get some results as early as possible. But that same management accepts the conventional wisdom that there is a long initial cycle before the first useful phase is delivered. Often project management believe that their 'phased' project does in fact give them the earliest possible delivery of something useful. My experience is that most such first phases can be sub-divided into anything between ten and one hundred smaller and earlier steps of useful delivery.

Phased planning asks a dangerous question: 'How much can we accomplish within some critical constraint (budget, deadline, storage space)?' Evo planning asks a very different question: 'How little development resource can we expend, and still accomplish something useful in the direction of our ultimate objectives?'

More formally, in evo planning today, we use the concept of selecting the potential steps with the highest user-value to development-cost ratio for earliest implementation. This is really like skimming the cream off the top of the milk.

Such 'user-value' may be financial. It may be of other kinds. It might prove to senior management that computer systems could be of some use in sorting out their pet problem. This obtains their support and goodwill for the rest of the system. It might be a try-out for a high risk part of the system in order to permit more time for redesign and evaluation of any difficulties.

I would like to stress that selection of high value/cost steps is a fundamental distinguishing feature in my own formal conception of evolutionary planning, in contrast to that which I have found elsewhere. Generally I find that there is little or no conscious thought about this 'cream' selection potential. On the contrary, I find that the first phases are often known to give little or no real value – but they are thought to be 'pathways to the future.'

In one case, in a European airline project, the first 50 planned work-years of a 250 work-year project were concerned with building a database system, which gave absolutely no value in the direction of the critical objectives! Of course it was rejected by the Board of Directors.

■ 7.3 Complete analysis, design, build and test at each step

One of the great time-wasters in software projects is detailed requirements analysis, followed by detailed design, followed by full coding and testing phases. If only we had the intellectual capacity, and the necessary knowledge, to do those things accurately! In reality, we have to admit that we cannot tackle such tasks adequately for any but trivially small projects. There are too many unknowns, too many dynamic changes, and too complex a set of interrelationships in the systems we build. We must take a more humble approach.

Even a large system development effort should be viewed only as an evolutionary increment in the life of the system. The introduction of the new system will change the environment. Such considerations point to the need for an open architectural framework, to be able to be open for change at all times.

We must set initial measurable objectives as far as we can reasonably have an opinion about the future. We must be prepared to modify these objectives as soon as experience (of partial delivery) dictates it. We must design a suitable general architectural framework (I call it the softecture, which is a short expression for software

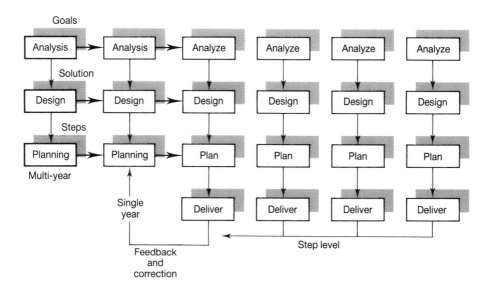

Figure 7.5 The evo cycle spread out. This illustrates the fact that with evolutionary delivery cycles, the various development activities are intermixed and spread out throughout the life cycle. Each activity feeds the others with practical insight and experience.

architecture) for enabling us to meet these objectives in spite of unexpected negative factors along the way.

We must set measurable objectives for each next small delivery step. Even these are subject to constant modification as we learn about reality. It is simply not possible to set an ambitious set of multiple quality, resource and functional objectives, and be sure of meeting them all as planned. We must be prepared for compromise and trade-off. We must then design (engineer) the immediate technical solution, build it, test it, deliver it – and get feedback. This feedback must be used to modify the immediate design (if necessary), modify the major architectural ideas (if necessary), and modify both the short-term and the long-term objectives (if necessary).

It is absurd to spend – in fact waste – so much time at the beginning of a project, to speculate on requirements and technical design attributes which can be measured much more cheaply and reliably if it is done while we implement a real working system.

The major objection to this line of action is the fear (based on experience) that we will 'paint ourselves into a corner', and that when we get negative feedback, it will be too late. We will have committed too many resources to the wrong solution. This objection is not valid.

Evolutionary delivery is devised to give us early warning signals of impending unpleasant realities. Unpleasantries do occur, but they never get a chance to become too large. We must learn to design far more 'open-ended' system architectures.

Up to now we have perceived our problem as one of analyzing things in enough detail, before any real construction takes place, to prevent construction errors. This is not as easy, or as productive, as the evolutionary alternative. Start with a basic design which is easy to modify, adapt, port and change; both in the long and short terms. Start using the system, and learn even more, even earlier – while being useful.

■ 7.4 User orientation

Software projects are not noted for their successful adaptation to what the market or user really needs or wants. The orientation is more often towards the machine, the algorithm, or the deadline – but too rarely the user. Many software developers literally never see their product in action with real users.

Most users never see the faces of the designers and programmers. They don't even know their names. Even if the developers did want to make a product which the users were really happy with, it is often too late and too impractical to do so by the time they find out what the user really wants.

With evolutionary delivery, the situation is changed. The developer is specifically charged with 'listening' to user reactions, early and often. The user can play a direct role in the development process. Neither the budget, nor the deadline are overrun. The overall system architecture is 'open ended,' and we are mentally, economically, and technically prepared to listen to what the user or customer wants.

The principle of selecting the highest available value-to-cost ratio step next is a dynamic one. User values can and should alter as users get experience. Valuable user ideas can give the planners a flow of new ideas, which were not in the original plans. If they are better ideas – we must find practical and economic ways of implementing them as soon as possible.

Every system developer should recognize the need for feedback, the inevitability of changes of ideas about value, and the learning of development cost estimation through experience. It is common sense. The need for applying learning and selection mechanisms earlier, more consciously and more frequently in the development process is clear from our everyday experience.

■ 7.5 Systems approach, not algorithm orientation

Many of our software engineering methods have a common weakness. They are exclusively oriented towards current computer programming languages. They do not even treat software, in the broadest (i.e. non-hardware) sense of that term. They do precious little about the Data Engineering (see Gilb, 1976a, and Gilb and Weinberg, 1984) aspects of software, and do even less about less obvious concerns such as documentation, training, marketing, and motivation (see 'Motivational Techniques for Reliability' in Gilb, 1976a). A contrast to all this will be found in the Apple Macintosh design effort – outstanding amongst other reasons because everything was designed in a fully integrated manner (see *Byte* 2/84). I often think that the real problem with software engineering is the lack of total architectural co-ordination of the system design process as a whole, of which software is merely a part.

Evolutionary delivery is a method which is not merely limited to software, in the narrow sense of that word. It is admirably suited to any creative process in which we are involved. It means that potentially 'ivory tower' programmers meet the real world early, often, and brutally, if necessary.

■ 7.6 Open-ended basic systems architecture

There is a clear need for both literature and teaching on open-ended technological solutions – the hundreds of them that exist. Not merely the 'pop' approach of standards, de facto standards, and structures. Old foxes learn by experience, but how shall we teach the young foxes what the old ones have learned so painfully – in time to avoid creating disasters?

Among the principal attributes of any system are those which allow it to survive and succeed under conditions which change with the passage of time. A good software engineer, or softect, should be making a continuous and detailed study of the many available design technologies which lead to systems which are more adaptable than others. There are a number of measurable technical properties here, such as maintainability, portability and extendability (see Chapter 19).

In terms of evolutionary delivery planning, open architectures are essential. Without them the effort will probably get caught in the all-too-familiar swamp of current software maintenance experience. The blame will be laid at the wrong door. 'We didn't plan in enough detail before we started coding!' they will say. The real truth is that it was

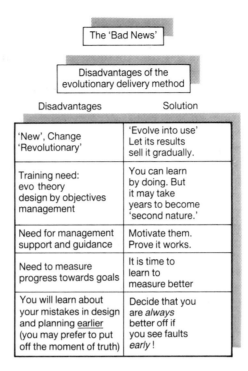

Figure 7.6 All methods have some problems and disadvantages to balance the positive aspects. Evolutionary delivery is no exception.

impossible in any case to know that much complex detail in advance of real experience. The real truth is that they didn't have a sufficiently open-ended structure to tolerate the change.

A good designer can always list at least ten reasonable ways to solve a design problem. In addition, the design engineer must have or find knowledge of the principle attributes of quality and resource, since these are the essential differentiators between the alternative solutions.

■ 7.7 Result orientation, not software development process orientation

In a traditional waterfall model software development cycle, the process itself seems more important than the result. I have often seen my clients' software engineering people paralyzed by the formalities of a process when there were no clear objectives towards which to steer the effort. The situation is so bad in this respect world-wide that I am

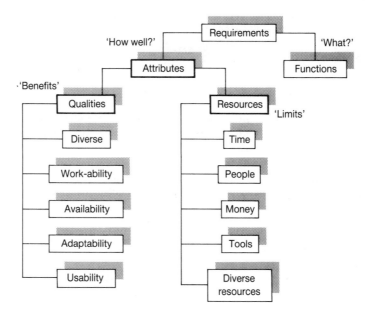

Figure 7.7 Some result requirements areas. The user-defined function and attribute requirements are the basic language for defining the results expected in each evolutionary step.

prepared to maintain that all large software engineering efforts at present have extremely unclear, unmeasurable and unstated objectives in critical quality and resource areas. You can try looking at 'usability' and 'maintainability' just for starters.

■ 7.8 On not knowing, and keeping it small and simple

You may well, after reading this book, arrive at the important conclusion: 'I don't know!' more frequently, and with less of a bad conscience than before. In fact there is no reason at all to feel uncomfortable about not knowing. On the contrary, you have just made one of the most important steps towards knowing.

Even in quite simple cases, the outcome of implementing our projects is difficult to predict with accuracy. Unexpected results or events become critical multipliers of the ultimate project attributes, and usually in the 'wrong' direction! There is a very generally applicable solution to this problem of result control. It is based on the principle of Schumacher (1973).

> **The 'small is beautiful' principle:**
> It is easier to see and deal with the effect of one small increment of the solution, than it is to understand the impact of the entire solution at once.

This is really no more than the basic principle of scientific experiment: keeping all factors but one constant, and examining the effects of varying the one. In this case we take a single small implementation step as the factor we 'vary,' and we look at the effects of that variation on our planned goals. The principle of keeping implementation steps small and simple has been appreciated for a long time (Lao Tzu in Bahn, 1980).

> **The principles of Tao Teh Ching:**
> That which remains quiet, is easy to handle.
> That which is not yet developed is easy to manage.
> That which is weak is easy to control.
> That which is still small is easy to direct.
> Deal with little troubles before they become big.
> Attend to little problems before they get out of hand.
> For the largest tree was once a sprout,
> the tallest tower started with the first brick,
> and the longest journey began with a first step.

Evolutionary delivery is about as basic as the way in which we walk about, or drive a car. There is a constant feedback from the environment telling us if it is safe, economic, and comfortable enough to continue towards our ultimate goal as we are presently doing.

We use such methods, up to a point, in our project implementation, for example 'phase two,' 'pilot test.' But our use of this magnificent (and purely common sense) tool is seriously underdeveloped. By conscious and full exploitation of evolutionary delivery ideas, we can not only exercise far better control over risk elements, but we can also gain many other important benefits as software engineering managers.

■ 7.9 The driving and chess analogies

Evolutionary delivery is very much like chess. You can have a strategy, but you have to respond to the immediate realities of the opponent's last move, or you will not survive. Any attempt to play out a grand strategy in spite of the realities is doomed. The Grand Master of Chess, the Cuban, José Raul Capablanca Y Granperra (1888–1942, world champion 1921–1927) is reported to have commented on people's interest in depth of search in playing chess, by a remark to this effect.

Capablanca's next-move principle:
There is only one move that really counts: the next one.

When driving an automobile, we must think ahead and plan our driving. But we are not absolutely committed to driving the way we plan, because something might unexpectedly get in our way and make such plans dangerous.

Can you imagine anything as silly as planning a drive from London to Rome, street by street, in great detail, and then trying to execute it, perhaps using a computer, without allowing for any deviations whatsoever in route or timing? Can you imagine the wasted planning effort trying to make sure that the plan would not fail at any point? For how many days would you have to plan to make a 'perfect' plan? Won't road conditions (weather, congestion, repairs) change by the time your plans hit the road? Isn't it obviously better, after a certain minimum of planning, to note the general route, making sure you have good road maps and extra time for contingencies, and to get into the car and start driving? Won't you in fact get there much faster if you go out there and confront the real situation, solving unexpected problems as they occur? Of course you will, and I would like to argue that exactly the same method is valid for complex problem-solving and project implementation.

Similarly, in playing chess, we certainly have our eyes on the goal of winning the game, or at least not losing it. Also, we may have thought out certain strategies and tactics of play. We may even have a clear notion of what we intend to do if our opponent makes certain moves in reply to our next moves. But, we neither have to commit ourselves to making these moves, nor do we.

Evolutionary delivery is very similar to chess, driving and many other activities such as management, games and sports. The un-expected is a natural part of the game, so it is not wise to plan in detail exactly what you are going to do. It is wiser to put your energy into being able and free to make an adequate reply no matter what the opponent does.

For example (as we shall discuss more fully in Chapter 13) in evolutionary delivery planning situations, we emphasize the necessity of creating an 'open-ended' system architecture. This simply means that we try to position ourselves so that any change, no matter how unexpected, is relatively easy to cope with, without major changes in the system we are evolving.

In conventional systems development, too much energy is spent trying to be sure what the user will need in detail – a hopeless task indeed – for the user is not in full control of his needs. Not enough energy is spent making an open-ended architecture, so that 'unexpected' user needs can easily be covered. I have found that it costs little or no extra to build open-ended systems in the short term. This is because you are not building specific logic and data to cope for specific events. You are merely putting the equivalent of 'electrical sockets' (or data interfaces, if you prefer) into the wall of your system – in order to allow new and different things, which may occur, to happen.

■ 7.10 Some characteristics of evolutionary steps

Only at the delivery of the first sub-step has the system some kind of reality, because now the first delivery step's implementation can give us some realistic feedback. We can now learn from this initial delivery stage in terms of its attributes. How long did it really take? How many other critical planned or budgeted resources did it consume (the unexpected and unwelcome side-effects)? Are we on a healthy path, or do we perhaps have a totally wrong global design?

Each step should have a planned and easy retreat path, in case we have overstepped our ability. One simple strategy for saving face here is to call each step an experiment until it is clearly successful: it is in fact an experiment! If it fails, declare the experiment to be a success in learning about what would not be suitable for implementation on a larger scale.

The Norwegian mountain survival principle:
You need never be ashamed of turning back in time.

Each step should be a useful step – providing some immediately useful results, ideally with the planned return-on-investment, or benefits, achieved. This shouldn't be too difficult to begin with, if you can pick the most promising things to implement first.

The juicy bits first principle:
If you deliver the juiciest bits of the project first, you will be forgiven for not providing all they dreamt about, or for not doing it as cheaply and quickly as they hoped.

'Juiciest' is a term used here to mean 'the most useful-to-the-user steps,' perhaps also in relation to their cost. The formal and measurable definition of this user value is defined by the 'quality' attribute requirements and the functional requirements specified by the user. It is worth noting that the initially specified requirements may have to change as time goes on, and thus the definition of exactly what is 'juicy' will change correspondingly. In effect, we have to recognize that it may be necessary to ask at each step, 'What is now the next best step?' It may not be possible to preplan the best set of steps since it is not possible to know which user requirements will change as time goes on. This is uncomfortable, but unavoidable, so evolutionary delivery just tries to find the best way of accommodating the dynamic situation.

Each step we take provides feedback, which should be used for the more detailed planning of the next and subsequent steps. This is not unlike what happens as we drive, and hear a radio report of a traffic jam ahead, whereupon we decide to find an alternative route, or even stop for a meal somewhat earlier than planned, in the hope that the jam will clear up before we continue.

Each step taken provides us with facts from the real world, which can be used in subsequent planning and implementation steps. If we had planned the project as a whole, in detail, before starting (the 'revolutionary' as opposed to 'evolutionary' method) we would now have had the effort of re-planning our detailed but 'unrealistic' plans for the project as a whole. Using the evo method, the detailed plans we do make are based on experience with the subject at hand, and are far more realistic than they otherwise would have been.

The mountain goat principle:
Take one step at a time up the slippery mountainside, and make absolutely sure that each hoof is on solid ground before you take the next step.

We can adjust our plans in accordance with realities, and this means that management gets a continuous and increasingly more accurate picture of the long-range resource-use, benefits (and snags!) to be expected.

Such adjustments of the global estimates might conceivably lead to recognition that the benefit-to-cost ratio of the project is of a doubtful nature. This in turn might lead to early major changes in the basic architecture of the solution ('get rid of that supplier'). It might lead to dropping the entire project, before it damages your reputation and uses too much of your resources. It is really very bad management to spend five years getting nowhere, as in the CIS project (Chapter 1),

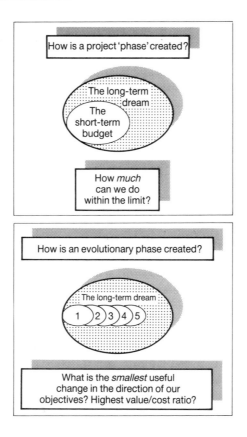

Figure 7.8 The key distinction between phased and evo planning. In phased planning, the phases are so large and complicated that true costs are impossible to estimate accurately. Evolutionary steps are, by contrast, much smaller and simpler to understand. Even if they are wrong, the scale of the error is small.

instead of finding out that you are on the wrong path, admitting it to yourself, and changing things, within a few weeks or months.

Traditional phased projects, which initially might seem to you to be 'evolutionary,' are created by asking that fatal question 'how much?' (of our long term dream can we do within some limit). Evolutionary planning always asks that 'small is beautiful' question: 'how little?' (i.e. how little work can we do and still produce high value for our users or customers).

The 'how little?' principle:
An ideal next evolutionary step costs as little as possible to
implement, and gives as much as possible in the way of results to
the end user.

■ 7.11 Example: the Swedish map-making system

A systems house client of mine had won a prestige contract with the
Swedish Government. It was small ($100 000, including off-the-shelf
hardware, and an estimated six work-months of software effort) but it
spelled the beginning of an interesting export business if carried out
satisfactorily. The contract fixed a delivery date (revolution, all at once)
three months hence. Two experienced people were assigned. There
was a fixed-price contract for labor and hardware.

When we made a formal attribute requirements specification, it
became clear that this system required far more documentation and
maintenance-support tools than anyone had envisaged. This was
because the software had to be maintained abroad, at the customer
site. The initial cost estimates were based on a similar system,
maintained domestically by the system builders themselves. Here is a
classic example of remembering the functional requirements ('a
geographical survey data capture system for drawing maps') but
forgetting to engineer and cost-estimate those attributes which
ultimately determine cost (like 'maintainability' and 'usability').

We decided to swallow the bitter pill of building maintenance tools
at our own cost, in order to maintain our reputation on the market. We
also noted that salesmen should never again be allowed to fix contract
prices on systems of unspecified quality, and without our engineering
design co-operation. This resulted in a higher quality ('maintainability'
was the critical attribute here) system design. And our estimates said
that it involved twice as much work (1500 more lines of code of
FORTRAN) than had been expected and contracted for.

We divided the project, as small as it was, into about ten
evolutionary delivery steps. Each step was useful to the government
customer. The first steps gave the fundamental automated systems.
The next steps built in more sophistication and automation. And, the
last steps gave the required maintenance aids and user-training
documentation.

After about two steps were delivered, our experience feedback told
us that the final increment would not be ready until about two or three
months after the contract delivery date. Not only that, but both our

team members were on sick-leave part of the time, and both got involved putting out 'fires' in earlier projects. The customer was consulted before we panicked into overtime, weekends, and before more (less knowledgeable) staff were brought into the project.

The reaction of the customer speaks a lot for the evolutionary delivery method. 'What do you mean, late?,' they said. 'You have already delivered things we can work with, early. We have more than enough to do just learning to use the system. Thanks for the warning, but the latter parts of the delivery are not critical to us at the moment, and we would prefer that you concentrate on doing a high quality job in whatever additional time it takes you.'

The final increments of the project were 'three months late,' but the client treated the project in public and in private as though it was delivered early!

> **The never-too-small-for-evolution principle:**
> When you think your project is too small for evolutionary step delivery, you have probably misjudged the real size of your project.

■ 7.12 Large-scale evolutionary delivery: industrial experience

This principle does not only apply to smaller projects. The author and his clients have personally used the method on dozens of projects, some of them involving several hundred work-years of effort in a wide variety of industries, as have IBM Federal Systems Division, System Development Corporation (SDC) and various defense projects.

7.12.1 System development corporation experiences

Carolyn Wong of System Development Corporation reported in *IEEE Transactions on Software Engineering*, November 1984, that using 'incremental build, implementation and test' gave a number of advantages. First it gave the result that 'all products were delivered within budget and within schedule.' Also 'by building identifiable and measurable functional capabilities incrementally, it provides earlier and more accurate progress measurement and control.' Further, 'critical or high risk software can be tested in an operational environment earlier in the project. Control software is continually tested and retested. Problem tracing is facilitated (limited controlled components are added

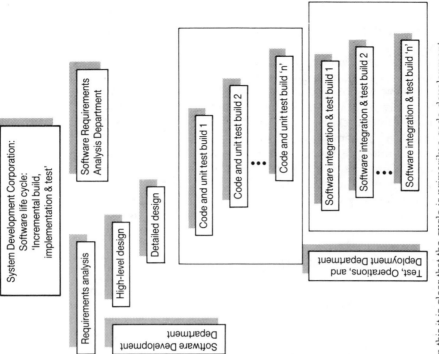

System Development Corporation:
Software life cycle:
'Incremental build,
implementation & test'

Software Requirements
Analysis Department

Requirements analysis

High-level design

Detailed design

Software Development
Department

Code and unit test build 1

Code and unit test build 2

•••

Code and unit test build 'n'

Software integration & test build 1

Software integration & test build 2

•••

Software integration & test build 'n'

Test, Operations, and
Deployment Department

SDC experiences with
evolutionary delivery
'incremental build,
implementation & test'

'ADS software...all products delivered
within budget & within schedule'

• A number of advantages
  over the traditional process
  of completing the coding
  phases before initiating testing.

• By building identifiable and
  measurable functional capabilities
  incrementally, it provides earlier
  and more accurate progress
  measurement and control.

• Critical or high risk software can
  be tested in an operational
  environment earlier in the project.

• Control software is continually
  tested and retested.

• Problem tracing is facilitated
  (limited controlled components
  are added incrementally).

• Requirements control, design, code development scheduling, integration, and testing are all conducted on the basis
  of functional capabilities. This provides high assurance
  that the final system will meet all requirements.

Figure 7.9 This is how SDC illustrates their software life cycle. From this it is clear that the cycle is primarily a code development evolution and does not include system analysis and design. Source: Wong, C, IEEE Trans. on Software Engineering, November 1984. (© 1984 IEEE)

incrementally).' Finally, she said, 'requirements control, design, code development scheduling, and testing are all conducted on the basis of functional capabilities. This provides high assurance that the final system will meet all requirements.'

It is worth noting that SDC's version of evolutionary delivery is not completely what we are recommending in this book. It seems primarily limited to code evolution, and functional steps. It does not explicitly include a systems evolution, open-ended architecture, evolution towards multiple measurable quality attributes or even direct hand-overs to final users (perhaps the most important single distinction). But, in spite of these limitations, it does show how powerful in practice the evolutionary development cycle is for helping them to meet fixed deadlines and budgets.

7.12.2 IBM FSD experiences

In *IBM Systems Journal* (No. 4, 1980) Harlan Mills, IBM's chief software guru, reports extensive experiences with evolutionary delivery. His model is closer to what we are recommending in this book, although it lacks many of the same elements that SDC lacked. It does seem to work on the basis of some sort of handover to users.

Here are some quotations which characterize the IBM Federal Systems Division experience:

> 'Management has learned to expect on-time, within-budget deliveries.'
> 'LAMPS . . . a 4-year . . . 200 person-years' (project was delivered) 'in 45 incremental deliveries. Every one of those deliveries was on time and under budget.'
> ' – NASA space program . . . 7000 person-years software development . . . few late or overrun (budgets) . . . in . . . decade, and none at all in the past four years.'

Comment: this would imply substantial experience with the method, and that it took six years to master the art of project 'course correction' so as to achieve perfect project delivery on-time and at budgeted cost.

Further quotations follow: 'evolution in . . . software engineering ideas . . .; evolution in . . . people using (them) . . .; evolution . . . not without pain . . .; programming . . . evolved to a precision design process . . .; software engineering has evolved from an undependable . . . activity to a . . . manageable activity for meeting schedules . . . budgets . . . quality.'

In the same issue of *IBM Systems Journal*, a close colleague of

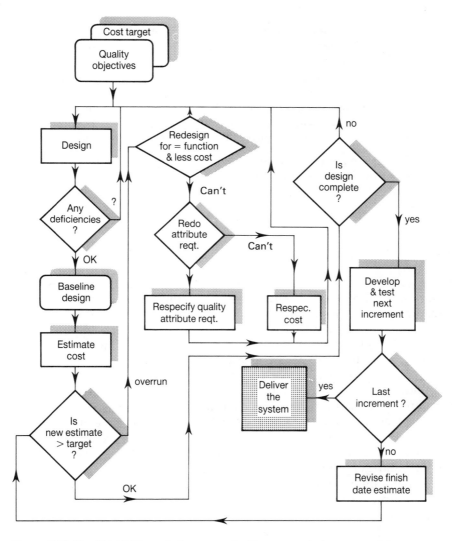

Figure 7.10 The IBM FSD evolutionary cycle. Every month the status of the cost and schedule is measured. If there is an indication that the project is out of control, technical redesign is attempted in a 'design to cost' mode. If this is not possible, then a sacrifice of lower priority quality or resource requirements is made, in order to keep the higher priority ones on track. Source: Quinnan, R., 1980, *IBM Systems Journal*, No. 4.

Mills', Michael Dyer, in an article on 'Software Development Practices' has the following comments:

> 'Integration engineering encourages . . . stepwise refinement . . . introducing ideas of incremental software development.'
> 'Each increment is a subset of the planned software product.'
> 'Structure phasing of incremental development to minimize modification of previous increments due to subsequent . . .'
> The software for each increment is instrumented for measurement of . . . system resources . . . as actual measurements become available . . . estimates should be . . . calibrated (for) fidelity.'

The IBM experience makes it quite clear that the method results in consistent on-time and under-budget delivery for all projects on which it was used. It is, in fact, the most powerful general risk control tool I know of.

■ 7.13 The objections

Naturally, if these results were so widely known and the reason they were arrived at was entirely self-evident, then you wouldn't need to read about it here.

You may be busy working out in your mind reasons why this does not apply to your particular case. That is what is holding you back! Of course, 'objections' to a new idea are a way of testing its validity.

The only truly effective way to convince skeptics of the general applicability of the evolutionary method is for them to create a useful evolutionary plan for their particular application. It has been possible to construct such a plan for every application which I have encountered in my 25 years of experience in this area. I am sure that in your particular case it is also possible to design a useful evolutionary plan. Try it, and don't give up until you succeed.

There are a number of reasons why people feel that they cannot use evolutionary planning in their environment. Since many of these objections to the method are commonly voiced, an elaboration of them here may help you to get a deeper understanding of the method.

7.13.1 Objection 1: 'Our system cannot be divided into smaller steps'

Answer: We have found that every problem with this objection, which we have attacked, was capable of being divided into interesting evolutionary steps in less than one day of planning effort.

Furthermore, we found that the people who initially said it could

Objection	Response
It can't be divided	It always can. Change solution, but satisfy goals
We are in a hurry!	Evo planning will get you there faster
Management won't	Wrong! They love it. They get control
Designers can't	Retrain your designers
Not traditional!	No, it isn't. Avoid traditional failures!
Change effort too big between steps	No problem if open architecture

Figure 7.11 Common objections to evolutionary delivery.

not be done, agreed with us that it could. 'I just never thought of it that way,' said our airline ticket calculation expert who initially denied that airline fare calculation could be delivered in a series of evolutionary developments.

Practical hint: *Sometimes it is difficult to construct all the functions of a new system and deliver them in partial steps. But the solution is often to make use of the existing system as a temporary crutch. You make a series of 'improvements' to the old system, and in the long run you end up with your new system. This is eminently practical, but some system developers have difficulty thinking in these terms.*

Sometimes, the initial solution architecture *is* wrong for evolutionary transition. In fact, our experience is that the best evolutionary solutions are made by first creating a totally different solution architecture. This does take skill, imagination, and often political deftness and diplomacy. But the rewards justify the effort.

Our answer to this first objection is that your problem is *always* capable of evolutionary delivery. But you might well have to change your solution architecture, while still keeping your high priority goals.

7.13.2 Objection 2: 'We are in a hurry'

This is the best possible objection, because if you really are in a hurry, there is no better argument for using the evolutionary delivery method.

Experience shows that it will be the surest way to deliver the most critical results much earlier, and that it will probably deliver the entire long-range solution earlier than you would otherwise have done. This is not to be confused with the delivery date you are currently estimating, which is probably over-optimistic and will never be met.

The IBM Federal Systems Division reported using the method on dozens of projects for four years. Not one of them was late (Mills, 1980). The System Development Corporation reported similar success (Wong, 1984).

In summary, all available experience indicates that the use of evolutionary delivery results in delivery time savings. 'We are in a hurry' is not only an invalid excuse for avoiding the evolutionary delivery method, but it is the main reason for using it!

7.13.3 Objection 3: 'Management won't like it'

Many of my clients are firmly convinced that their boss will not like evolutionary delivery plans, because we do not expect to do detailed long-term planning and cost estimation initially. Only rough planning for the long-term project, and detailed planning for the initial delivery step are required.

The fact is that management, the higher the better, is usually particularly enthusiastic about this method.

Why? First because nobody is asking them to commit large resources to a doubtful result, in the long term future. The message in an evolutionary plan is: here is a framework for meeting your long term goals; here is what we will accomplish in the short term; and here is how much it will cost.

If we fail, you have lost little but you know we couldn't be trusted with anything bigger. If we succeed, and make genuine progress for our organization, we will be on the pathway to the future we want.

If we make some mistakes, then hopefully we will make them early enough to learn from them, and avoid them in the longer term. The managers have a constant stream of proposals asking them to believe in long term results at great risk to their reputation. They have probably been 'burned', and they don't like it.

Here are planners who say, 'judge us on our results.' The economic benefit from early results is music to a Financial Director's ears. Not only that, but the project suddenly seems self-financing. It begins its payback shortly after it starts. No large capital expenditures are necessary for many evolutionary plans. Some can even be financed from current operating expenses. This is important when capital is tight or when interest rates are high.

In summary: make a realistic and interesting (high value, low cost first) evolutionary plan, and your management *will* like it!

7.13.4 Objection 4: 'Our designers cannot make evolutionary plans'

This may be true, in which case you should be very worried. Your planners, managers, system designers and design engineers are incapable of giving you low risk, fast results? You may be letting people with a 'bricklayer' education, try to play 'skyscraper architect.' It just isn't going to work. There is nothing so pitiful, and we have seen it far too often, as to have hundreds (literally!) of people grinding away at the wrong solution, simply for lack of the right architectural idea.

If you need to bring in outside people with the deeper professional qualifications, and the broader perspective required to be good solution architects, do so. If your solution providers complain that they cannot find evolutionary solutions, then that is a sign that they are the wrong people to do so. If they are trying, and eager to improve their ability to do so, then perhaps there is hope for them. Train them. Motivate them.

Evolutionary delivery planning requires knowledge of the open-ended architectural possibilities, so that you can modify your plans as you evolve, without too many problems. It is the ability to select 'open solutions' which is the key to successful evolutionary architecture, and not every engineer is an architect.

In summary, if your designers can't do it, get yourself some other people at the top level of design, or retrain your present people so that they can. It is not easy, but it is worth it.

7.13.5 Objection 5: 'It is not the traditional way to design and plan in our company'

No, it is very unlikely that your staff exploits evolutionary delivery planning fully at the moment. I think you will find that the old foxes in your company do make use of it to some degree, but they may not be making full use of its power. They were never taught all the rules for doing so, and they simply matured to the point where they know they have to try to do things evolutionarily, because that is the only way to survive.

There is a worse problem with the many youngsters in your organizations, who want to make their mark on the world as fast as possible. But if the plan fails, they will simply find another employer. They are dangerous (without any ill intent), and evolutionary delivery planning will force them to come to terms with the reality of your company, before they get a chance to job hop.

Evolutionary delivery planning is really an old tradition which needs to be taught in new contexts, and perhaps needs to be given some powerful communication tools, like quality attribute measurement, to make it work well.

In summary, if it is not a tradition in your environment, then you should make it one now!

7.13.6 Objection 6: 'The "extra effort" to move from step to step will cost much more than doing it all once'

This objection is very real in the 'experience' of some people. Unfortunately those experiences are irrelevant, because they are usually based on defensive efforts to maintain badly-designed systems which have a 'closed architecture,' i.e. an architecture which, by definition, makes it very hard to modify the system and deliver new increments. Thus, the 'extra effort.'

Well-practiced evolutionary architecture presupposes that you know from the very beginning that you are going to evolve the system for the foreseeable future, into uncertain and uncharted waters. You are going to make certain, in your choice of solution strategy, your 'high level architecture' (infotecture, softecture and software engineering, in some combination) that you will survive the storms you may encounter. You will not be able to forsee all such needs for open architecture, but in the early evolutionary stages of delivery you will get some useful experience in changing the system.

If it is difficult to do, then you should, and can economically, find a new more-open basic architecture straight away, because you are otherwise going to suffer for a long time from the bad softecture you have got. It is in fact a very good school for solution architects to try to deliver evolutionary steps. They can learn how well their design adapts to real change, and they should have the realistic possibility of modifying that architecture at early stages of development and planning.

Our experience is that this pseudo-problem, of 'extra cost for evolutionary delivery steps' does not exist in reality, not least because it shows up early and can be cleaned up early. This is not true of phased planning where too large a commitment has already been made to design ideas before there is any feedback about the modifiability aspects of the solution.

In summary, the transition effort between steps will only take more effort if you have the wrong solution architecture. Normally it is far less of a problem than the risk you run for wasting resources by taking too large an implementation step.

■ 7.14 Revising estimates

Evolutionary delivery, and the feedback it produces, often lead to management acceptance of revised estimates for time and money at early stages of the project. This removes unpleasant and unreasonable pressure on the implementers. It gives management more time to find any needed extra resources. They are able to release and redeploy resources which are not required as or when originally planned.

In general, the method leads to dynamic planning. Based on experience readily at hand, estimates are constantly being improved during the many implementation steps. As a consequence, management can and will have justifiable confidence in such estimate refinements.

It follows that since 'final' estimates are refined throughout the project, then the 'real' final results will correspond increasingly closely with the latest adjusted estimates. The familiar gap between realities and our original 'guesstimates' is minimized.

You might feel intuitively that this is 'cheating' somewhat on the difficult task of predicting the future. But I would maintain that you are only cheating yourself of real control, if you use the more conventional 'big-bang' estimation techniques.

As a simple exercise in evolutionary planning: take a current project and try to extract a critical and useful tenth of it for earlier delivery. What problems, if any, do you encounter? It is sometimes difficult, but never impossible. Don't give up too easily!

The self-fulfilling truth principle:
Evolutionary development estimates tend to come true, because if they were false, but become critical, we can correct the project trajectory to hit them.

■ 7.15 What can evolutionary delivery do for you as a manager?

Evolutionary delivery planning is, like the other tools in this book, a management perception tool. It will help you understand and control the complex tasks which are your responsibility. It does this by means of the oldest of management strategies, 'divide and conquer.'

Evolutionary delivery breaks your task down into many smaller deliverable results. The benefit is that the deliverable results are put into some kind of use by someone trying to do real work with them. These results have to be tailored to available realities, and do not imply full-scale user release.

The important point is that the system constructors must complete *all* the necessary details of training, handbooks, user interface, reliable databases, recovery systems, performance, and motivation which 'programmers' too often leave out.

This facing of reality forces you to see the true costs of the system at an earlier stage. This in turn leads to revised planning and budgets which are more realistic. So, instead of getting the bad news late, you get it while it is still cheap to act on.

The fact of giving your hungry 'users' (people and organizations who make use of a change which you are managing) early results, has some useful effects:

- They are happier with your activity and are thus more supportive and cooperative.
- Your subordinates are confronted with the realities of your users at an earlier stage of design and planning. They grow up faster.
- If your team is unable to produce anything useful, it is quickly exposed as being incompetent. You can do something about that before it becomes a bigger problem.
- You will get experience in estimating at very early stages, which will be invaluable in making early estimates of budgets, delivery dates, work-power requirements and other resources needed for later stages.
- Your activities will gain in political credibility in the competition with other groups for company or outside resources.
- Sudden budget cuts or supporting management changes cannot deprive you of a chance to demonstrate ability to deliver results: you will already have done so.

■ 7.16 Summary

Successful planning is planning which gives the results we have planned for, both the long-term ones and the more immediate ones.

Planning is something that happens in people's heads and on paper. This is *not* the same thing as the implementation of the plan in the real world.

Planning is like a model of the real world at a particular point in time. Like all models it is both idealized and simplified.

All the tools in this book can be regarded as helping us to define what we want and helping us make 'closer to reality' models of what might happen if we implemented the proposed solution.

But we must not lose sight of the fact that these models are not the real world. They will not scream, or threaten to strike, when presented with a poor design. Evolutionary planning alone closes the gap between theory and reality. It puts planners and managers alike in contact with the effects of their planning on the budget, the performance of their staff, the allocation of resources, and the satisfaction of their clients. As such it is a very healthy medicine.

The evolutionary planning method closes the circle of

what we want, (requirements)
how to get it, (solutions)

and

what will happen if we do it this way? (evolutionary delivery feedback).

Lindbloom's scientific muddling principle: The iron law of incrementalism (Lindbloom, 1980):
If a wise policymaker proceeds through a succession of incremental changes, he avoids serious lasting mistakes in several ways.

The software engineering community needs to take a long hard look at the evolutionary delivery method. It needs to teach it to software professionals, to managers, and to the new people entering the ranks.

System development must function in a total systems environment. Software is not an island of self-sufficiency. There is a need for clear goal setting and multidimensional analysis techniques. Good design principles and design data should be collected in evolving software engineering handbooks. We must learn to gradually evolve documentation, data designs, interfaces, hardware hosts, and not least people.

■ References and further reading

Bahn, A.J., (translator), 1980, Tao Teh Ching, Frederick Unger
    Publishing Co., NY

Boehm, B.W., 1981, *Software engineering economics*, Prentice-Hall, N.J.

Byte 2/84, 'The wizards behind the Mac,' *Byte Magazine*, 1984, February,
    p. 63

Deming, W.E., 1986, *Out of the crisis*, MIT Press

Fagan, M.E., 1976, 'Design and code inspections to reduce errors in
    program development,' *IBM Systems Journal*, **15**, (3) pp. 182–211

Gilb, T., 1976a, *Data engineering*, Studentlitteratur, Lund, Sweden, (out
    of print)

Gilb, T., 1976b, *Software metrics*, Winthrop, (out of print)

Gilb, T., 1979, 'Structured design methods for maintainability,' in
    Infotech State of the Art Report on Structured Software Development,
    Pergamon Infotech, Maidenhead, UK

Gilb, T., 1981a, 'Evolutionary development,' *ACM Software Eng. Notes*,
    April

Gilb, T., 1981b, 'System attribute specification: a cornerstone of
    software engineering,' *ACM Software Eng. Notes*, July, pp. 78–79

Gilb, T., 1981c, 'The software engineering handbook,' *ACM Software
    Eng. Notes*, October, pp. 30–31

Gilb, T., 1984a, 'The impact analysis (estimation) table in human
    factors design,' in Proc. IFIP conf. on *Human Machine Interactions*,
    London, September, pp. 104–113

Gilb, T., 1984b, 'Software engineering using design by objectives,'
    ACM Software Eng. Notes, April

Gilb, T., and Weinberg, G.M., 1984, *Humanized input: techniques for
    reliable keyed input*, QED Inc., Wellesley, Mass.

Gilbert, P., 1983, *Software design and development*, SRA Publishers

Lindbloom, C.E., 1980, 'The science of muddling through,' in *The book
    of laws*, Faber, H. (ed.), Sphere Books, London

Mills, H.D., 1980, *IBM Systems Journal*, (4)

Quinnan, R.E., 1980, *IBM Systems Journal*, (4)

Schumacher, E.E., 1973, *Small is beautiful: a study of economics as if people
    mattered*, Abacus-Sphere Books

Wong, C., 1984, 'A successful software development,' *IEEE Trans. on
    Software Engineering*, November

See also Chapter 15 of this book

PART TWO

How to do it

8

Functional specification

■ Introduction

If you have read, or even skimmed through, Part One of this book, some of the main software project management problems (and even some non-software ones) should be clearer to you, as well as the general outline of how to deal with them using the methods and principles in this book. Part Two tells you *how* to do it, how to apply these ideas to your own projects. Part Two is therefore more like a handbook. One particular illustration – a real case history – is used throughout.

Chapter 8 will begin with an introduction to the case study which is used throughout Part Two. The second half of the chapter will discuss functional specification.

The main purpose of functional specification is to identify those system functions (what the system does or will do) involved in the software and systems engineering process. Functional requirements are usually recorded in the form of a simple list of requirements to be fulfilled by the users or clients.

This is in contrast to attribute requirements which have a much richer scale of demands and possible tradeoffs depending on their priority. It also contrasts with the technical solutions we decide on, in our attempt to meet the attribute requirements. These solutions are never demanded by the user or customer. They are the result of an engineering process. As such they must be kept separate from user requirements. Functional requirements must be clearly separated from attribute requirements (quality and resource, Chapter 9) and from the technical design solutions for meeting those attribute requirements (solutions, Chapter 10).

■ 8.1 Organizational productivity planning: the IBC case study

8.1.1 Introduction to the case study

While 'fictional' cases may be clearer and tidier, and the solutions more elegant, they have a certain artificiality about them. This real-life case history includes all the imperfections and even the personality problems which play a large part in such projects in our everyday lives. Its background is as follows:

The Project Manager of IBC (let us say that this stands for the International Banking Corporation) attended my course in Rio de Janeiro, for a week's lectures about the ideas discussed in this book.

IBC is primarily in banking, but is also involved with a number of non-banking subsidiaries and their data processing operations. During that week the Project Manager used his current project ('making a better systems handbook') as an example in class exercises. It became clear that he would be interested in having my further assistance at his office in Sao Paulo. We agreed that I should meet his bosses and get their approval and initial support.

The next Monday afternoon a lunch meeting was set up for me with the Director of IBC systems development. They had about 300 employees in the IBC Computer Center Systems Division. The lunch was attended by the Project Manager, his boss who was a Division Manager and three other Division Managers reporting to the Director. I was to undertake to show how the ideas in this book could be integrated into their plan for a systems handbook, and how the ideas could be used as a planning language to express the plans for the systems handbook project (which was how the Project Manager's project was popularly referred to at the time).

I undertook to make a management presentation during the last half-day of the two, and work began the next morning.

8.1.2 The two-day study

The Project Manager and his Division Manager were assigned to me for the two days, and we sat alone in a conference room during most of that time. They both made it quite clear to me that 'our proposals must not touch the organizational aspects, but be strictly limited to technical suggestions.' This was said to be the direct wish of the Director.

8.1.3 The original project

The original idea had been to improve the productivity of the three hundred people working on computer programming and system design. The aim was that they should be less dominated by maintaining the old computerized systems, and thus devote more resources to meeting the new and dynamically changing needs of the Corporation in data processing.

An improved 'Programming Standards Handbook' was therefore to be written. However, when the Project Manager was given the project about six months earlier, his experience (as an Arthur Andersen consultant) told him that the project had to be broader. He suggested, and got approval for, the concept of the project as making a 'Systems Development Handbook.'

8.1.4 Clarifying the real goals of the Director

We used the first morning to make a formal attribute specification for the problem we were trying to solve. (Attributes specifications are discussed in detail in Chapter 9.) This concentrated on the technical and economic aspects of the computerized systems which the company was producing and maintaining. By 11 a.m. we had a very full page of ideas, and then the Director dropped in on us unexpectedly.

8.1.5 The Director's correction

I asked him if he could spare a few minutes to give us some feedback on our goal setting. After all, if we were wrong on that, the rest of our work for him would be wasted.

The Director read our attribute specification (see Figure 9.1) for future organizational change objectives: 'This is very interesting. Can I really express all my wishes in this form?' Then, after further minutes of study, he asked: 'I have some needs which don't seem to be on this list. What about such things as job satisfaction, reducing employee turnover in my division, our ability to make use of the organization as a training ground for future executives of the Corporation, and so on. . . .?' He reeled off a list of hitherto suppressed wishes (which were noted accordingly).

I replied that we had by no means included these factors. In fact we had intentionally avoided them, giving priority to a purely technical and economic viewpoint. 'No! If anything these factors are more important in my view than the technical considerations,' he replied.

We deduced that he had made some sort of a deal with *his* boss to train future executives, and that his future road to the top of the Corporation was through showing himself to be a manager of people, rather than computer programs. We thanked him for his time. It had taken him less than 30 minutes.

8.1.6 The lunchtime revelation

Over the following lunch the Project Manager revealed that both he and his boss, the Division Manager, had been severely shaken by the corrections from the Director. The Project Manager admitted that they had given me quite different directives about the project than those that the Director was actually interested in. They had been working on the project for months, and had until now not understood what the essential goals of it really were! And the Director himself was clearly surprised that we had not already included those goals.

My experience was, I told the Project Manager, that management goals are rarely communicated in a clear and complete written manner. They are even more rarely collected on a concentrated page or two. And they were rarely stated in measurable and quantitative form, with a few obvious exceptions for time and money goals.

My explanation for the Project Manager and the Division Manager's 'shocking experience' was simply that the Director had never realized that they did not fully understand his strong views on the human and organizational aspects of his planning for improvements. When he saw that the organizational goals were completely missing from the formal plan, he was forced to an immediate reaction. I explained that it was quite normal to get surprising new goals stated by management at the stage of trying to get them to approve a measurable attribute specification.

After lunch, we made two new pages (see Figures 9.2, 9.3) of attribute specifications as additions to the technical and economic goals. We made sure to use the exact terms of the Director when stating these goals, so that he would recognize what we were doing as his own wishes.

8.1.7 Would the Director think we were crazy?

On the second day of the study we had progressed through the several levels of design: policy, major organizational changes, detailed specification of the changes. (See Section 6.1, Tables 10.2–10.5, Figure 10.2.)

We agreed that we didn't want to use the extremely short time we had that week to perform detailed analysis of the quality of the suggestions. But I felt we should at least give the Director some vision of the fact that there was a possibility of evolutionary implementation for these ideas. The previous project was clearly revolutionary, all at once, in nature. The entire handbook was to be developed and implemented more or less as one big package, in about a year or two, or whenever it was satisfactorily finished.

I drafted a simple one-page evolutionary implementation plan showing possible implementation steps and sub-steps. Of course these were not merely 'development' stages for the project, but were changes which would begin to immediately deliver the improvements desired to the 300-person organization, and through them to the entire Corporation affected by data processing. (See Tables 13.1, 13.2.)

The Project Manager and his boss told me that they were afraid of a negative reaction from the Director about the evolutionary plan. It was so unconventional to plan so many delivery stages, and I was not including estimates for final cost and delivery dates. The Director, they claimed, would *insist* on those estimates.

I reminded them that cost and time estimates for the entire project were not as critical as with old-style revolutionary planning. Deliveries were in such small result-increments that management would have control all the way through. Good estimates could be developed at very early stages of the project, based on actual experience of the early deliveries. I also reminded the Project Manager of what I had said on the course he attended – that people of his level rarely believed that the 'big boss' would like evolutionary planning. But, in fact in my experience, the bigger the bosses, the more they loved it.

They maintained that although they understood and agreed with evolutionary planning, they knew their boss much better than I did. They were not only afraid of his disapproval, but they thought there was a real risk that all three of us would be thrown out of his office as lunatics if we dared present such a revolutionary planning concept. (They nevertheless agreed to let me present the plan as it stood.)

8.1.8 The presentation to the boss

About 5 p.m. that second day we started a delayed meeting with the Director and his five Vice-Directors. We presented the material, and it was obvious by the questions and remarks from the Director that he really liked the ideas and the way of expressing them.

We had found a clear language for expressing his problems. We had a much broader attack on the problems than a purely technical handbook would have given (it was difficult to find any trace of the handbook idea in our proposals by this time). We had a plan which guaranteed short term results and the possibility of getting some 'action' this year.

8.1.9 Presenting the evolutionary development plan

Then the moment of truth came: the finale of presenting the draft of the evolutionary plan, so the Director could envisage how all these many new suggestions could be implemented early and under very controlled practical conditions.

To the Project Manager's and the Division Manager's great relief we did not get kicked out immediately. On the contrary, the Director obviously warmed to this way of thinking, and discussed it with us in detail. He clearly liked the possibility of setting changes in motion that same day (by giving approval to the policy and asking for attribute specifications for his various major projects the next day).

Finally the presentation was finished. It was 8 p.m. in the evening and we had had an intensive two and half days together. The Director had not sat there with an 'I'll let you know later when I've evaluated it' attitude. He had given clear signals throughout the meeting that he was in full support of these ideas, and was giving his 'go ahead' then and there (to refine the proposals to more realistic detail than could be achieved in the two day study).

Then he picked my last presentation foil from the darkened projector. It was the evolutionary steps plan. Some of us held our breath, for a moment. 'This,' he said as he waved the evolutionary plan, 'this is what I really love!'

8.1.10 Postscript

The initial reports I received from the Project Manager and the Division Manager by mail told that they were successfully carrying out the plan, and would even enjoy sharing their experiences with others internationally.

In discussions I had with them in Rio de Janeiro a year later, they gave me an impressive piece of work that the Project Group had carried out. They had defined over one hundred measurable attributes of the organization and the products and services they provide. They intended to select the most critical attributes for proper long term measurement and control.

The work they had done was better than anything I have seen done anywhere in this area. But I had to give them a firm reminder that they had fallen into the trap of doing too much theoretical work, and not delivering results to the users in the short term.

They explained that there had been some organizational shakeups in the previous year which made it difficult to carry out those changes. I told them that nevertheless, they should have given more attention to evolutionary delivery of results in the short term, and they agreed to do so. In any case it was clear that the Director had invested something in getting measurable control over his operation.

This case study story forms a background and a source for illustrations for the following 'how to' for the various tools of this book.

■ 8.2 Specifying what you want – functional requirements

Some general principles of functional specification are

> **The functional requirements principle:**
> The functional requirement specification lists essential things which the product must do, and which must be delivered at specified times. It is different from the quality-and-resource attributes required, and from the solutions selected to reach those attributes.
>
> **The binary function principle:**
> A functional specification is 'present' or 'absent' from a plan or a real system. There is no such thing as a degree of presence or absence of a function.

If a function F(1–4) consists of four planned subfunctions F1, F2, F3 and F4, but only F1 and F2 are implemented, then F(1–4) is 'absent' (not implemented fully). A subfunction of it F(1&2) is implemented fully and the other subfunction F(3&4) is not. We could say that 50% of the planned functions of F(1–4) are implemented. This is an attribute of the implementation process and does not change the binary nature of the functions in plans or implementation.

> **The explosion principle:**
> Functional ideas can be defined in more detail by exploding them into constituent ideas.
>
> **The delineation principle:**
> A functional specification is not necessarily a specification to *build* something new. It can be used to *delineate* the existing functions whose attributes are to be impacted by planned changes at planned points in time.

■ 8.3 Distinguishing between specifications and requirements

A functional specification is not a requirement, unless we explicitly make it a requirement. Functional specification may be used for a wide variety of purposes aside from stating requirements.

8.3.1 Example

A functional specification for purposes of delineation

IBC-SYS: The IBC Systems Development Group.

A functional *requirement*:

IBC-SYS-ROTATE: We shall implement a job rotation plan.

IBC-SYS-ROTATE-PERS: The personnel department shall have responsibility for planning and implementing the job rotation (ROTATE) requirement.

■ 8.4 Functional specification: rule one

Be sure to separate functional ideas from attribute ideas. If, for example, the specification 'Readable User Handbook' were given, then we should separate it into its main component ideas: 'Readable,' a benefit, a measurable quality requirement, and 'User handbook,' a function, with no measurable degrees of existence – only presence or absence.

Keep this function on a separate function list. Do not mix it with the attribute requirement. We will of course attach attribute requirements to their functions at some point (see Chapter 9), but we must do it in an unambiguous and systematic way.

■ 8.5 A useful analysis method for any plan or design

It is an interesting exercise to take any piece of project documentation and mark, with F and A for example, the different functional requirements (F) and attribute (A) requirements, and even suggested solutions (with an S). This exercise will show you how far these specification ideas are usually mixed together. But it will also serve to clarify the absolute requirements (functions), requirements with some degree of flexibility (attributes), and solutions, which might be useful as ideas for later use, but which are not goals as such.

8.5.1 Example (from IBC case)

We (IBC Systems Department) = F(unction)

want (goal implied)

to write a systems development handbook (solution not a real goal)
= S

to improve development productivity substantially (attribute = A
= undefined)

■ 8.6 A caution – solution specification may be an indirect statement

Be careful. Solutions stated at this stage are often a user's way of telling you which attributes are wanted. You are responsible for translating these solutions back into the attribute goals which the user really wants. For instance if the user demands 'standardized,' you will have to ask them 'why?.' You will probably translate this into what they really want; 'ease of maintenance', 'personnel interchangeability,' or other benefits which are what typically lie behind such words.

In the IBC case study, the project was described simply as 'making a new systems handbook.' When I asked 'why?,' the real objectives became clearer. They wanted to increase productivity of systems and programming staff, so that they could do more of the work which was piling up. The function was implicit. But we could state it formally:

IBC-SYS: The IBC systems development organization.

■ 8.7 How detailed does a functional specification need to be?

In many cases, there is no real need to go into detail about the functions within the main functional area to be treated. It is often a fairly clearly defined organizational or product unit. The important thing is to improve it, by improving its quality and cost attributes.

If we were creating an entirely new organization or system, we might need to know more. If we were going to automate an existing set of functions, we would need to know more. If we were planning to add substantial new functional ideas to an existing organization, we would also need to know more about the planned functional detail. This may surprise people who have been taught that most of the effort needed to define a new system should be put into a detailed study, or mapping, of the current system, its processes and data flows.

Personally, I have time and again found this to be an unnecessary effort. It is sufficient for you to identify the function at its highest level (like IBC Systems Organization) and to treat it as a dynamically changing, but self-defining, set of sub-functions. This means that you do of course analyze the existing system as the need dictates. You only need to look at the parts you are changing. When you do look at them, even if it be several years into the change process, you know that you are looking at the real thing and the updated system (including data and human practices). You do not risk basing your judgement on an outdated analysis.

■ 8.8 Functional specification: rule two

You will need to explode functions for more detail (i.e. divide them into smaller subconcepts).

In this case the method needed is a straightforward list of interesting functional areas, probably with a hierarchical relationship to one another. Sometimes overlapping functional descriptions are useful too.

For example in doing an analysis of our IBC plans we found it useful to 'explode' the organization into smaller groups of people like this:

IBC-SYS

> IBC-SYS-PROF: Professional employees
> IBC-SYS-MGT: Management
> IBC-REST: All other (non prof. and non mgt.
> employees)

■ 8.9 Reasons for functional breakdown

The reasons for the functional breakdown ('decomposition' if you prefer) in the example above, IBC-SYS, were:

1. to allow us to analyze our plans and solutions in more detail.
2. to make sure that particular groups of employees at IBC were not inadvertently overlooked.
3. to allow us to communicate our plans to those employee groups regarding plans that impacted them.

What we were not concerned with, was the invention or construction of these functional groups. They already existed. We were using the functional specification as a means of delineation.

Time and again, functional specification can be simplified to a low volume (less than a page) of specification. It becomes primarily a way of saying of which functions you want to improve the attributes (delineation). You are not making a functional requirement, because that requirement has already been met by the existing system. It is implicit that the function will be kept intact when you improve attributes.

You are less interested in describing the system in detail. You are more interested in delineating which are the functions of the system of which you are going to try to improve the attributes. You can do this in spite of having a complex system. But you must be prepared to use the system itself as its own living definition. You must also be willing to tackle change by means of evolutionary steps. We can then use most of our design and analysis effort to identify improvement areas (attributes), and potential solutions for reaching desirable attributes, for those functions we have delineated.

There are however situations where you need a great deal more functional requirement definition, because you must construct the system in detail, and be able to systematically test that all required functions are planned and implemented. However my main concern is that we should not get so deeply involved in a detailed functional analysis and specification process when this is not really necessary. In particular, we should not get involved in detailed functional analysis and specification processes at the expense of concentration on our users' primary objectives.

Users are as a rule concerned with quality and cost (attribute) improvement, and already have whatever functions they really need. Some of these functions may not yet be computerized, and this leads computer people to the illusion that the functions do not exist. They do.

■ 8.10 Tags

We make use of 'tags' for identifying functional concepts, as well as attributes, solutions and evolutionary steps, for later reference. I find that in software engineering projects, where there may be hundreds or even thousands of individual functional specification ideas in the planning documentation, there is no systematic tagging of the individual elementary functional ideas. This makes them much more difficult to inspect and test in a mechanical manner. It is here we begin to fail to deliver what somebody thinks we have promised.

Practical hint: *I recommend that every single function idea or function specification begin on a new line, and be tagged by a unique identification of some sort.*

8.10.1 Example of breaking these rules

2.1.3 The software shall be compatible with Zenix Version 4.2, and have a window/mouse/pull-down menu support in addition.

8.10.2 Example of following the rules (by re-editing the above)

2.1.3 SOFTWARE REQUIREMENTS

COMPAT: Zenix Version 4.2 compatibility is required.

WINDOW: window support is required.

MOUSE: mouse support is required.

PULLDOWN: pull-down menu support is required.

It is now mechanically simpler to check that each elementary functional item is included or considered in all other planning (code, documentation, tests, for example).

Is 'top-down' or 'bottom-up' functional specification best?

Each of these has advantages in certain situations, so there is no rule of 'best.' There may be situations where it is natural to start with specification of lower level, more detailed, concepts which are of great current interest or importance. These more detailed concepts may later be grouped together and given a common higher-level name for easy reference in later planning.

The process of explosion of functions into many sub-functions is also a promising method for identifying ideas for the evolutionary building-and-delivery steps of our solution, as discussed below.

■ 8.11 How do we divide a project into functional categories?

You can, if it suits your purposes, explode functional specifications into any functional sub-concepts which you find useful. There are, however, some reasons which might force you to choose particular explosion strategies. The choice of functional explosion depends on the principal goals you want to accomplish:

- if you want to optimize *performance*, then decomposition must be along lines of 'frequency of usage';
- if you want to optimize *delivery schedule*, it will be by separating essential early functions from those than can be delivered later;
- you want to optimize *maintenance ease*, then those functions which are more likely to be subject to change need to be separated from those which are inherently more stable;
- if you want to minimize *risk of failure*, then you will probably separate high and low risk functions, and will probably also want to keep the functions themselves small, thus leading to greater functional detail;
- if you have many *conflicting high-priority goals*, there will be some compromise. You won't be able to apply any of the above rules in a simple way.

■ 8.12 Functional explosion principles

Here are some principles for functional explosions which will work well in many situations:

The essentials-first principle:
Divide functions into 'things which can be implemented early,' and 'things which can be delivered later.'

We have elsewhere, in discussing evolutionary delivery planning, stressed the need to avoid doing everything at once. The division into essentials is based primarily on user needs and priorities. It must however consider logical pre-requisites, political realities, and cost factors as well. You have to make your own set of rules for this.

This functional decomposition process will make it much easier to create evolutionary delivery plans at a later stage. These plans, in turn, will be a way of getting some earlier results delivered. The same rule applies to dividing up technical 'solutions' in preparation for evolutionary plans. In fact many of the rules which apply to solutions, also apply to functions, because they are of similar nature to the implementor – only their source (i.e. the *user* gives functional require-ments, the *designer* gives solutions based on attribute requirements) is different.

> **The divide-to-communicate principle:**
> When making functional explosions for purposes of presentation
> or analysis, you can divide them into simple categories such as
> existing groups within your organization or other categories
> which may make it easier for other people to understand your
> plans.

■ 8.13 Conclusion

System functions need to be delineated both to understand a system
and to demand new functions. They can be divided into sub-functions
which can be implemented earlier and later respectively, in order to
prepare the way for evolutionary delivery planning, or to help us meet
other attribute targets.

It is critical that the functional requirements are formally separated
from the corresponding attribute requirements, because attributes are
quantitative, and require translation into a design solution.

Attribute specification

■ Introduction

Chapter 9 is a detailed tutorial on how to specify quality and resource attributes in a highly structured language.

■ 9.1 The general principles of attribute specification

The attribute requirements specification is the cornerstone upon which the other ideas in this book are built. It expresses the objectives for a system. The specification can be used to express future requirements as well as to describe existing systems or past achievements.

An attribute is a quality concept or resource concept which describes a system quantitatively.

An attribute specification is a list of attributes.

The attribute specification presents a dynamic picture of our thinking on attribute levels. It can show a series of changes in quality and resource usage through different points in time on your planning horizon. Additionally, the attribute specification is the natural place to record modifications in the plans which are the natural results of a more-detailed planning and design process, as well as the results of early partial delivery of the system.

Attributes are characteristics of our systems which represent constraints. We are trying to reach a certain minimum level of the quality attributes. We must avoid using more than a certain maximum level of the resource attributes. In both cases this method uses the concept of the 'worst acceptable level' as a way to express the constraints.

The quantitative specification of attributes gives us the necessary clarity of purpose in finding solutions to our problems.

Attribute definitions must be tailored to the project purposes at hand. Often we can use everyday notions to describe attributes, such as those in Chapter 19. For example 'reliability' or 'development cost.' However just as often, it will be worth constructing a set of attributes whose definition is tailored for your particular project. For example 'Fleet Tracking Database Consistency,' might have a special and local definition to a military group.

The following are some initial general principles of attribute specification:

> **The critical control principle:**
> All critical attributes must be specified and controlled throughout the project and product lifetime.

Critical attributes are those which can kill the entire system or project, if they go beyond certain limits. We refer to those limits as the worst acceptable case.

The measurability principle:
All attributes can and should be made measurable in practice.

Attributes can always be made measurable. This frequently seems difficult, but there always is a way of achieving it. People invariably speak about attributes as though they were on some kind of scale. An example is 'an extremely user-friendly system.' The key words are 'high, low, very, extremely' and other similar scalar adjectives.

People all too often fail to define a scale of measure because their culture does not demand that discipline of them. It is our objective here to encourage a change in that culture. Attributes must be made measurable because this will demand clear thinking among customers (users), management (of the engineering process), designers (engineers) and implementors. Measurability will also allow us to monitor progress in design and delivery of the system in an unambiguous way.

The attribute hierarchy principle:
It is often convenient to express attributes as a hierarchy of attributes and sub-attributes.

Major attributes can be defined by specifying or 'exploding' them into their sub-attributes. Such a hierarchy of attribute ideas gives us an overview – when we need one – without going into too much detail. A hierarchy allows us to handle a very long list of interesting attributes of a complex system, in a manner that is easier to understand than a simple list of such attributes.

Attribute hierarchies allow us to concentrate our attention on a particular group of attribute goals – such as 'performance' – when we need to. And, finally, attribute hierarchies reduce our temptation to accidentally oversimplify the realities with which we are faced.

The result-oriented attribute principle:
The attributes should be specified in terms of the final end-user results demanded.

The language which is used to specify the attributes should be easily understood by everyone involved in the project, especially the ultimate consumer of the product of the project. It should certainly not be in terms of computerese, using terms like 'complexity metrics.' This enables everyone to communicate effectively about the attributes and to take responsibility for the results of the project. People can react appropriately when attribute specifications do not adequately represent their end-user needs.

The real test is that the user-management should be able to sign off on the attribute requirements specification as representing what they want.

The prerequisite principle:
The initial attribute specification must be made early (day one, hour one) in the project, before any attempt is made at solution specification.

Solution alternatives can only be judged in the light of all attribute requirements. The quality of your design process is dependent on the explicit clarity of those attribute requirements. Do not waste time evaluating solution ideas until the attribute requirements are written, quantified, and agreed upon by all concerned. Do not constrain designers needlessly by specifying solution ideas before they have had a chance to find their own ideas based on your real requirements.

For example 'an integrated database' prejudges the technical solution. Express the real requirements. 'Integrated' may be an indirect way of asking for some combination of adaptability for change and high performance. The database may only represent one possible solution. Indeed some database solutions may defeat your real goals here.

The fluid attribute-level principle:
Don't ever try to freeze exact attribute requirements. You must expect changes by the user during development, and because of the uncontrolled side-effects of your real system.

Even after the system is operational, the attribute levels achieved will change with time and circumstance. There is no final answer. But this does not mean that the attributes to be aimed at should not be carefully quantified. The current state of the measurable attributes should be determined, and then consideration given to the future levels, and the time scales for their achievement. Use of the evolutionary delivery method will give some measures of your future attribute levels based on early experience.

The overview principle:
The attribute requirement specification should be written on one page, and in a consistent language.

It is necessary to have a complete overview of all critical attributes, so that we can see the trade-off possibilities, and account for significant side-effects on other critical goals.

■ 9.2 The basic rules for attribute specification

Make a list of the most critical quality and resource attributes for your project. 'Critical attributes' are those attributes which, if they did get out of control, would be destructive of the entire project.

■ 9.3 Attribute hierarchies

If the list of your critical attributes is more than about seven to ten, then you will probably find it convenient to create groups of them under single names. For example, you might choose to group together those attributes which show some common idea of, for example,

system performance:
  weekly work-load capacity
  system availability
  response time to questions

The attribute name chosen should be a short one – for easy reference at later stages. It should also be a name to which users of the system can relate easily. Ideally, you should pick up and use the exact terminology of the top executive who is asking for this particular project result. The definition of each attribute name is given by the definitions below it. This is either as a measurable attribute or as a set of attributes.

It is common for people to start by identifying the 'low level' goals first. They are more pressing, more visible, more immediate. But if we fail to identify the real reason why we want to achieve certain goals, then we may never get what we really want.

The 'high level' attributes are what 'lie behind' the low level goals. The reason for trying to identify high level goals is to help us to avoid getting side-tracked into merely achieving the lesser 'indirect' goals. These are the ones which *may* lead to achievement of higher level goals, but will not necessarily do so. If you want to get at the heart of the matter, you should ask yourself, and your colleagues, questions which lead towards the most important high level, attribute goals.

There is a very simple but powerful way to do this. For each attribute you have identified, ask 'why?' Why does this attribute seem critical to us? What is the real reason behind our asking for it?

For example, it is all too easy to say we want high 'reliability,' when we really want system availability. Availability is a function of reliability, but also of maintainability and integrity. Controlling reliability alone will not give us what we really want.

It is also, for example, tempting to say that we want 'compatibility' or 'standards' when we really want ease of transfer ('portability'). Portability is a function of the degree of compatibility, but is also dependent upon the people and tools needed to do the transfer. If you want to ease the transfer, you have to control it directly at the portability level. The compatibility and standards ideas are really only the means to the end. See Chapter 19 for more details on these concepts.

Identification of high level attribute requirements will help to avoid diverting resources into less important areas.

There is another reason for identifying high level goals. It puts us in a position to see many other possible solutions to our problem. We can often solve our real problem – which we can see better when we define our higher level goals – in a much faster, easier, more economical way than we first thought possible.

Using the 'system performance' example, if we ask 'why?' of the performance goals, we might get the answer 'better customer service.' If we ask 'why' again, we may get 'keeping our customers away from competitors.' And a further 'why' may give us 'protecting our income base . . .' and so on.

Notice that for each higher level attribute goal which you identify, you will be able to think of a number of solution possibilities which are not directly related to the lower level goal expressed first. (How many ways can you think of to give better customer service, apart from increasing the performance of the service itself?)

■ 9.4 Exploding towards lower level attributes

9.4.1 The IBC case objectives as initially stated

Sometimes it seems more natural to work in the opposite direction, towards more-detailed goal ideas. It may seem natural to identify the

Subject: Management objectives for systems division (tech./eco.)

Definition / Satisfaction	Scale	Test	Worst limit	Plan	Best limit	Now	Reference
Value	CR$ val/month	set by user	25% ROI	>25% ROI	>50% ROI	? not eval.	BHP Australia
Development cost	plan ±	% diff.	±10%	±5%		not known 100% ± ?	
Operations cost	plan ±	% diff.	±10%	±5%		not known 100% ± ?	
Planned quality	plan ±	% diff.	±10%	±5%		not known 100% ± ?	
Maintenance cost	min/ loc/yr		0.2 new 0.5 old	0.1 new 0.3 old		0.5 min/ loc/year	5000 Pr x 5000 L 70%/250
Portability	salvage value –> COBOL	calculate		95%			
Reliability	logic & data wrong	errors/ line/ year		<0.1/ Kloc/ year			
Updatedness	reality to update	days average sample	next day	same day	same hour	? 30 days	
Availability	% of planned uptime	oper. logs	95%	98%	99.9 %	no plan	
Security						see security explosion for detail	
Friendliness	ease employee learning	days on job to solo	1 –> 7 days	<1 day	<2 hour to solo	uncontrolled 10 – >100 days ?	

Requirements

Reference data only

planning ability

product qualities

Figure 9.1 IBC management objectives.

Table 9.1 IBC organizational improvement objectives (initial draft).

SATISFACTION: (this is an ID tag for objectives below)
(These 4 items (Value . . . Planned Qualities) are a measure of planning ability)

VALUE: (Value is an ID tag for the parameters below)
SCALE = (scale of measure of the ideas) = value in ROI (return on investment) = actual savings or revenue per month generated/(monthly costs + write-offs); as %
TEST = (how to measure in practice) = value estimated monthly by user, costs from official accounts
WORST(by now + 3 years) = (worst acceptable case) = 25% ROI
PLAN(now + 3 years) = (planned level) = > 25% ROI
BEST = (best imaginable or state-of-art limit) = >50% ROI
NOW = (present status of the function IBC-SYS) = not evaluated by IBC or known to the planning group
REFERENCE = Broken Hill Pty., Australia uses this method for DP projects

DEVELOPMENT COST:
SCALE = +/- % deviation from initially planned costs
TEST = official accounting data compared to official cost estimate
WORST = 10% negative deviation
PLAN = < or = 5% negative deviation
NOW = not known, probably often 100% negative deviation

OPERATIONAL COST: (similar to DEVELOPMENT COST)

PLANNED QUALITIES: (similar to DEVELOPMENT COST)

(the next group of SATISFACTION sub-objectives are deemed to be the critical product qualities for the bank systems)

MAINTENANCE COST:
SCALE = minutes/line of non-commentary source code maintained/year
TEST = logged maintenance minutes for system/estimated code lines
WORST(new code, created by new process) = 0.2 min./LOC/year
WORST = (old code, existing today) = 0.5 min./LOC/year
PLAN(new code) = 0.1 M/L/Y (based on Fagan's inspection experience)
PLAN(old) = 0.3 M/L/Y
NOW(estimated overall for IBC today) = 0.5 M/L/Y
REFERENCE = now estimate is based on 5000 programs, avg. 5000 LOC/program, 70% of 250 programmers in maintenance)

PORTABILITY:
SCALE = salvage value vs. new-build cost estimate when ported to IBM COBOL
TEST = calculation and samples of conversions
PLAN(now + 3 years) = 95%

RELIABILITY:
SCALE = errors reported per line of source code in system per year
TEST = reported logic and database errors in official log vs. official size data
PLAN(19xx) = less than 0.1 errors per 1000 lines of code per year

Table 9.1 (cont.)

UPDATEDNESS:
SCALE = time from event until update is in our database
TEST = measure one day's sample at random of at least 10 (prefer 50) cases
WORST = next day
PLAN = same day
BEST = same hour
NOW = don't have a measure. Guesstimate = within 30 days

AVAILABILITY:
SCALE = % of planned system uptime
TEST = operational logs versus operational plans
WORST = 95%
PLAN = 98%
BEST = 99.9%
NOW = no plan or control

SECURITY:
Critical factor identified, but no specification made during the initial session, among other things because it is considered complex (many security objects and levels)

FRIENDLINESS:
SCALE = days on-the-job for bank employees to learn tasks supplied by a new system
TEST = 90% successful completion of assigned tasks in employee test for system within factor two times experienced operators' average time
WORST = 1 to 7 days
PLAN = less than 1 day (to passing test)
BEST = less than 2 hours
NOW = uncontrolled in design requirements. Guesstimate 10 to 100 days

most critical attribute goal ideas or directions without regard for the total picture. In fact a top executive frequently does exactly that for us, and little more. We are left with the practical task of finding out what the boss really wants. A practical case of this happening is presented in Figure 9.1. The detailed text format of the figure is given in Table 9.1.

This SATISFACTION specification was the initial attribute specification for the future IBC organization characteristics.

We specified them in two hours of discussion, using a shorthand format to give a one page overview of all these characteristics. I have also used the long format (Table 9.1), in order to give readers a better ability to interpret our specifications. After the Director had reviewed this, and given us feedback on missing objectives, we made brief sketches of his additional goals (Figure 9.2).

Subject: Employee qualities (What the Director also wanted)

Definition Name :Quality	Scale	Test	Worst limit	Plan	Best limit	Now	Reference
Professional job satisfaction & motivation	%			95%			
Turnover rate (internal)	%/ year			10%			
Turnover (us − >outside)	%/ year			≥10% less desirable < 1% desirable			
Training investment	%/ year			10%			
Company supported higher education	% budget			5%			
Promotion −>outside mgt.	%/ year			3%			
◄———— What the Director told us he wanted							

Figure 9.2 IBC employee qualities as we outlined them in reality. We did not take time to give all the parameters ('Worst' etc.).

Table 9.2 Employee qualities.

MOTIVATION:
SCALE: % employees responding positively to survey of satisfaction with job
PLAN = 95%?

TURNOVER.IBC:
SCALE = annual turnover rate IBC.SYS employees to other IBC groups
PLAN = 10%

TURNOVER.EXT:
SCALE = annual turnover rate IBC-SYS to outside of IBC employers
PLAN(less-desired employees) = 10% or more
PLAN(desirable ones) 1% or less

TRAINING INVESTMENT:
SCALE = % of employee time
PLAN = 10%

EDUCATION:
SCALE = higher education employee subsidy as % IBC-SYS budget
Plan = 5%

PROMOTION:
SCALE = promotion outside of IBC-SYS to management positions in IBC
PLAN = 3% (employees per year)

The attributes of the organization shown in Table 9.2 were identified by the Director after reading the first set of objectives and discovering that we had clearly forgotten to include these other vital objectives. The detailed specification given in the table was prepared for the purposes of this book.

The Director had another group of objectives he revealed to us, which we grouped under the heading of individual adaptability (Figure 9.3). This has been expanded for the purposes of this book in Table 9.3.

We have now illustrated how we defined three major goal directions for the organization: (user) satisfaction, employee qualities, adaptability.

All these are now more than mere words. They are backed up by specific measurable ideas at a fairly detailed level, even after less than one day of work to define them. Of course IBC went on to devote more attention to detailed analysis of these goals later. But, an entirely new 'language' had been demonstrated for specifying software attributes and software organizational qualities. It was taken into practical use as a communications tool, in a single day.

Subject: Adaptability of employees (What the Director also wanted)

Definition / Name :Quality	Scale	Test	Worst limit	Plan	Best limit	Now	Reference
(Tag) 1.1 Headcount — Employee growth				30%		40%	
1.2 Maintenance — Servicing ability high priority	days to do			1 – >2 days		25 days	
1.3 New — New project start ability	days to useful			30 days		700 days	via evo
1.4 Languages — New language learn-ability				5 days		5 – >30 days	Ex. APL

What the Director told us he really wanted

Figure 9.3 Adaptability of employees as we outlined them in reality.

Table 9.3 Adaptability objectives.

ADAPTABILITY:

HEADCT:
SCALE = net employee growth rate in IBC-SYS yearly %
NOW = 40% (last year)
PLAN = 30% (while still achieving all other objectives)

MAINTENANCE:
SCALE = days delay before maintenance service given to high-priority new projects
NOW = 25 days
PLAN = 1 to 2 days

NEW:
SCALE = delay from conception until first results of new projects are available to the bank
NOW = 700 days
PLAN = 30 days

LANGUAGES:
SCALE = time for employees to learn new software languages
NOW = 5 to 30 days
PLAN = 5 days

9.4.2 Attribute explosion into a hierarchy

We need to give more-detailed definition to important ideas like 'adaptability.' Better definition means that your colleagues will understand the ideas in the same way. If ambiguity of interpretation is allowed, then people will work in conflicting directions. This process of definition by means of sub-attributes is called 'attribute explosion.'

Bear in mind that the explosion of a term is simply a 'special case' definition. For example, in the IBC example the term 'satisfaction' refers to the entire set of more-detailed goals ('value' through 'friendliness').

The only 'right' definition is the one that the *people involved agree to use*. The 'true' interpretation of the meaning of the high level name (satisfaction, employee qualities, and adaptability) of the exploded definition, depends entirely on the set of sub-ideas (sub-attributes) defined within it. The high level attribute name itself means nothing. It is merely a convenient way of referring to the set of attributes which it headlines. The details define the name 'officially.' Nobody is allowed to misinterpret it in their own private way, as is so easy with less formal definitions.

■ 9.5 The scale of measure

Scale = (the units of measure defined).
The icon for the Scale concept is $-|-|-$.

All attribute requirements can and must be measured in some way. We suggest two types of attribute measurement definition. One is theoretical, like a volt. The other is practical, like a voltmeter. We call them the 'scale' and the 'test' (see Section 9.6 for details on the 'test'). The scale says something about *what* we are trying to measure. The test says something about *how* we intend to measure it in a practical, economic and accurate way.

9.5.1 Higher level measurement:

> **The 'set' principle of hierarchical measurement:**
> The lowest measurable levels of attribute specification are the sets of measures which define all higher level attribute names which group them.

The higher level names do not normally have or need their own scales, they 'borrow' the set of scales below them.

For example:
FRIENDLINESS:
    LEARNABILITY: SCALE = minutes to learn, PLAN = 5
    PRODUCTIVITY: SCALE = tasks per hour, PLAN = 20

In this case friendliness is defined by means of the set of the two sub-concepts learnability and productivity. If the system as delivered takes five minutes to learn, and one can carry out 20 tasks per hour, then the friendliness objectives have been met.

9.5.2 At which level of a hierarchical definition do we apply measures?

The general strategy for making vague concepts measurable in practice, is to repeatedly explode them into sub-concepts, through several levels, if necessary, until it becomes obvious how to measure them. Put another way, if you find it very difficult to define a measure for a concept, then this could be because it is really a high level concept, composed of many sub-concepts. Make a simple list of the concepts it is composed of, and then try again to define each one of these with a scale of measure.

For example 'user-friendliness' usually needs explosion. Any one scale of measure like 'speed of learning to use the system' is immediately unsatisfactory, because we intuitively know that it is only part of the concept. It helps to break 'user-friendliness' down into a handful of components. For example, 'speed of learning,' 'educational level for entry to training,' 'speed of working when trained,' 'errors made when working at normal speed,' and 'opinion survey; % who like to work with the system.' See Sections 19.2.4 and 19.3.4 for more detail.

Even this may require a further level of breakdown by type of user, when users are of widely varying capability or type; for example: beginner, child, daily full-time user, and occasional executive user.

How far do you go in this explosion process? You should go as far as you want to, to communicate essential ideas. There is a cost associated with designing a system to meet each specified objective. So, the value of achieving that objective has to justify the cost of catering to it.

The principle of detail:
You must define things to whatever level of detail is necessary to control the critical parameters of your system.

If you are in doubt about how detailed to get, detail 'too much' initially. It is a fairly cheap process. Then stand back from your specification, and simplify it to fit the reality of the cost of development. If you find this difficult to judge, then design and deliver your system in small evolutionary steps of less than 5% of total project effort. This will give you early feedback about value and cost, and allow you to determine whether you have in fact gone too deep (or too shallow) in specification detail.

9.5.3 Exploding attributes at many levels: the IBC example

For example in the IBC case, the initial attribute idea is (if you think about it):

0. A better-quality product, and a more-productive organization

This is exploded initially to three major ideas:

0.1. SATISFACTION (of users of the bank computer systems)

Table 9.4 Product attributes.

Number	Abbreviation	Description	Measure
18	AtLeg	Systems legal currentness	?
19	Audt	System auditability	VMP/CMA
20	ConfOper	System operational reliability	ABENDS/Job steps submitted (per month)
21	ConfInfo	Information reliability	AtInfo,%ErInfo, DspInfo
22	AtInfo	Information currentness	User eval. (Satisf, No)
23	%ErInfo	% errors on outputs	Inconsistencies, sampling
24	DspInfo	Data availability	User managers assessed

0.2. EMPLOYEE QUALITIES (of computer systems department employees only), and

0.3. ADAPTABILITY of employees.

These three ideas were then broken down into the concrete measurable ideas in the Tables and Figures 9.1, 9.2 and 9.3.

9.5.4 The initial IBC implementation of attributes

No further explosion was deemed necessary during our initial IBC study. However, one year later the IBC had in fact done a detailed study of attributes for controlling their systems work and had many more measurable attribute ideas. A sample page of that larger study is reproduced in Table 9.4.

■ 9.6 The test

TEST = (some way to measure along the scale specified).
ICON: '?'

Specification of the practical test to be used while initial objectives are being specified is recommended. It is wise to specify measuring tests which are already in common usage, such as 'employee time accounting' or 'cost accounting systems'. This is partly to ensure that the numbers will be available in practice, and partly to give people confidence in the independence and reliability of the measuring tool.

A rough measuring tool is better than no tool whatsoever. Specify the best measuring tool you can think of initially, however poor it

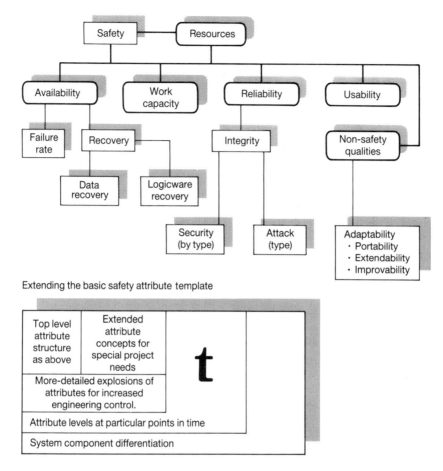

Extending the basic safety attribute template

Figure 9.4 An example from practical work, of defining the concept of 'safety.' The top half of the figure shows how the general template ideas (Chapter 19) are tailored to the safety attribute. The lower half shows different ways of tailoring the attribute specification to particular project needs. The major tailoring concepts are extension, explosion, time specification and differentiation of level for system components with different needs.

might appear. The specification can be improved upon and updated later, and it is always easier to work with something written down.

> **The iterative specification principle:**
> Write down your first thoughts, then improve upon them
> continuously. (It is easier to refine writings than thoughts,
> especially when other people are going to help you.)

Usability Specification
Subject: Software quality attribute specification

Definition Name : Quality	Scale	Test	Worst limit	Plan	Best limit	Now	Reference
Input/output media integratedness	min. to swap 10 device	Sample new	15	5–10	1 ?	not avail.	
Training need	hours to solo ability	sample of <20 new	<1	.1	–>0	–	
User productivity	% user time lost due us	sample real/ideal	50%	10%	–>0	–	
User error rate	% acts changed	by computer logging	<10%	<3%	<1%	–	
Users min. qualification level	% OK answer native	built-in 15 min. test	90%	80%	40%	–	Note: remember to design the test
User-less-ness	% tasks un-attended	manual estimate	50%	–>100%	–	–	
Coherence	% percieved = our product image	sample opinion survey	95%	–>100%	100%	–	
User opinion	%++ feeling for it	survey <50 users	–	90–>99%	100%	–	

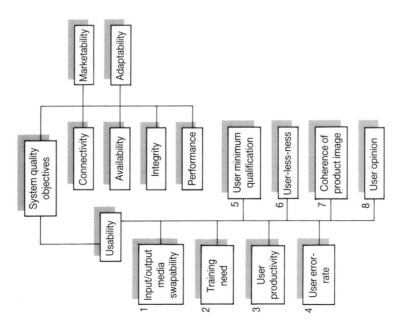

Figure 9.5 An example of explosion of the usability attribute in a particular case.

The main motivation for forcing you to document the measuring method, the test, to be used is:

- to make you recognize that the cost of measuring might have to be included in the budget or schedule;
- to ensure that everybody involved knows that the actual achievement of the required objectives can and will be measured. This motivates them to take the objectives more seriously.
- to prepare a preliminary outline of the formal test plan for the attributes required.

There can be many possible stages in a project where you will wish to be able to measure or test an attribute. Unless otherwise specified, however, the measure implied must be one that should be able to be carried out in acceptance tests, or at the time where the changes planned by the project start to have an impact.

TEST = the official company accounting data
(the implied point in time where the test applies is when the system is initially used in operation)

The points at which the test procedures apply can be defined in parentheses. For example:

TEST (design phases) = use Fagan's inspection method data
TEST (coding phase) = use unit test procedures (Standard ISO 1234)
TEST (quality assure) = use data collected from previous system use.

An attribute specification is not and cannot be chiselled in stone. It is a highly dynamic method for recording your goals and your constantly improved and more realistic understanding of what they really are. We can start with ideals, but we must work our way towards realities.

You cannot begin to judge the effects of any solution ideas in a complete and safe manner unless you are capable of measuring the effect of those ideas in all critical attribute areas. This may sound obvious, but the mistake of trying to judge solutions without adequate measuring concepts is surprisingly normal practice. Take a look at almost any specification of objectives and their corresponding test plans; the explicit test of critical ideas is normally missing.

■ 9.7 'Worst case level' specification

WORST = (the worst acceptable level under any circumstances)
ICON: |←|

The worst case is the worst *acceptable case*. Anything less constitutes an official failure to meet minimum acceptable requirements for the project.

It may well be that in reality, the user might tolerate something worse than the 'official' worst case, but a line has to be drawn somewhere to provide motivation to reject all solutions which will not push us safely over the worst case level. The idea, after all, is to get to the *planned* level.

9.7.1 Determining the worst case specification level

How do we determine the worst case level for any particular attribute? It can be set at the level of the present system (the 'now' level.) It can be set higher than the now level, an essential improvement. It can be set without regard for other attributes. It is the level we cannot tolerate lowering, no matter how good other attributes are.

> **Practical hint:** *Imagine some level which is obviously totally unacceptable under any circumstances. Imagine improvements along the scale until you begin to wonder if the level you are imagining might be acceptable to some users, under certain conditions. You are now in the right area. If necessary, define several worst case levels, using the qualifer (in parentheses).*
>
> For example:
>
> *Worst(for beta test site users) = 80%*
> *Worst(for initial paying customers) = 95%*
> *Worst(one year after initial customer delivery) = 99%*

9.7.2 Sharing the worst case level with others

The worst case level can form the basis for a *legally binding contract specification*, which, if not achieved by the supplier, constitutes legal non-delivery of the entire system. If not achieved, it constitutes moral non-delivery, responsibility for delay, and even failure of the entire venture.

Table 9.5 The borders of attribute specification.

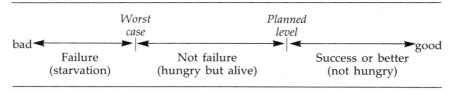

It is of great practical importance that worst case levels are included in formal (signed) agreements with representatives of those who are going to use the system – such as trade unions, consumer representatives, and employee groups. If they are not involved in this procedure, they will feel no obligation to 'live with' initial versions of the system.

Such early versions may be at near-worst-case levels for some attributes – but, we hope, with possibilities of future improvement. If users feel cheated or left out, they can destroy active support and co-operation. They can threaten the solution's long-term future.

■ 9.8 The 'planned level' of an attribute

9.8.1 Basic concepts of the planned level

PLAN = (the level hoped-for together with all other planned
            attribute levels)
ICON:'(?'

While the worst case attribute level represents the border between failure and non-failure, the planned level represents attainment of formal success. Real success may depend on meeting planned levels which have moved faster in the real world than you have been able to respond to!

9.8.2 Budget analogies

The planned level is where you have decided in advance to stop developing, and to start delivering and living with the solution. The planned level is never perfection. It is simply the level of the attribute in question which is 'good enough.' But in terms of goal setting, it must be a level which can be attained together with all the other planned levels. It must be consistent with them, otherwise both they and it are unrealistic.

The planned level for resources, such as money and time, is conceptually identical to an official financial budget. The planned level for quality attributes can be thought of as a 'quality budget.' The planned level for qualities can be thought of as more like a sales quota than an expense budget. We want to get to it, but we don't mind if we exceed it within the same resource budget.

We will see that impact estimation tables (Chapter 11) will give us a tool for viewing our progress towards finding a balanced set of solutions to reach all planned attribute levels.

9.8.3 How do we set the planned levels?

The answers are the same as for any budgeting and estimating process. At first the planned levels may be desired benefits with stated (wished-for) cost and delivery dates. It fact we may deliberately set ambitions a little higher than strictly necessary so as to see how far our solution designers can stretch themselves and the system before they scream 'impossible!'

For example if we know that:

AVAILABILITY:
NOW(our old system) = 90%
BEST(competitor) = 95%

then

WORST(initial delivery) = 90%
WORST(one year after initial delivery = 95%

now we have defined our minimum ambitions, we can afford to stretch our designer's imagination. So, we try the definition:

PLAN(initial delivery) = 95%
PLAN(within 5 years of delivery) = 99.9%

Maybe this will prove too difficult, in conflict with other attribute requirements. But we will at least expect to get the worst case requirements fulfilled. We will also try to meet the planned levels, and only give way on them after consultation with the user, in order to meet higher priority requirements.

An attribute specification is by no means static. It is a living reflection of our progress in providing solutions. You should not hesitate to put some numbers down on paper for fear that someone will commit you to achievement of those numbers. But since not everybody is familiar with these particular rules of design, it might be wise to include a disclaimer on the document in question such as:

> 'The levels set in this document represent the best estimation efforts at this stage (insert date and design stage here). They do not represent a commitment by anybody to achieve any or all of them until such a commitment is explicitly undertaken. They serve as a basis for finding out about feasible solutions.'

9.8.4 Planned levels must be achieved at one time

The difficult thing about planned attributes compared to the other attribute specification levels, is that all planned levels of the various attributes must be achievable at one time in the real world. The worst case level, by contrast, can be viewed in isolation from all other attributes of the same system. If the worst case requirement is violated, then it doesn't make any difference how well you have done in other attributes. Your system is 'dead,' by your own definition.

It is not all that difficult to set a planned level for something, nor is it all that difficult to achieve a single one of them, if you are not bound to achieve any other attribute goal at the planned level too. This is a variation of Weinberg's Zeroth Law of Reliability, that states: 'If a system doesn't have to be reliable, it can meet any other objective.' (Gilb, T., and Weinberg, G.M., (1984) *Humanized input: techniques for reliable keyed input*, QED Information Sciences Inc., Wellesley, Mass.)

9.8.5 Nobody knows exactly what planned levels are realistic

Of course nobody can know exactly which ambitious planned levels will balance with all other planned levels in advance of finding design solutions, and in advance of real experience. The initial statement of planned levels should be as realistic as you can make it. But, it should also be intentionally ambitious.

As you progress into design phases, you can use the impact estimation technique to understand what a more realistic set of planned levels will look like. At the same time, you can use evolutionary delivery experience to adjust your perception of realistic planned levels. Planned levels can be expressed as a series of levels in time or on various sub-products. For example:

PLAN (initial release) = 89% or more
PLAN (by release 2.0) = 95% or more
PLAN (real time components) = 99.9%
PLAN (one time configurators) = 90% or more

■ 9.9 The 'best case' specification

BEST = (the best known level achieved anywhere under any
        circumstances. Synonym: RECORD
ICON: $|\rightarrow|$

The parenthesis qualifer can also be useful for giving a number of reference cases.

For example:

BEST(Competitor XYZ, last year) = 80% (*Computer Weekly*, 8 Nov.)
BEST(Competitor XYZ, future) = 90% (Advert. claims, Feb. last)
BEST(our research labs) = 92% (Tech. Report 23.45)

The use of a 'best case level' specification is a useful option. It has an informative value, because it tells clients, managers, and users that there is an unexploited potential in this attribute. It has a provocative value, because it challenges the holders of the purse strings to give developers the necessary resources to move away from previously planned levels, and in the direction of the best case levels. It may entice the setters of planned levels in other areas to give ground, to sacrifice some of the attributes desirable to them, in order to attain more of this particular one. If they fail to react to this challenge, it remains documented that they were once faced with it, but failed to act.

The best case is the state of the art limit, also called the 'engineering limit,' for that attribute in an environment corresponding to your own. The best case is not some unreal idea such as '100% reliability.' Of course the user wants it. But the user has no right to want something he will not pay for. His resources are not infinite, and this is the present cost of the state of perfection. Do not waste your time with totally unrealistic ideals. The best case will do more useful work for you as a tool if you put something appetizing *and* realistic in front of the user. Remember: it is not a requirement, only a reference.

■ 9.10 The 'now level' specification

NOW (reference to system, date) = (level of the attribute in a
system we want to compare
our plans with)

ICON: ')('

This icon is the Blissymbolic for 'now,' being made up of Past ')',
and Future '('. I would like to recommend the Blissymbols as the basis
of a notation for system development. More details can be found in
Semantography-Blissymbolics, by Charles K. Bliss, Semantography Trust
Fund, 13 Warrington Ave., Epping, NSW 2121, Australia.

The specification of the present level of the attribute in the current
environment provides useful comparative information. It makes
evaluation, and approval procedures of the planned and worst case
levels, easier to understand for managers and users who 'have a feel
for' the system, but who rarely have accurate measures for most
attributes in their heads.

The numeric difference between the now level and the planned
level is a measure of the change which the new system or solution will
be expected to give in this particular attribute area. Many people give
up too easily when trying to create a comparative standard (the 'now'
level) from which to help the manager or user evaluate the new
solution proposals. A little determination and imagination will produce
a now-level measure for most critical attributes.

You may not think you have an 'old' system. But, there is
invariably some older system which you are planning to replace. It
maybe is not automated, and maybe it is not your system – but the
functions are probably being done somehow, and you can probably
find a level of the attribute to serve as a comparison.

The now level may, like the best case, have a number of
references, using a parenthesis condition, such as:

NOW(compet. XYZ, last year) = 0.5 errors/1000 customers/year
NOW(our product bcd) = 0.6 errors/1000 customers/year

9.10.1 The difference between 'now' and 'best'

The essential difference between the 'now' level and the 'best' case
level is that the 'now' level refers to our departure point, usually our
own old system; sometimes a competitor's system. The 'best case' is
neither 'where we were,' nor 'where they were.' The best case is 'the
best level ever experienced in reality.' An exception is when our plan

aspires to beating the best ever known (pushing the state of the art forward). In this case our planned level is better than the 'best.' 'Now' is not a requirement only a reference point.

■ 9.11 The 'authority' specification

> ICON : '←'
> SYNONYM : PA = (parent is)
> AUTHORITY = the President's speech (23 Nov., p. 23), 'best'

It is useful to include references to sources of measures directly on the attribute specification document. This will help in quality control through cross-reference checking (see Chapters 12 and 21). It will often lend authority to the specifications whenever it can be documented that they were properly derived from people in authority. If nobody with proper authority has made the specification, then at least the person who has suggested it should make this plain, and challenge someone in authority to revise or approve the specification. For example:

> AUTHORITY = Pat Analyst (29 Nov., during feasibility study,
> needs user approval before we take it seriously).

If multiple sources can be cited, so much the better. For example:

> Authority (bd. of dir., 23 Nov.) = 'highest competitive quality'
> Authority (group quality handbook) = '90% min. availability'

■ 9.12 Summary

If you insist on using the goal clarification discipline described here, you will be rewarded with a more efficient decision-making process.

If you fail to create crystal clear and complete goals for your people to work with, you will suffer from an ineffective problem-solution process. You will get results which are quite different from the ones you should have specified in the first place.

Save time. Spend the first one per cent of your problem solving process on making a clear goal statement.

■ 9.13 Exercises

1. Take some plans from your current work situation and extract all words or terms which hint at benefits or costs. Try to find

appropriate scales, tests, authority and levels (now, best, worst, plan) for each.
2. Use both the templates (Chapter 19) and your professional knowledge, to identify any missing objectives from the plans you have examined.
3. Try to get a group of colleagues to approve your interpretation of the goals.

10

Solutions: how to find and specify them

■ Introduction

The previous chapter was concerned with a language for specifying one type of requirements, 'attribute specification.' We will now turn our attention to a disciplined process for finding a suitable set of solutions to meet those objectives.

The term 'solution' here is defined as one of those many design decisions which are required to enable us to meet our attribute requirements.

In order to meet all our planned quality attribute levels within all our planned resource limitations, we will need a set of design solutions. None of these solutions will be specifically stated as required by our users. If they were, then they would be 'functional requirements.' By definition, here, the solutions we will be looking for are entirely the province of the design engineer. The user or client of the system will be the only judge of whether the attribute requirements have been met (by the use of our chosen solutions), and whether the functional requirements are delivered.

This chapter includes practical detail for the general process of finding solutions, specifying them, and cross-checking them against the design requirements. It cannot include advice on specific solutions for specific design objectives. This is a matter of detailed and specific technology, which is continually changing.

> **The solution determination principle:**
> Attributes determine solutions.

A solution is a set of design engineering ideas to meet the user's attribute requirements specification.

A solution is determined by an engineering process, and it is dictated by the levels of user quality-and-resource attributes required. A particular set of attribute requirements can often be met by many different possible sets of technical solutions. There is no one single 'right' set of solutions.

Technical solutions (e.g. 'use C language'), if dictated by the user or client, are not 'solutions.' They are not the province of the design engineer. The design engineer is, in my view, responsible for ensuring that such user-specified solutions are really the wish of the user. Very often they are a user's way of expressing attribute requirements (e.g. language C might be a requirement for portability). It is then the responsibility of the design engineer, in the interest of the client, to constructively challenge such demands.

Finding and evaluating solutions is not a simple process. There are a number of methods which can help us do it better, many of which are discussed here in Part Two: impact analysis, impact estimation, inspection and evolutionary delivery. There are many stages of development at which a decision to use or not to use a solution can be made. It is certainly not as simple as assuming that all solutions are found during a single design phase. There are many cycles of refinement in the design process.

It is also worth nothing that there is no fixed sequence for the use of these tools, any more than there is one for a carpenter's saws, hammers, chisels and screwdrivers. There is a constant iteration between them, as you move between different levels of detail, and as you try out the design ideas in a practical environment.

You can use the attribute requirements as a checklist of items which need some solution specification. The simple tool for keeping track of this initial brainstorming is the use of impact analysis tables (Section 11.13). A simple example of this method is given below. This will give you about half of the design solution ideas you need. A harder discipline, impact estimation (Chapter 11) will give you most of the rest of the design ideas you need, while you try to meet planned quality levels (with a safety margin), within resource limitations.

Inspection (Chapter 12) will help you to see inconsistencies in your thinking and documentation process. The defects found by inspection will undoubtedly lead you to rework your solution specification.

The design solutions which are not identified by this process need to be identified in the practical realm. Evolutionary delivery is the tool to use. When things do not turn out as expected during a particular delivery step, you will be forced to re-evaluate your solutions to correct the situation.

There is a hidden assumption in the process of finding solutions to match your attribute requirements. It is that you know the multiple quality and resource attributes of each solution idea. If you know these then you can pick out the solutions relevant to the requirements.

The concept of handbooks containing a list of technical solutions, with information about their expected attributes, is imbedded in all engineering disciplines, except for software engineering. There are no real software engineering handbooks available at this time (1987). It will be some time before we are at the same level of maturity as other disciplines in this respect. Therefore, I have eliminated discussion of software engineering handbooks in this book. I have decided to stick with what is currently achievable, rather than what seems to be the logical way of organizing our discipline. The equivalent today of a formal engineering handbook is the data that resides in the heads and personal notebooks of the designers.

Table 10.1 The basic structure of an engineering handbook using a
hypothetical attribute list.

Solution idea = 'binary search (on a sequential file on disk or other direct
                    access device)'
Portability = (expected range and scale of measure)
Ease of implementation = (expected range and scale of measure)
Availability = (expected range and scale of measure)
Development cost = (expected range and scale of measure)
Operational cost = (expected range and scale of measure)
Storage cost = (expected range and scale of measure)
Notes on exceptions and conflicts with other solutions.

Solution idea = 'Smalltalk programming language'
Portability = (expected range and scale of measure)
Reliability = (expected range and scale of measure)
Ease of maintenance = (expected range and scale of measure)
Learning ease = (expected range and scale of measure)
Maintenance ease = (expected range and scale of measure)
Execution speed = (expected range and scale of measure)
Notes on exceptions and conflicts with other solutions.

The impact analysis table (or chart) is a practical tool for
stimulating and checking that you have enough solutions to meet your
objectives. List your major objectives on the left hand side of a page,
for example:

OBJECTIVES . . .   (SOLUTIONS, next step)
Market share
(over 50%)

Perceived quality
(best of all competitors)

Production costs
(variable and lowest)

then indicate which of your strategies, design ideas, tactics, policies (in
short 'solutions') contribute to the objectives. For example:

OBJECTIVES . . .   SOLUTIONS
Market share   Written 3-year guarantees
(over 50%)   100 extra salesmen

Perceived quality   Advertising about our quality
(best of all competitors)

Production costs   ?
(variable and lowest)

There must be a reasonable balance between objectives and the specified solutions for meeting them, even at this informal level of analysis. By using this impact analysis chart, you might, for example, realize and be able to get others to realize that

1. We have some interesting solutions for 'market share.' But we now need to know such things as: will they provably do the job?; are they perhaps unnecessarily costly?
2. The solution we have for 'perceived quality' looks hopelessly optimistic. Our competitors will all be claiming the same. Maybe we actually have to do something to change the real quality of our products?
3. We haven't done anything at all for production costs. We need some solution ideas right now for that item.

■ 10.1 Solutions: the initial search

10.1.1 Finding solutions using attribute requirements as a stimulant

> **The principle of full coverage:**
> You must have enough solutions to meet all your objectives.

Solution ideas come as a result of focusing your attention on your specified objectives (attributes and functions).

10.1.2 The relationship with functional requirements

Functions determine the attributes of interest.

The separation of attribute requirements and functional requirements is an important concept. It leads to creative solutions and prevents the problem of software engineers merely automating existing systems. People (software engineers or end-users) always start with functions because they can easily envisage them. There is always some functional system already in existence, automated or not, corresponding to the one which is being considered for software engineering. The software engineering task is usually part of an effort to improve the attributes of those existing functions.

Knowing the function and its environment, we determine the attribute requirements. It is the attribute requirements which pose the software engineering problem of finding appropriate solutions.

> **The principle of what really determines the solutions:**
> Attributes determine solutions. But functions and their
> environment determine attribute requirements.

A current problem in the software industry is that software engineers concentrate too much on functional specification. They pay little, if any, attention to the attribute requirements. But it is actually the attributes which determine the technical solutions. Attributes and their solutions are the primary material of real software engineering. It is not necessary to know whether an automobile is going to be used as an ambulance, a police car or a bank robbers' get-away vehicle in order to design its motor to the speed and fuel attributes required.

■ 10.2 Using attributes as the major stimulant for solutions

Here is an outline of a process for finding solutions:

1. Focus on one attribute at a time and brainstorm solution ideas which would contribute to meet its planned level.
2. Estimate side-effects (using an impact estimation table, Chapter 11) on other attributes which were not considered in the first phase.
3. Eliminate those solutions which have such large undesired side-effects as to cause the worst case levels to be threatened for any attribute requirement.
4. Repeat the cycle until you estimate that all planned attribute levels have been met (using impact estimation tables, Chapter 11) or until you have no further design solution ideas.
5. If you estimate that all planned attribute levels will be met, you have in theory finished designing. (Not really, go to step 7.)
6. If you have no further design solution ideas, but you have not reached your planned benefit levels (or stayed within your planned resource limits) then you must either
   (a) Access more design expertise (then go to step 1) or
   (b) Change your planned attribute levels to reflect your best design (then go to step 7).
7. You can now test your design hypothesis by
   (a) Fagan's inspection process (Chapter 12).
   (b) Evolutionary delivery and measurement (Chapter 13).
   (c) Other analysis tools such as impact analysis, solution comparison or solution handbooks (Chapter 11).
   (d) Any other appropriate method or tool you find useful.

8. This process is a never-ending cycle of improvement when you
   have competition, or the technology cost and effect is
   changing.

Here are some principles which seem to apply to the above
process.

The S = f(A) principle:
Solutions are a function of all attribute requirements.

The infinitely complex principle:
The process of finding a complete set of solutions for all attribute
requirements is complex and is never perfected.

The imperfect design principle:
The perfect design solution will never exist. You won't ever have
time to find a perfect design solution, but you can continue
working towards one for the system lifetime.

The moving target principle:
Since real attribute requirements will be forced to change in
time, the design must be correspondingly adaptable to be able to
meet them in the future.

Practical hints: *Don't worry about getting the design solution
complete or perfect. You can't, anyway.*

*Do a reasonable job, so that you reduce wasted time in
evolutionary implementation steps.*

*Be prepared to learn from evolutionary implementation
experience, to change your design whenever necessary in order
to keep it in accordance with the real needs and the real
technology.*

*You can't get it right the first time, but you can get a good start,
and then you can get it more right as you evolve the system.*

*The most important design effort initially is to place a large
number of open-ended (see Section 13.4) design strategies in
place, so that your learning and change process will be
comfortable.*

The search for solutions can be automated (Figure 10.1).

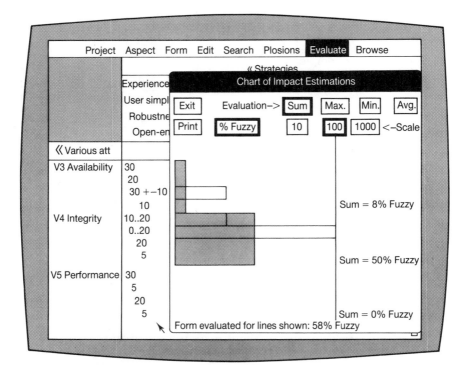

Figure 10.1 Automating the search for solutions. The figure shows a screen image from a prototype system for automated software engineering, called the ASPECT Engine, by Lech Krzanik, of Krakow, Poland. It can automatically search for solutions which match its attribute requirements and evaluate them multi-dimensionally.

V3, V4 and V5 represent various major attribute requirements and their sub-attributes defined in detail elsewhere. On the top, strategies such as 'experience' represent tags for suggested solutions to the required planned level of attributes. The 100% planned level of all attributes is represented by the vertical line down from the box with 100 in it. The bars represent the estimated impact of the selected and defined strategies on the required attributes. The hollow bars are the estimated impact (100% for integrity) and the shaded bars are the estimated degree of uncertainty (50% for integrity).

4.   DEVELOP: ('Planned Professional Competence Development')

4.1   PATH PLAN: A written approved career path plan shall exist for each professional.

4.2   ROTATE: Job rotation shall be planned for on average once a year.

4.3   EXPERIENCE HANDBOOKS: We shall collect technique lists and their attributes in centrally published handbooks (so that all professionals have accurate and complete knowledge of possible techniques and experiences).

4.4   PERSONAL FEEDBACK: Our work-reporting system shall provide each professional and manager with cumulative statistics on their personal use of time and their activities. (This shall be used to help improve their time usage and productivity.)

4.5   PRODUCT QUALITY FEEDBACK: Measured attributes (costs and quality) of all projects which an individual is associated with shall be regularly made available to that person for his evaluation and improvement.

4.6   CLASSIC TRAINING: At least 50% of each individual's training shall be directed to subjects with long-term value which are not 'IBM Product Oriented'. (Examples, English, Design by Objectives, Management subjects.)

4.7   PERSONAL TRAINING BUDGET: Each professional shall have a personal time budget for training. It shall be at least three weeks yearly. This is to be obligatory and to be cumulative if not used. We will pay all travel and tuition costs for training or study which may be suggested by the employee.

4.8   USER CONTACT: All professionals of type 'analyst', 'designer', 'project leader' should be required to spend at least one week a year working directly in the departments with their system.

4.9   COMPETITION: For programming, maintenance and design tasks, there should be regular opportunity for direct competition between teams for the tasks, based on lowest time bid or best design.

4.10   TEAMS: The normal working environment for all tasks shall be based on joint team responsibility: less senior people should be mixed with more senior people to help the learning by both parties. We should never be too dependent on single individuals alone.

Figure 10.2 An example of solution specification from the IBC case study. This is an exact specification used in the IBC case study to define the solution strategy, DEVELOP (planned professional competence development).

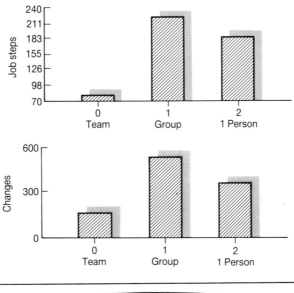

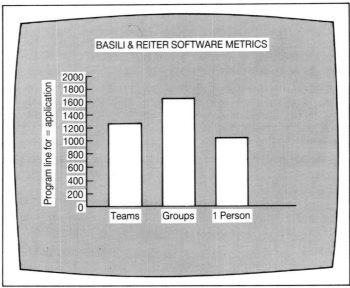

Figure 10.3 Measuring team effects. The productive effect of a cooperating team is measurable, as this data indicates. The cooperating team required only about 80 job steps (top) to complete the task, while non-cooperating groups or individuals required over 200 job steps. Similarly (middle) the team required substantially fewer changes, or corrections, to get things right. Finally, in the lower chart, the teams were better than groups in terms of the total program lines of code required to complete the application. Source: Shneiderman, *Datamation* 1–80. (© 1980 by Cahners Publishing Company)

■ 10.3 Solution specification

Here are some initial rules for specifying the solution:

- keep it brief,
- be as unambiguous as possible (but you can still detail it later),
- put new ideas in a new statement (new line and new sentence).

■ 10.4 Solution tagging

All solution ideas should get a unique identification tag of some sort for future reference and cross reference.

The most elementary levels of a documented design specification should be assigned their own unique tag. For example: 'TAG-A: The screen should be in color and of the highest available pixel resolution,' has two design specifications but only one tag. It should be broken down to the elementary ideas, like this:

'COLOR: The screen should be in color.
RESOLUTION: The screen should be of the highest available pixel resolution.'

The example above (Figure 10.2) has two forms of tagging. A number (4.9) and a mnemonic (COMPETITION).

Sometimes both a name and a number are useful. They can even be considered as one single tag (4.9 COMPETITION).

The structural design of the tagging I will leave up to the reader. The essential point is that each distinct solution idea should have a unique reference tag.

I personally prefer a mnemonic tag ('TEAMS' not '4.10') because it does not get obsolete (as numbers do) by additions or removals from the list of design solutions, and it conveys more meaning when cross-referenced from other documents.

There are many uses for tags. They are useful, for example, to summarize the gist of an idea and headline it, to be a convenient cross-reference pointer to the idea (which helps in inspection of design, of test plans, and even of logic). They also allow the ideas to be summarized on evaluation tables (such as impact estimation tables), and act as a basis for software configuration management: keeping track of multiple versions of software.

Software configuration management is a design and maintenance process, modeled strongly on corresponding hardware disciplines. These are primarily from the aerospace and military fields. The basic idea is to keep track of the set of design and implementation components which make up any one complex system. The purpose is to be able to analyze faults and the effects of changes on particular unique configurations, which might be in the hands of customers, by knowing exactly what their configuration is composed of.

10.4.1 Hierarchical tagging

Tags can be used in conjunction with each other to indicate that the ideas are members of a group. For example:

> IBC.DEVELOP.TEAM which indicates that TEAM is a subset of the DEVELOP ideas, and that DEVELOP is a subset of the IBC ideas. This device can be used to ensure unique tags in spite of the fact that another group may be assigning tags to another part of the project. For example:

> IBC.POLICY.TEAM references a totally different solution, which may bear no resemblance to IBC.DEVELOP.TEAM. When we are within a particular context of discussion, the shortened version (TEAM or POLICY.TEAM for example) can be used unambiguously.

10.4.2 Temporal tagging

In the evolving and dynamic systems we are trying to deal with here, the detailed definition behind a tag may be changed, for updating, correction or improvement. It must be possible to indicate explicitly which version we are referring to. We can use a simple qualifier like TEAM(810902, Draft), TEAM(860311, 1st revision) to pin down a precise definition.

We can do this at a higher level of reference, perhaps once and for all by, for example, IBC(sysplan).DEVELOP(860311).TEAM, where TEAM is now = TEAM(sysplan,860311), because of the high level qualifiers appearing after IBC and DEVELOP. We don't necessarily have to write the temporal qualifier every time we use it, as long as it is clearly defined in the document at hand.

10.4.3 The tag principle

> **The tag principle:**
> Untagged ideas never die, but they do just fade away.

Practical hints: *In large systems you will want automated support to keep track of tags and find their cross-reference. A data dictionary system or database may be a useful start. Some users will want to extend this design control concept to a longer term configuration control scheme, for multiple delivered and maintained versions of the software.*

If the documentation you have to work with does not have tags, then create them for your own protection: create tags for the most elementary design statements; use a hierarchical design statement and tagging method.

The most powerful motivator for thorough use of tags is the use of Fagan's inspection method (see Chapters 12 and 21). When you have to cross check a number of voluminous specifications and designs for detail, then the tag saves you a lot of time scanning many documents to find what you actually want.

■ 10.5 Solution hierarchies

Get the architecture right first.

We need a method for clarifying the main architectural areas of a software system in relation to the more-detailed engineering design decisions. Hierarchical representation of our technical solution provides such a device.

10.5.1 The top ten solutions on a page

Although an initial solution brainstorming process may provide a mixture of high-impact and low-impact solution ideas you need to concentrate on collecting the high-impact (on attribute requirements) solutions first.

Concentrate first on getting a single page of high-impact solutions. In the IBC case, they looked like Table 10.2 overleaf.

10.5.2 The solution hierarchy detail

Once the main architecture ideas are in place, you can proceed with a systematic process of detailing them. You can, if you wish, explode solution ideas into a hierarchy several levels deep. There are several

Table 10.2 The top-level of solutions for the IBC case study.

POLICY (basic decision-making rules for IBC-SYS, also known as IBC.POLICY. For detail see Section 6.1

PERSON (professional personnel resource-control systems; formal and detailed)

DEVELOP (see Figure 10.2)

INFOTECT (information systems architect)

DBO (use design-by-objectives methods). See Table 10.3 and Table 10.4 for details

BUSINESS ANALYST (have a filter between end users and systems development)

AUTOMATE (maximize computer support of development function)

STANDARDS (have result-oriented quality and cost standards)

RESPONSIBILITY (increase the degree of team joint responsibility)

consequences of a solution hierarchy:

1. When a high level idea is removed, all lower level ideas are also removed.
2. All detailed explosion serves to define the higher level concepts more unambiguously.
3. Our ability to estimate correctly the impact of the ideas-of-the-higher-level increases in proportion to the level of detailed definition below it.

This is a well known principle of what the building business calls quantity surveying (UK), where architectural designs are broken down into numbers of bricks and door installation work operations, to be given to potential contractors for cost estimation purposes.

■ 10.6 Solution modularization

How do we 'best' break down a larger solution idea into more detailed ones?

The answer to this is the same as to any similar question of modular explosion. It depends on our objectives and their priority.

10.6.1 Example of explosion rules

For example, if our highest priority is to control risk of failure or of deviation from plan, then surely we must explode into small visible

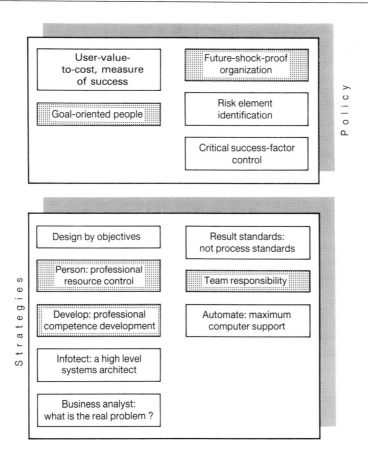

Figure 10.4 Elements of a first-cut solution. This is an overview of the major solutions for meeting the IBC objectives (Chapter 9). The shaded solutions were initially forbidden since they were organizational in nature, but were later encouraged when the objectives were clarified.

understandable modules, and modules of high risk and low risk separated from one another.

If our highest priority is to meet deadlines, and to get critical things delivered early, then our explosion must try to:

- separate those solutions which must be delivered early, from those that can tolerate late delivery;
- keep initial solution modules small so that there is no major delay on any early delivery, even if problems are encountered.

If ease of maintenance and change is highest on our list, then those

Table 10.3 The IBC case explosion of the DBO solution.

.SFS	System Function Specification see Chapter 8
.SAS	System Attribute Specification (detail in Table 10.4). See also Chapter 9
.STS	System Solution Technique Specification
.T/A	Handbook (techniques handbook with their attributes) see Section 11.16
.IA	Impact Analysis tables, see Section 11.13
.IE	Impact Estimation tables, see Section 11.2
.SC	Solution Comparison method, see Section 11.14
.INSPECT	Fagan's Inspection method, decomposed in Table 10.5
.EVO	the Evolutionary Delivery method, Chapters 13 and 15

ideas which are most likely to need change should be separated from those which will likely remain static. A sequential file is a stable design concept. But the access mechanism for getting into that file may be changed – for example, from sequential seek, to binary search, or to indexed sequential.

I make no attempt here to be thorough, but merely to illustrate that the explosion of solutions should be done with the dominating objectives in mind. If solution ideas are not exploded into enough detail, then we risk the practical penalty of having to drag less useful ideas along with the useful ones. This might result in a delay in getting useful things done.

10.6.2 An IBC example of explosion into solution specification

For example: in the IBC case study the IBC.DBO (design by objectives) solution would require several years of development before it was fully available. Indeed the original plan was to use at least three years to develop better methods before any real change was made to the software development environment.

The initial explosion of DBO was by the major techniques in it (Table 10.3). This explosion is dictated more by convenience than anything else. The methods are described separately in the literature, but they can be largely implemented independently of each other. Some of them are far easier to implement than others, and some would have considerable pragmatic and political value compared to others. So we have a number of choices when it comes to the sequencing of implementation of the sub-functions. We are consciously looking for evolutionary ways of delivering the solution ideas.

Table 10.4 The explosion of the attribute specification solution SAS.

.BIG4: The four largest existing projects will get an approved top ten measurable attributes on one page

.STANDARD: an attribute specification standard will apply to all projects

.INSP: attribute specs. will be used in inspections (high & low levels)

.TRAIN: training courses will be given for attribute specification

.TEMPLATE: attribute templates will be provided (see Chapter 19)

.CHECKLIST: checklists for Fagan's inspection will be introduced for SAS

.TEST: test plans will be checked against SAS 'TEST' specs.

We chose to implement the IBC.DBO.SAS (measurable attribute objectives) specification early, because we realized that it would have great immediate value (getting project objectives better understood). We also realized that since the Director of IBC had already experienced the use of this method dramatically, two days earlier (see Section 8.1.5), we would get political management support and understanding for the early stages of implementation of the solution.

However, changing a development culture to master fully the use of quantitative multiple objectives can take many years in a large shop. We are now into the third year of changing a 23 000 person organization, and there is a long way to go, even though it is official company policy. See Chapter 20 for ways to motivate people.

Therefore, we can further divide the SAS specification into sub-solutions which make it easier to swallow, a bit at a time (Table 10.4). From this explosion, we are given the opportunity to do high impact and low cost items like SAS.BIG4 before we go through the bureaucracy of proper introduction of the method into the organization (things like SAS.TRAIN and SAS.TEMPLATE). This explosion is the one we actually used to generate the evolutionary IBC organizational development plan.

Of course, just because you have decided to do something like SAS first, doesn't mean you have to do the entire SAS explosion before anything else. Some of those items may provide less result-value at higher cost than the best items in an explosion of something else, for example of IBC.DBO.INSPECT (Table 10.5).

For example, you might want to combine INSPECT.Q&D with SAS.BIG4 in the early implementation steps of the plan, since they both have high immediate value and low implementation cost. Then you could proceed to select the cream, in various combinations, from all other exploded solution plans.

Table 10.5 IBC.DBO. INSPECT explosion.

.IBM: adopt IBM inspection rules as basis

.PR-LD: full-time project leader for INSPECT implementation

.DATA: collect inspection statistics as part of work report scheme

.MOD2W: moderators shall have two weeks training (partly on job)

.P = Mt: preparation time shall approx. equal inspection time (or cancel)

.3HR: up to one hours free discussion scheduled company time after meet.

.DOC: the high level documentation design and specs. shall be brought up to easily inspectable standard (for example with cross-referencing)

.AUTO: computer-aided inspection shall be done as far as possible (cross-referencing)

.Q/A: quality assurance dept. is responsible professionally for moderators

.WHAT?: all written documentation will be inspected at earliest possible time

.STAT: full inspection statistics shall be collected in computer base

.DEMO: all data collected may be required back from source projects or people

.Q&D: inspect code against pseudocode as quick and dirty start of inspection

The point at this stage is that your ability to identify 'juicy' starting points, is dependent on the degree to which you have taken the trouble to explode solution ideas into some detail, and the degree to which you have also managed to separate juicy ideas from the 'whistles and bells.' The term 'juicy' is defined here as implementation steps which have relatively high positive impact on stated quality objectives, and also have low consumption of budgeted resources attributes.

■ 10.7 Solution cross-referencing

In order to be able to check the correctness of a solution implementation, and in order to make correct changes to complex software documentation, you need to cross-reference the solution tags (Section 10.4) in other forms of documentation.

For example, the following documentation will benefit from systematic cross-referencing of the solutions:

- test planning,
- detailed individual test cases,
- user documentation drafts (not final copy, necessarily),
- higher level documentation and specification,
- attribute specification,

Table 10.6 Examples of imbedding cross-references in systems documentation.

A TEST CASE
1234 ABC (Test No. 1 of solution 'IBC.DBO.INSP.Q&D')

A TEST DESIGN
USER.DOC.FEAT.COLOR: All 256 colors can be displayed at user command in
any combination of 16 at a time.(Design Spec. = COLOR.SCREEN.USER.CT)
Notice that the test design has its own tag COLOR for cross-referencing

IN PROGRAM CODE
DO SUBPROGXYZ; (tested by design USER.DOC.FEAT.XYZ)

- module and interface planning,
- pseudocode (in comments),
- marketing plans.

Briefly the cross-reference needs to be imbedded in the documentation somehow. Then when changes are made, in either the solution or the other cross-referenced documentation, it will trigger notification that 'you can't change one without the other'. For example, see Table 10.6.

The point of these examples is to illustrate that we must explicitly take the effort to include the cross-references, as comments, at the same time as we generate the documentation. In some cases it has not been done already, and cross-references must be written in afterwards, but this is frequently worth the effort in terms of preventing errors.

Readers should experiment with cross-referencing so as to convince themselves of its value in detecting inconsistencies (through inspection) or the need for changes (as a result of maintenance elsewhere). Remember that without consistency checking we can expect about 34% to 74% (according to Thayer *et al.*, 1978, *Software reliability*, North-Holland) of our operational software errors to be the result of design documentation inconsistency (before coding took place).

In another large software development effort (see Chapter 21) we found about four thousand design documentation defects, using inspection, in material which was already on its way to the program coders. Since we had inadequate cross-referencing and other inadequate support methods in place at the time, we reckon we were about 30% effective (when we should have been at least 80% effective). This group decided to develop and implement extensive cross-referencing tools as a result of their experiences without them.

Both cross-referencing, and follow-up mechanisms (inspection and automated support for the cross-references) are necessary to avoid the error content we must otherwise expect.

The software engineering manager has to ensure that these mechanisms are in place. The programmers and testers will, without your intervention, quite happily satisfy themselves that the defective specifications are coded and tested 'correctly.'

■ 10.8 Closing remarks

Technical solutions are the engineered design-specifications for meeting the users' attribute objectives.

They are the province of the engineer, not the user. It is important to treat them separately from user-dictated requirements, if the engineer is to keep the attributes under control. The engineer needs to be free to modify the solution technologies in use, in order to increase the chances of meeting the attribute requirements.

11

Solution evaluation

■ Introduction

How can we know that the solutions suggested will satisfy our requirements? This is really the most fundamental question of engineering management.

The answer is complex, and it includes a number of interconnecting tools, not all of which are the subject of this book. The answer is also one which addresses the moving target of users' changing requirements. The difficulty of estimating the value of the solutions is also compounded by the changing technological cost and availability.

The impact estimation (IE) technique gives us a better overall picture of design progress than anything used by most software engineering managers today. It has a very general utility in giving an initial answer to the question of solution satisfaction, and can also stimulate our search for a more-complete set of solutions. It is simply a method for estimating your design progress towards your design targets. In principle, it is similar to an attempt to estimate the total cost of a series of design components in relation to a fixed-cost budget.

For example, if the budget was $1000, and three proposed design components cost $100, $200 and $500 respectively, then we would estimate that we have 'used up' 80% ($800/$1000) of our design cost budget.

Impact estimation uses a similar language to this (% of planned level) for estimating the impact of proposed solutions on all the attributes we are designing towards.

■ 11.1 Basic impact estimation

Let us take as an example a single design solution (4.1 PATH PLAN from Figure 10.2, the IBC case) and try to estimate its impact on a single objective (HEADCT, from Table 9.3).

PATH PLAN: 'a written approved career path plan shall exist for each professional'

HEADCT: Scale = net employee growth rate in IBC-SYS yearly percentage
NOW = 40%, PLAN = 30% (while still achieving all other objectives)

The language to be used is simple. If we think PATH PLAN has no impact on HEADCT we estimate zero per cent (0%) impact. If we think PATH PLAN, by itself, leads to the exact achievement of the ability to maintain a 30% growth rate, while keeping all other objectives at planned levels, then we will credit it with 100%. If we think the truth lies somewhere else, we simply indicate it with the most appropriate number relative to these two (0% and 100%) estimates.

In this case I made a quick round-numbers estimate of 5% for the impact of the PATH PLAN solution on the HEADCT objective. This is my way of saying it doesn't solve the whole problem, but it makes an interesting contribution. If we had a couple of dozen such ideas, we might just get there.

You might like to call this guesstimation. It is. However the estimates can be as solidly based as any estimate, if you care to take the trouble. Even when the estimate is quite rough, it serves a useful purpose, one which cannot be served with mere words.

■ 11.2 The impact estimation table

> **Practical hint:** *The IE table can be nicely put onto a conventional spreadsheet program on a personal computer. It can also be used then to produce charts of design progress. See Figure 11.2 for sample.*

The IE table is a tool for expressing our design progress of multiple solutions (from left to right) upon multiple objectives (from top to bottom). The IE table in Figure 11.1 is only a part of the total IBC case study objectives and solutions. If our estimated numbers are roughly correct – and they should be if we have any useful levels of professional knowledge about the problem at hand – I would make the following observations.

- the total set of solutions (4.1 to 4.8 + diverse) are not adequate for meeting the planned levels of any of the objectives.
- the contribution made by the set of solutions (4. DEVELOP) is interesting (ranging from 15% to 60%) and cannot be lightly discarded.
- there is no documentation on the table as to the source of the estimates – either person or evidence. This should have been included for credibility and for testing the solidity of the estimates.
- We would need similar tables for the other IBC case study objectives (Tables 9.1–9.3), in order to evaluate the effect of the

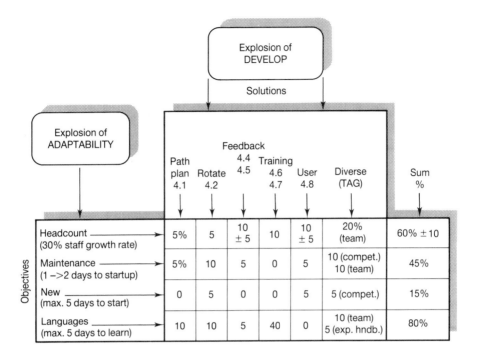

Figure 11.1 An impact estimation table for the IBC case.

DEVELOP solutions on them. For all we know they might be unacceptable due to severe negative effects.

- We need similar tables for evaluating the effects of the other already suggested solution areas (Table 10.2 POLICY through RESPONSIBILITY).

■ 11.3 Limitations of impact estimation

The impact estimation itself is filled with possibilities for errors. These are unavoidable. In fact it is well to keep in mind that there is no question here of substantial accuracy. We are mainly interested in getting the approximately correct order of magnitude, so that we can spot design objectives which are insufficiently covered by adequate design solution thinking.

When an estimate is obviously uncertain, and we want to indicate this to the reader of the IE table, you will notice that we use plus-

Requirements \ Solutions	Planned level =	Tag = .Exper.Co. .Selfmetric.	User simplicity	Robustness Stab., Surv.	Open-end ! re-eval !	File descriptor	Cmnd. intrf. & mgr. Dialect	TOTAL %	Deviation	
Profitability	20% ROI	5	10	10	10	20	20	75	– 25	Underdesign
Usability	30 minutes	30	60	25	20	20	40	195	95	Overdesign
Connectivity	5 minutes	10	40	0	40	40	40	170	70	Overdesign
Availability	99.98%	30	20	30	10	20	20	130	30	Overdesign
Integrity	99.99%	10	10	20	5	20	– 10	55	– 45	Underdesign
Performance	>12 Tr/S	30	5	20	5	5	5	70	– 30	Underdesign
Marketability	12 langs.	40	40	40	20	30	40	210	110	Overdesign
Adaptability	10 years	30	30	10	10	30	30	140	40	Overdesign
Dev. resources	$12mill.	20	30	30	10	30	30	150	50	OVERBUDGET !
Mkt. cost & res.	$1mill./yr	5	10	20	10	5	15	65	– 35	Underbudget
Value/cost	Ratio =>>	1.85	1.34	0.78	1.5	1.32	1.03			
		Best solution	not best	not best	not best	not best	not best			
Average value/ cost ratio = 1.3										

Figure 11.2 Usability example: a spreadsheet top-level impact estimation.

minus symbols (for example 40 ± 30, meaning 10 to 70% impact, probably 40%). Notice also that we cumulate the plus-minus estimations algebraically to give some total estimate of the uncertainty of the estimate.

It is not always necessary to use explicit uncertainty estimates, even though we are aware of the fact that there is some uncertainty. It is mainly a device to communicate the concept of uncertainty to people who otherwise might assume the estimates are more certain than they really are.

Uncertainty in estimates is not a new engineering management problem. Here are some of the reasons why uncertainty is unavoidable:

1. Sometimes we are intentionally making a quick estimate. In such cases it is not worth the effort to dig for facts which would increase the accuracy of the estimate.
2. The facts which would allow us to make accurate estimates are simply not available (especially true for software engineering).
3. Our systems are composed of many other design solution ideas which may have a synergic (2 + 2 > 4) or a thrashing (2 + 2 < 4) effect on our results. These may be uncharted and unknown, or at best difficult to know about until we build the system or a pilot version of it.
4. Many design solution specifications which will be a part of the final system are not yet made at all. It is thus impossible to consider how these solutions will act when put together with the ones we are estimating for just now.
5. Many design solution ideas are not yet exploded into sufficient design detail to make an accurate estimate. The general solution idea may have a wide range of impact degrees, depending on exactly how it is finally exploded into detail.
6. The softcrafters making the practical implementation can influence the outcome considerably, depending on their professional ability.
7. The final result might be sensitive to small changes in some resource (such as available storage space – impacting performance) and the amount of resource available might be unknown at present.

The principle of impact estimation tables:
Estimating the impacts of many solutions on all objectives is filled with sources of error, all of which together amount to a smaller error than the error of not trying to estimate at all.

■ 11.4 The concept of the 'best' solution

Just as a good chess move is partly characterized by the number of squares it does or can exercise control over, a good solution specification is characterized by the number and level of positive impacts it has on attributes. A simple way to characterize this is to add the effects (algebraically) on all attributes. The bigger the sum for quality attributes, the better. The smaller the sum for resource attributes, the better. The ratio of impacts for a single solution is the sum of all impacts on qualities divided by the sum of all impacts on resources (and is a rough measure of the goodness of a solution).

> **Practical hint:** *We have at times used spreadsheet software to calculate the above measure, and to give some impression of the strong solutions and weak ones. Remove the weakest ones first. See Figure 11.2 for example.*

■ 11.5 The evaluation of side-effects

One of the strengths of the impact estimation method is that it forces us to do something we don't normally even have a language for: the evaluation of the side-effects of solutions.

We seem only to recognize the side-effects of a 'good idea' when some really disastrous side-effect is already well-known from past experience. Generally, we just seem to let the side-effects accumulate, and surprise us.

Side-effects may be unintentional or intentional, and negative or positive. From a designer's point of view, we want to maximize the positive side-effects, even though we only become conscious of them through our attempts to chart them on the impact estimation table.

> **Practical hint:** *Impact estimation side-effects can serve as a systematic argument for or against a particular solution when making presentations to colleagues.*

> **The principle of side-effect estimation:**
> Side-effect estimation brings out the good news, *and* the bad news, early.

■ 11.6 Summing up the effects of a single attribute

The impact estimation table shows the total effect of a series of design solutions by simple algebraic addition of the individual estimates. This, of course is not entirely realistic. It is an intentional simplification. Such a simplification is justified because the estimates are necessarily rough, as pointed out in Section 11.3. The main point is not 'to get accurate estimates,' but to spot objectives insufficiently designed-for. Sometimes the impact sum, if over 300% to 500% or more, indicates 'overdesign' and an opportunity to trim the fat.

You might well object that the effects of many solutions do not simply 'add up' in so simple a way. Correct. However, in most cases it is not really worth the trouble to build a more complex model. In general, if accuracy is essential, it will be cheaper to obtain accurate estimates by building the system to some extent. This is, of course, what engineers frequently have to do.

The impact estimation method earns its keep by forcing us to think more systematically. We consider all objectives for side-effects. We are forced to estimate the degree of impact.

The impact sum merely gives us a signal that we ought to do more, or we have perhaps done too much. We are after extremes. The things in between the extremes, which seem okay, may well have their hidden problems. We expect to see these problems surface in early evolutionary delivery steps, where there will be time and budget enough to correct them.

To try to get the design perfect at such an early stage would not be economic. Our objective is to improve the design, but not to perfect it. Our objective is to make sure that every method used is a good investment of our precious **calendar** time and people resources.

■ 11.7 Safety factors

It is quite possible that the sum of impacts estimated for solutions exceed 100% of a quality target (like '230%') or are lower than' a resource budget (like '50%'). In both cases this gives us a good margin if our estimates have been too optimistic. It also helps us to cope, when at later stages, unknowns creep into the development work or the design.

Even in engineering disciplines which are far better developed than software engineering, the providing of a safety factor is a strong tradition. Software engineering is still so lacking in solid experience that only time can give, that we need a larger safety factor than other disciplines. Only experience will tell you how large a safety factor you need. The answer will vary according to need and competence, and is a matter for management judgement. Management can demand a particular safety factor, and is responsible that it is adequate.

Remember that the degree to which you make use of evolutionary delivery management and design methods will influence how much of a safety factor you require. For small controlled incremental growth, large safety factors are not necessary at impact estimation time.

> **Practical hint:** *Most managers seem to feel comfortable when the safety factor is two or better. This implies a minimum of 200% for quality attributes and a maximum of 50% for resource attributes, in the impact estimation sum. Use these as starting safety factors until you get more experience.*

> **The safety factor principle:**
> To hit the bull's eye at least once, use a better bow than seems necessary, allow three arrows at least, and borrow Robin Hood if you can.

■ 11.8 Hierarchies of impact estimation

Impact estimation tables can be made for any level of detail or overview which you find desirable.

A one-page overview of the impact of the top architectural decisions on the top objectives, is useful for presentations to management. (See Figure 11.3, for example.) More detailed tables, such as the one shown earlier for IBC DEVELOP solutions and ADAPTABILITY objectives (Figure 11.1) allow us to focus in more detail on debatable issues.

Detailed tables can also be used as supporting evidence as to how the higher level tables were estimated. The sums from lower level tables are directly used in the higher level ones. This is illustrated in Figure 11.3, where the estimate at the intersection of DEVELOP and ADAPTABILITY is a direct citation of the average (45%) and sums from the more detailed table (Figure 11.1).

> **Practial hint:** *Be prepared to backup the detailed numbers in the top level presentation with lower level estimates. This level of presentation is suitable for graphic bar chart presentations.*

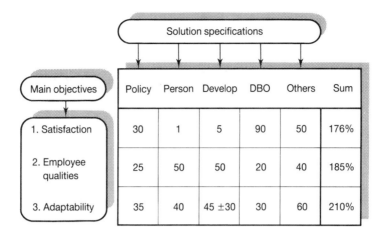

Figure 11.3 A top-level impact estimation table for the IBC case. This figure shows that the proposed set of solutions meets the main objectives with a safety margin of about two.

The estimation hierarchy principle:
Deeper estimation gives better generalization, or the more trees you actually count, the more sure you are about the woods.

■ 11.9 Supplementary estimation methods

Chapter 16 of this book gives an in depth view of estimation techniques in software engineering. The most important messages are:

1. If estimation is really so important to you, then you had better take an *active* approach to reaching your targets (like design to target, and contract guarantees).
2. Early estimation techniques (such as impact estimation) are better than no estimation, but cannot replace the accuracy of later estimation techniques such as inspection statistics, testing statistics and evolutionary delivery step measurements and predictions based on them.

The fundamental principle of estimation:
Perfect estimation of complex systems costs too much.

You cannot normally estimate any complex system attributes perfectly. You can, however, manage your priorities in the face of threatening realities. If you actually estimate anything perfectly, it is either an accident, an illusion caused by ignorance, or you are cheating.

'If I could have only been right more than half the time, that would have been an improvement' (Alfred P. Sloan, in *My Years With General Motors*).

Practical hint: *Don't ever look back. Do not attempt to compare your impact estimation numbers with the real system results. You will cause yourself unnecessary grief. The main point is to motivate you to change your design, not to predict its attributes. The only thing you want to compare with reality is your high-priority targets.*

Of course we need to learn from past mistakes of estimation, but the impact estimation table is not the right place to do this because it is at too early a stage of design. Too many changes are made after the estimates are made.

■ 11.10 Justification of an estimate

Most impact estimates are not justified (defended by written comment for each estimate) for the reasons cited above. It is only an order-of-magnitude guesstimation method anyway. However, the estimator must be prepared to justify estimates to colleagues, management and inspectors.

If the estimate is of minor impact (under 5% of plan) or is uncontroversial (everybody concerned would not question it) then no written documentation is necessary. You should however be prepared to explain any number, if challenged. Sometimes a written note on the basis for the estimation is useful to help estimators remember their own exact thinking and assumptions.

If the estimate is a significant component (say 25%–50% or more of the planned level), or if it is not likely to be understood by managers or colleagues or outside consultants who review the impact estimation table, then explicit written documentation is called for. This justification documentation is basically a footnote containing at least keywords and references to facts.

For example: in the following table the footnote explains how the 30% was arrived at.

| 4% | 0% | 30%† | 10% | (a row of impact estimation numbers) |
| ? | 0% | 5% | 10% | |

†based on the Omega project averages for 4000 hours of inspection.

Practical hint: *Your system design standards should contain rules for when you require justification of an estimate in writing. Inspection checklists (see Section 12.4) for the impact estimation should ask questions like:*

1. Are all estimates obviously reasonable?
2. Are all controversial or large estimates (over 5%) satisfactorily justified in writing?

Get at least one independent person to sign off on any impact estimation (inspector, peer review or a manager).

Who should justify the estimate?

If you cannot justify the estimate in writing, you have no business making it. If it is a random number taken out of thin air, say so. And then delete it until you have some better way to justify it. If you really do not know how whatever you are suggesting impacts the critical objectives, don't suggest it. If you know everything except the impact on one single critical objective, maybe you had better take the trouble to find out, or at least clearly state the fact in writing, that you do not know yet but are taking steps to find out. Use a question mark '?'.

TRW Systems in their 'Requirements Properties Matrix' *Characteristics of Software Quality*, North-Holland, or Boehm, B., IFIP Proceedings 1974, Stockholm) have a special code in their impact tables for the situation 'under analysis.'

Whatever you do, don't begin to destroy your professional credibility by pretending you know what you have no evidence for. It is difficult to be right even when we do have some evidence of the past history of effects. It is professional suicide to pretend we have no problems where they might well occur. Believe it or not, nobody expects you to know everything in your field of expertise. But they do hope you won't mislead them about your knowledge. 'I know I don't know' is a badge of professional responsibility, not of ignorance.

■ 11.11 Inspection of impact estimation

The impact estimation documentation is a most important subject for using Fagan's inspection method (see Chapters 12 and 21) at high levels of design and software engineering.

The inspection method is based, on comparing two or more written sources which should be consistent with each other. A prerequisite for effective inspection is clarity of documentation. Impact estimation gives quite clear and systematic documentation for the assertion that a particular set of design solutions has a particular degree of impact, with a degree of uncertainty, on critical system objectives.

One management option therefore is to institutionalize the inspection of the impact estimation tables, or some part of them. This will ensure that estimators take their numbers more seriously and can justify them to colleagues. It will delegate the evaluation to where it belongs.

Practical hint: *Get a thorough inspection done at least once on an impact estimation table, then review the experiences with your team before deciding whether you have time to do this or not. Look for the indirect side-effects of this process to give the clearest benefit, such as getting goals clarified and definitions of solutions clarified.*

The principle of early estimation:
You don't *have* to estimate the impact of design suggestions – but if you don't, you'll find out when you implement them just how bad they are.

■ 11.12 Who estimates impact?

11.12.1 Making the 'suggester' estimate the impact too

Anybody who seriously champions an idea should do so only when it is clear to what degree that idea impacts all critical success factors on the project.

The assertion that 'we should do this idea,' should be accompanied by estimates of how that idea impacts all the agreed-upon, planned, and worst case levels of the objectives. Anything less is irresponsible.

You should reserve formal judgement on any 'good' idea until the multiple effects have been estimated.

At the softect and software engineer levels, where creative solutions are generated, it is essential that the generators of such ideas take responsibility for estimating impacts on all critical objectives immediately. How often have you seen the keen technologist, enthusiastic about a single attribute, totally ignoring the other (negative) effects, especially unmentionable things like cost and time.

If software engineering management does not direct designers to respect the written measurable objectives, i.e. the critical success factors, then they are not responsible managers.

A practical tool for directing the attention of technologists to the real objectives driving a project is to insist that all technological ideas be estimated on an impact estimation table, and then inspected by peers. If they cannot make an estimate, even with a plus-minus deviation estimate with a wide range ('10% to 80%') then they are showing evidence of their incompetence as designers.

Excellent! Now you can train them in more depth to be able to understand the impacts of their technology. They cannot be trained to know all the answers, but they can be trained to know how to find the answers, and when to admit that they cannot. They can be trained to state their uncertainty, in no uncertain terms. This is what other professional disciplines have developed for a long time, and it is time that software engineering followed suit.

11.12.2 The expert test

Real experts can and will, make and credibly justify impact estimates, or at least fearlessly admit their ignorance. Fools will make excuses and equally credibly justify them.

The expert principle:
Experts know they don't know, the others try to fool people that they do.

Practical hint: *Demand that everyone who proposes an idea ensures (not necessarily by doing it personally) that an impact estimation, with justification, is available for at least the 'top ten' attributes, before they seriously push the idea or suggest it to others. If they don't, you will have to.*

Don't let this stop creative brainstorming – but do let it be the brainstorming filter.

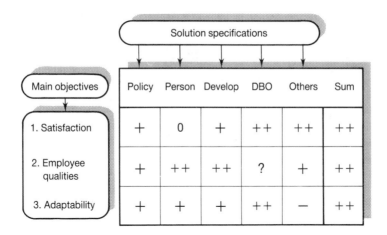

Figure 11.4 Impact analysis. Codes: 0 = little or no impact; + = interesting impact; + + = large or significant impact; ? = impact undetermined or unknown; − = negative impact.

The estimator principle:
Design solutions alone have no value except when we can estimate contribution to our design objectives.

■ 11.13 Relational presentation: simple impact analysis

It may be useful to make or to show a simplified version of the impact estimation table. This can be done without having to make numerical estimates. This can be useful for some of the following reasons;

- because you don't have time to make credible estimates,
- because you don't want people to quibble about the estimates,
- as a simple prelude to later filling in estimates,
- for management overview presentation.

On occasions I have found it quite useful to use units of measure other than the percentage of plan units.

For example, in the case of one multinational chemicals corporation the major objective was to reduce staffing levels in an office environment. The plan was to reduce the headcount by something like 65 people. We found it quite natural to express the impact of the solution areas directly in probable reduction of headcount, rather than percentages of the 65 person plan. For example: solution X will reduce by 5 to 10 people (probably only 6).

There certainly is nothing holy about the percentage-of-plan units. But, they have stood the test of time and popularity, and by far dominate the practical use of the impact estimation method.

Practical hint: *If people hesitate to commit themselves to numbers, initially, use the impact analysis language to get them moving, discussing and communicating.*

This idea can be used at detailed levels of the hierarchy of design objectives, to make sure that all objectives are being reasonably addressed. In particular, it can chart whether some design objectives have been entirely forgotten or not.

A further refinement is to analyze the system in various functional dimensions, or major subsystems. Use a series of charts for, for example, Applications Software, Systems Software, People and Organization, Hardware, Communications, Marketing Aspects. This can be useful for allowing specialists in these areas to participate and to focus on areas of special interest to them. It will also help you avoid narrow overspecialization in your particular areas of expertise.

The impact analysis principle:
Even superficial systematic analysis of solution completeness will turn up many defects in our design.

■ 11.14 Solution comparison and analysis

11.14.1 Identifying the best solution alternative

A frequent software engineering problem is to select the best solution from among several acceptable alternatives. The balanced way of doing this is to select the one solution which gives the highest contribution to your critical objectives planned levels. This can be done by evaluating the percentage contribution for all planned attribute levels, and looking at the ratio: sum % qualities divided by sum % resource usage. The solution alternative with the highest ratio is probably the one you should pick, if you must pick one only.

It is not necessary to 'weight' the various attributes, since they are effectively already weighted by the planned level itself. Achievement of individual planned levels has equal weight. No one planned level is more critical than another.

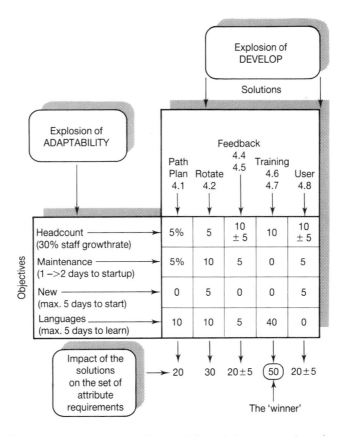

Figure 11.5 An impact estimation table, used for solution comparison, from the IBC case.

11.14.2 What if the decision becomes political or emotional?

There may be political factors which influence the final decision. By using a multidimensional and quantitative approach to evaluation of alternatives, a more rational and professional deliberation is possible.

If the scores of the two leading alternatives are similar, then little harm is done by letting someone follow their prejudices and choose their favorite alternative. But, when someone tries to argue for the selection of a solution which rates very low compared to the alternatives, they will be seen to be openly defying both the evaluations and the objectives.

Who knows? Such discussions might show that either the objectives set, or the evaluations, are somehow wrong. Somebody's

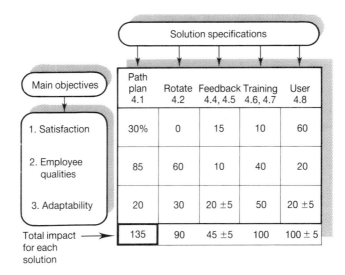

Figure 11.6 Solution comparison for the top level of benefits, IBC case. The overall viewpoint, compared with ADAPTABILITY alone, points to PATH PLAN as the first choice.

gut feeling might be more sound than earlier less-informed attempts at formal estimation methods. If they manage to present a convincing case for change of objectives or change of evaluation of the attributes of the alternatives, you should consider allowing for that change. Don't however discard the formal method and let mere emotion reign. Translate that gut feeling into something official and acceptable to the parties involved.

Figure 11.5 (derived from Figure 11.1) illustrates the principle. Let us say that someone says that the solution areas are mutually exclusive alternatives. We are going to have to pick one and only one (at least to begin with). The TRAINING area seems like the winner. But since the conclusion in this case is strongly dependent on our 40% impact estimation in one single area, we need to assure ourselves that this single estimate is as credible as any other estimate.

The point is that the conclusions may be debatable, but the evidence upon which they are based is auditable by anyone wishing to do so. We are not limited to someone *else's* conclusion that 'TRAINING investment is the best alternative.' We can challenge the conclusions by challenging the basis on which they are made. We have, what I in earlier years called 'decision documentation'.

Table 11.1 A simplified resource specification (teaching example, not real case).

---

*MONEY.*CAPITAL
SCALE = initial capital budget requirement
WORST = 200.000
PLAN(this year) = 50.000
PLAN(total all years) = 100.000

*TIME.*CALENDAR
SCALE = months from project budget approval and funds release to accepted delivery of evolutionary increment
WORST ACCEPTABLE(final increment, this budget) = 12 months
PLAN(first customer payable increment) = 6 months
PLAN(last increment, this budget) = 10 months

11.14.3 An overview table for solution comparison

The impact estimation table illustrated in Figure 11.5 clearly shows that the conclusion is based only on the evaluation of a third of the overall goals (ADAPTABILITY, but not SATISFACTION and EMPLOYEE QUALITIES). So, another way of examining the selection of the TRAIN-ING alternative would be to do a similar evaluation against the other goals, and to perhaps summarize the overall findings on an overview table (see Figure 11.6).

11.14.4 Considering the benefit-to-cost ratio

Up to now our model has only considered the benefits of the alternative solutions, not their costs. The 'best' solution in terms of benefits might turn out to cost far more than it is worth. We can treat the costs separately, if we wish. There may be sound reasons for doing so.

It can be useful to shed more light on your selection of alternative solutions by looking at the benefit-to-cost ratio. I am using the word 'cost' to mean 'resources' – any resources which we consider to be limited, such as people, time, money and space.

Let us introduce some resource specifications, in order to illustrate the point (see Table 11.1).

11.14.5 Estimating impact on all attributes

We can now estimate the impact on both benefits and resources, as shown in Figure 11.7.

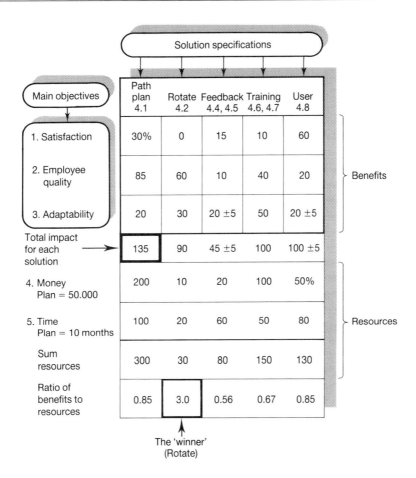

Figure 11.7 Solution alternative selection based on benefit/cost ratio. In this case, the solution alternative ROTATE (job rotation) comes out on top simply because it is ten times cheaper than the otherwise attractive PATH PLAN.

11.14.6 Is the winner really picked on this evaluation?

This way of selecting alternatives may totally exclude the losing alternatives from further consideration. But it is just as likely to provoke a proponent of the losing alternatives to revise the design, so that it becomes more competitive. For example, if we could find some alternative way to implement PATH PLAN more cheaply than initially envisaged, it might win.

We can see from this model that we would have to reduce the resource sum to 45 or less to meet the challenge and to win. This clearly implies finding a solution for under 20.000 MONEY UNITS (40% of the plan) and two weeks to implement (5% of the ten month TIME plan), or some other combination of resources. The important point here is that the nature of the challenge – exactly what is needed to win – is clearly visible, and therefore more likely to be acted upon.

Given the challenge, an imaginative designer might well come up with a solution.

11.14.7 The basis for evolutionary step selection

It could be that this mode of selection does not exclude the other options from later consideration. It can be used to make a formal decision objectively on the 'juiciest' next step for evolutionary delivery. It can be used as a long range step sequencing mechanism – the highest benefit/resource ratio steps are planned earliest – assuming they can be implemented independently of each other.

11.14.8 Static versus dynamic evaluation

I have found that the most fruitful use of this method is not to use it in a single static evaluation, but to be prepared to give proponents of other solutions a fair chance to improve their impact estimates, either by improving the designs, or by gathering better facts to estimate the impact. I have found this particularly when the alternatives are from competitive companies looking for a contract. It is possible to get real concessions in price and contract conditions when impact estimation is used to communicate to such companies that they are losing, and by how much they need to improve to win. It would be nice if they all gave their best final bid initially, but they don't, and it is to your advantage to give them a clear motivation to improve on their offer.

11.14.9 Requesting alternative solutions based on objectives

My personal preference is to publish the planned levels and worst cases in any request for proposal, together with the information that bids will be judged by these criteria. This makes outside suppliers communicate with you in a way more tailored to your objectives. Otherwise they may waste their time and yours overwhelming you with irrelevant facts about their products.

11.14.10 Communication to top management

I have experienced that these models of evaluation should be communicated to top management and to committees, such as Boards of Directors, together with your recommendations, when the selection of an alternative is either highly political or of major economic significance.

The estimates should be independently audited in advance, in writing, for such managers, and the documentation should be complete enough to allow those managers to conduct their own independent audit of your conclusions. Sometimes they will be satisfied with a random sample of one or a few estimates to judge the solidity of your estimates. Be prepared to explain how the estimates have been arrived at.

Practical hint: *Keep it public. Keep the solution comparison model and its evaluations and their basic facts open and available to everyone. There will always be forces which push for secrecy, but my experience is that openness is the best stimulant to discover the best solutions.*

11.14.11 The principles of solution comparison

The principles of solution comparison:
Solutions must be compared on the basis of their impact on all critical objectives. Anything else is a false comparison.
or
The best solution is the one that is best for your objectives, there is no generally best solution.

■ 11.15 Worst case analysis

Up to this point we have based the impact estimation technique on the 'planned level' of the objectives. This is the most common and useful variation.

It should be pointed out that this is not a limitation of any kind. You can estimate the percentage impact against any levels which you feel are useful, for example,

- the worst acceptable case,
- other planned levels (long term as opposed to short term),
- a mixture of all these levels,
- the best (state of the art) case level

Feel free to do what seems useful to you.

■ 11.16 Solution handbooks and attribute tables

Note that if you wish to store information about the multiple properties of methods or technologies, you can use the impact estimation format, and choose either special purpose attribute definitions or generalized ones (such as the examples in Chapter 19) as reference points.

This would be useful for sharing experiences about qualities and costs in a large scale software engineering environment. It could form the basis of a software engineering handbook. It could also be used as a format for storing data about technologies, in a computer, for information retrieval and automated design engineering.

■ 11.17 Summary

Impact estimation is a tool for systematic quantitative exploration of many ideas and their impact on your many objectives.

It is a useful early discipline for finding weak areas in your design at an earlier stage of the project than otherwise.

It imposes a discipline on team members for communicating the reasons behind technological ideas in a disciplined, credible, and inspectable manner.

It is not an attempt to predict results accurately, but merely to identify the weakest areas in engineering design at the earliest possible stage.

The basic format of impact estimation can be used for a variety of impact estimation purposes, such as:

- selecting alternatives,
- determining evolutionary step sequence,
- communicating and storing technological facts in general,
- presenting proposals to management or empowered committees,
- allowing independent audit of suggestions,
- helping a design team to work together as a team.

■ Further reading

Boehm, B.W., 1974, *Requirements properties matrix*, Proc. IFIP conf., Stockholm

Gilb, T., 1979, 'Structured design methods for maintainability,' in *Infotech State of the Art Report on Structured Software Development*, **2**, Pergamon Infotech, Maidenhead, UK

Lano, R.J., 1979, *A technique for software and systems design*, North-Holland

12

The inspection process: early quality and process control

■ Introduction

This chapter describes the main rules of Fagan's inspection method. It will give additional background and perspective on the method. For a practical example of implementation of inspection in a software engineering environment, see Chapter 21. These chapters should be sufficient to enable readers to begin to apply inspection in their environment, but for a large-scale implementation effort the reader should study the literature references and be prepared to learn evolutionarily exactly what works in practice for them.

■ 12.1 The basic rules

Inspection is a technique originally developed by Michael E. Fagan of IBM.

Inspection ensures that project documentation, at all levels and at all stages, is clear, self-explanatory, unambiguous, and consistent with both all other documentation on the same project, and with the higher-level goals of the organization.

Its rules are strict, and people may initially react against the idea of what they see as more bureaucracy. But it has been repeatedly found that the net savings using inspection are directly proportional to the extent to which these rules are carefully observed in practice.

The principle of Fagan's inspection rules:
Fagan developed inspection at IBM, therefore his inspection rules had to contribute to net profit in order to survive.
and
If you think an inspection rule is unnecessary, you have probably misunderstood the method.

The following is a summary of inspection procedural rules, followed by an account of each one in greater detail.

1. Inspections are carried out at a number of points in the process of project planning and system development. (See Figure 12.1.)
2. All classes of defects in documentation are inspected; not merely logic or function errors (see Chapter 21).
3. Inspections are carried out by colleagues at *all* levels of seniority, except the big boss.
4. Inspections are carried out in a prescribed series of steps, such

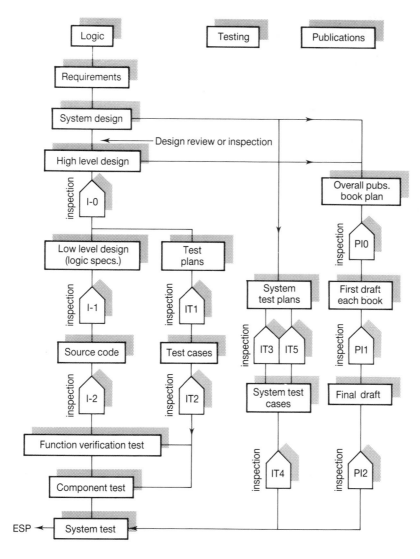

Figure 12.1 The inspection process map. This map shows the use of eleven inspections in use at the IBM development laboratories, Kingston, New York, on Project Orbit, a 500 000 line of code networked operating system. The project was delivered early and had about one hundred times fewer errors than would normally be expected.

Process aspect	Inspection	Walk-through
1. Formal moderator training	✓	No
2. Defined participant 'roles'	✓	No
3. Who leads process?	Moderator	Owner
4. Use of 'how to find defects' checklists	✓	No
5. Statistics analysis: by type	✓	No
6. Formal follow-up to reduce bad fixes	✓	Varied pract.
7. Fewer future errors because of error feedback to sources	✓	Accidental
8. Systematic QC process improvement via statistics	✓	No
9. Analysis → process problem → fix	✓	No

Figure 12.2 A comparison of key aspects of inspection with walkthroughs. Source: Fagan, M., 'Design and code inspections,' *IBM Systems Journal*, **15**, (3), 200.

as individual preparation, public meeting, error rework, etc. (see Section 12.3).

5. Inspection meetings are limited to two hours.
6. Inspections are led by a trained moderator (see Section 12.2).
7. Inspectors are assigned specific roles to increase effectiveness (see Section 12.5).
8. Checklists of questions to be asked by the inspectors are used to define the task and to stimulate increased defect finding (see Section 12.4).
9. Material is inspected *at a particular rate* which has been found to give maximum error-finding ability (see Section 12.7).
10. Statistics on types of defects are kept, and used for reports which are analyzed in a manner similar to financial analysis (see Section 12.6).

Practical hint: *Follow inspection rules completely until you can prove that dropping them or varying them gives better measurable results. If you simplify or modify the method before you can measure it, then you won't understand why Fagan did it that way.*

■ 12.2 The trained moderator

The moderator is the leader of the inspection meetings and the processes that immediately surround it. This is a part-time job even in large organizations, and in smaller ones the moderator may be the project or departmental manager. At IBM, for instance, moderators are trained on a three-day course, but elsewhere they have generally been self-trained, using whatever experience is available. The real training of the moderator consists of being guided through a series of inspections by a senior leader of moderators, often a quality assurance person.

The role of the moderator is:

1. to organize all practical details surrounding inspections, the documentation availability, who, when and where, etc.
2. to lead inspection meetings;
3. to ensure that the participating inspectors follow the procedural rules decided upon;
4. to pace the inspection process at a productive speed;
5. to note defects and classify them;
6. to assign the defect list to an individual for rework;
7. to check that all assigned rework has actually been done and passed as satisfactory.

Practical hint: *Make sure that the introductory year of using inspection in your environment is led by champions of the cause. Make sure that the champions are well trained. Send them on a public course on the subject. Make sure they are well read in inspection literature. Make them responsible for seeing that the moderators do their job properly, as reflected in the statistics collected about effort and effect.*

The moderator principle:
Inspections without trained moderators will only have moderate success.

■ 12.3 Inspection steps

The following are the basic inspection steps:

1. *Planning:* The moderator, on being given project documentation (at whatever stage) for inspection, decides who will inspect,

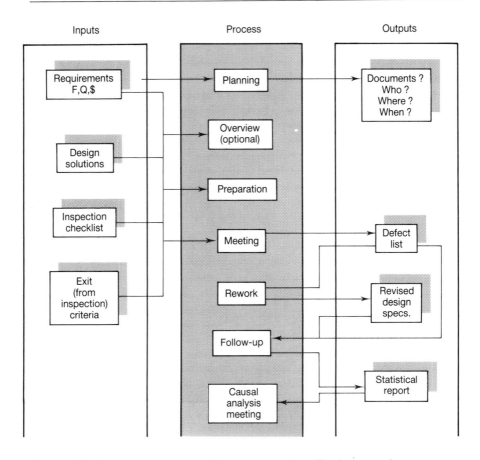

Inputs   Process   Outputs

Figure 12.3 A process overview of Fagan's inspection. The inputs to the preparation and meeting are the high level (inputs to last definition process) documentation, and low level (output from the last definition process) documentation. The inspectors are also given specialized (for the low level type of documentation) checklists and corresponding work standards. Exit criteria include the prerequisites for declaring inspections officially complete, such as 'all defects corrected' and 'statistics documented.'

where and when, and distributes documentation accordingly.

2. *Overview:* This step gives an overall view of the project before any detail is inspected. It might take the form of a 30–60 minute presentation for the inspectors, and it can be omitted when the overall project is familiar to them.

3. *Preparation:* Inspectors work alone for about 1½ hours, during which time they familiarize themselves with the material and

prepare to put forward a maximum of discovered presumed defects (inconsistencies between two sorts of documentation) during the coming meeting. While this phase might appear time consuming, it has been shown to give a net increase in productivity of the actual inspection meeting.

4. *Meeting:* The meeting is attended by all inspectors including the moderator. Normally there are three to five participants, though there may be more (in the interests of getting a number of points of view) at a very high level 'architectural' meeting. The volume of work to be handled during each meeting is limited and specified.

    Generally speaking, inspection ability seems to fall off after two hours, which may often mean that not all material ready for inspection on a particular project will be discussed at a single meeting.

    The originators of the documentation in question are normally not present at the meeting to explain or defend it, though one of the originators can be included as a communication link back to this team. A major purpose of inspection is to ensure that project documentation is self-explanatory to those who have to use it.

    Inspectors can all be members of the same larger project, but they should mostly be members of a different small team than the originators. During the meeting, inspectors point out suspected defects to the moderator, who always notes them in writing. No discussion as to whether a purported defect is 'real' is allowed. The reason for this is that if an inspector *feels* that something is wrong or unclear, then from the point of view of unambiguous documentation, it *is* wrong. The lack of clarity must be corrected by 'rework', to prevent someone involved in its implementation from misunderstanding the real intent.

5. *Rework:* After the meeting, the defects list is assigned to some one person for repair. Better solutions are not discussed in the meeting because this is found to be neither productive nor necessary.

6. *Follow up:* The moderator is personally responsible for ensuring that defects in documentation have really been reworked. If they have not, the documentation in question is not allowed to be used in any further work as it has known defects. Rework completion is one of several necessary 'exit' criteria for inspection completion.

    The moderator can judge these corrections, but is not obliged to do more than determine that the rework has been carried out completely. The correctness of the rework process will in any case be judged by later inspections and tests.

7. *Third hour meeting:* Participants at the above two hour inspection meeting are not allowed to discuss solutions or improvements, so in order that good solution ideas should not be lost, a third hour meeting can be held at which inspectors may express their more personal views on errors and improvements.

Practical hint: *Some companies plan inspections up to the lunch hour or end of office hours, hoping that people will get together in their own time for this purpose. Those who have instituted this on company time report that it pays off in terms of constructive and creative ideas.*

12.3.1 Inspection phases

A complete list of possible inspection phases is shown in Table 12.1.

The inspection-steps principle:
If you think some of the inspection steps are too time consuming, and you drop them, you are in danger of losing more time than you save. (You can find out for sure by analyzing your statistics.)

■ 12.4 Checklists

Inspectors are always given checklists to increase their effectiveness. Such lists are built on experience (assimilated inspection statistics). They also give the inspector a clear definition of his role and an instant course in inspection work. Checklists are almost 'standards' for work process, which are rephrased as a series of questions.

We have found that all checklists can be written on a single page (maybe 25 questions) for a single type of inspection (for example for unit test design, or for 'quality objectives'). Anything more than the single page becomes too much to deal with in practice.

12.4.1 A test plan checklist

The following is a test plan checklist which I provided for a client. A checklist question normally contains the defect type code beside each question. For example question 3 below, could be classed as M(ajor) M(issing) QU(ality). The categories are in three dimensions: 1. major/

Table 12.1 Possible inspection phases.

Step name	Description	Done by
Planning	Administrative, practical setup	Moderator
Overview	Familiarize new team with project	Whole team
Preparation	Participants study documentation	Individuals alone
Meeting	Participants tell moderator about presumed 'defects' which are noted	Whole team
Rework	Somebody corrects the defects	A re-worker
Follow-up	Check that rework is completed	Moderator
Third hour	Safety-valve session for ideas suppressed at the meeting	Whole team
or Causal analysis	Meeting statistics are analyzed	Whole team

minor; 2. missing/wrong/extra/unintelligible; 3. a statistical class of error created by each company on site using inspection.

1. Is there a plan to meet all parts of the test plan standard?
2. Do all individual specifications include estimates for time and cases, including totals? Have the most recently available experience data from actual time used to test, been used to make the estimates.
3. Do the tests go beyond conventional function and performance tests, and test all quality and resource objectives as well?
4. Is there a plan to test the corresponding (to this source code) user-documentation and maintenance-documentation?
5. etc. (This should be about 20–25 questions.)

The single page principle:
If a subject is really important, and you understand it really well, then you can state it on a single page.

■ 12.5 Roles of inspection specialization

The assigning of specialized roles tends to increase team productivity. Each individual has their particular responsibility, and nobody else is going to carry it for them.

Specialist roles can be defined by corresponding specialist check-lists (in addition to the general checklist). But this is not generally done in practice, since the struggle to get a good set of checklists for many inspection areas is difficult enough. The specialist roles need to be defined in relation to the exact stage of development being in-spected. For example, a system test integration design might assign roles of moderator (always a special role), non-functional quality testing, user-interface testing, adherence to testing and quality standards.

Types of specialization might include people with interests in outside contracting, publication, future extensions, maintenance, planning, etc.

■ 12.6 Inspection statistics

The collection and analysis of defect statistics is a recognized part of quality control in engineering. The use of inspection statistics is as important to the cost-effective management of planning and develop-ment as cost accounting and financial reporting is to company management in general. Collected statistics serve to seek out weak areas in the development process in general, and show the need for such things as better training and other technical and organiza-tional changes. They give an indication of the level of errors left, and they help to measure the net value of the inspection process itself.

A practical example of this in action will be found in the Omega case study of inspection, Chapter 21.

> **Practical hint:** *Statistics about costs of finding and fixing defects are vital for defending and improving the method of inspection and other software engineering methods in your development process. If you fail to collect and analyze them, you risk leaving bad methods in too long, and risk not recognizing and selling better methods to colleagues and management. Don't fail to collect and use the statistics; it is a necessary overhead.*

> **The statistics principle:**
> Inspection without statistics is like night driving without headlights; you may not see obstacles or opportunities until it is too late.

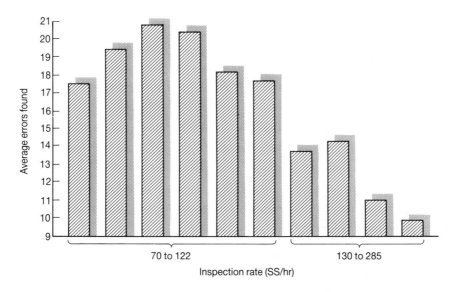

Figure 12.4 Inspection rate vs productivity as determined in the IBM inspection classes using a student problem. SS/hr is the number of source statements inspected per hour. Notice the dramatic drop in the number of errors found as a result of increasing the inspection rate by only a little above the optimum. It pays to stick close to the optimum rate. Source: Frank Buck, 1981, *Technical Report 21.802*, September, IBM, Kingston, New York.

■ 12.7 Rate of inspection

Carefully recorded experience has shown that the productivity of inspections, measured in defects found per hour of time used, is critically dependent on conducting both preparation and meetings within a narrow range of rate of inspection.

For example, by driving an inspection at 35% more than the optimum speed, the absolute number of defects found might drop by one third or more. You might have saved 40 minutes out of 120 for inspection, but it could easily cost your same people 200 minutes or more to find and correct those same defects. You will be either delaying project delivery or delivering shoddy quality to users.

The saving of potentially wasted time by using inspection is probably its most valuable feature. Don't drive inspections so fast that you miss defects which will only cause you much bigger problems later on. We are usually under a lot of deadline pressure, so it is tempting to drive inspections faster than we should, but it is important to try and organize the work process so that this temptation is avoided.

This implies:

- *training* inspectors to respect the speed limits;
- *keeping statistics* which allow rates of speed, defect-finding effectiveness, cost of fixing errors at later stages, and moderator identification to be analyzed – so that erring moderators can be shown the loss they cause for the whole group if they do not respect the rates in practice;
- *motivating* inspection teams to maximize defects found (offer prizes for the best defects found performance by teams).

Tables, based on your own experience, of optimum rates are made and given to the moderator, who becomes responsible for maintaining those rates. If this is not done, it will show in the inspection statistics as a low rate of defects found compared to the norm.

Practical hint: *Publish optimum rate curves on your internal newsletters, and publish examples of estimated and real losses due to inspections being conducted outside the best rates of speed. Tell people where information about optimum rates can be found, and give an idea of the valid rates.*

The inspection-rate principle:
Inspection rates are to defect-finding efficiency what automobile speed rates are to fuel efficiency: too slow or too fast are both wasteful – and you have to measure carefully to find the optimum speeds for different conditions.

■ 12.8 More detail

This summary of the inspection method should serve to give a **management overview and definition**. It does not, however, contain sufficient detail to allow you to successfully practice it. You and your colleagues will require more detailed texts. The most authoritative of these are available as *Technical Reports on Inspection*, published by IBM, Kingston Laboratories, New York.

Fagan's 1976 *IBM Systems Journal* article is perhaps the classic. The 1985 (No. 2) *IBM Systems Journal* articles show the state of the art at that time. IBM will be possibly the richest source of inspection knowledge for some time to come. Freedman and Weinberg's book *Handbook of Walkthroughs, Inspections and Technical Reviews* (Little Brown) is an

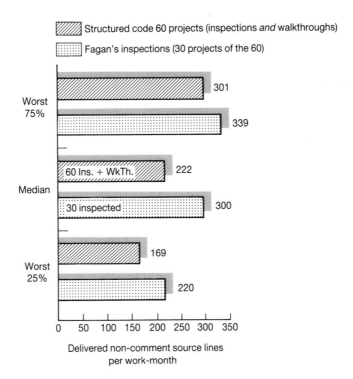

Figure 12.5 Inspection productivity compared to walkthroughs. The 60 projects all used structured coding. About half the projects used inspection, and about half used structured walkthroughs. So the difference between inspections and walkthroughs is greater than the 35% median seen here. Source: Walston, C.E. and Felix, C.P., 1977. 'A method of programming measurement and estimation,' *IBM Systems Journal*, **16**, (1), 54–73.

excellent background on the organizational and human aspects of conducting inspections.

For a deeper study of the method as it exists today, you might like to read *Quality Control Handbook* (McGraw-Hill) for an impression of the rich professional knowledge available on the subject, when we are mature enough to exploit it.

■ 12.9 Benefits of inspection

The expected benefits, shown in Table 12.2, are given in very general terms, since they vary according to the area applied. The comparison is with reviews, structured walkthroughs and other less stringent forms

Table 12.2 Benefits of inspection.

Benefit	Effect expected with inspections (see Figure 12.6 for supporting data)
delivery	earlier delivery, control over schedule (25–35%)
cost	reduced development costs (25–35%)
maintenance	reduced maintenance costs (10 to 30 times less)
reliability	substantial increase in correctness (10 to 100 times fewer defects)
productivity	increased for development and maintenance people (reflected in above results)
testing	time and machine time reduction due to better organization of tests (85% improvement)

of quality control. All numbers are based on statistically valid industrial experiences, mainly at IBM, but which have been replicated in large and small environments elsewhere, all over the world.

Figures 12.7 to 12.9 illustrate further aspects of the benefits of inspection.

> **Practical hint:** *If you collect inspection statistics and compare them with test statistics and operational statistics, you will be able to measure the benefits of inspection yourself, very quickly. See the Omega project example (Section 21.16) of very early-in-initial-use attempts to quantify the benefits of inspection.*

■ 12.10 The economics of inspection

The main reason for the effectiveness of inspection, in spite of the use of scarce human and calendar-time resources, is 'earliness.' The key numbers are these:

- Over 60% of the bugs which will occur in your operational software will be there before the code is ever written. They exist when code is written because we are so human at creating them and so poor at removing them.
- Code checking, even inspection of code, and thorough testing, will only serve to confirm the existence of these bugs in the real software!

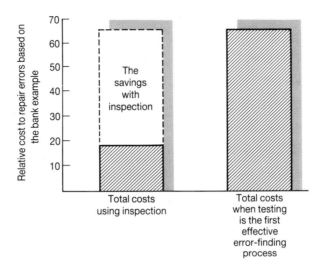

Figure 12.6 A stitch in time saves nine. Inspection, because it discovers errors at an earlier point in the development process than conventional program testing, reduces the development cost, because the correction costs are lower. Source: Standard Chartered Bank.

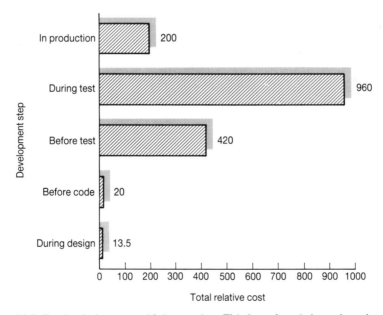

Figure 12.7 Total relative cost with inspection. This bar chart is based on data from a bank. It shows that in spite of the fact that most errors are found during inspection, they only account for about a third of the total repair costs.

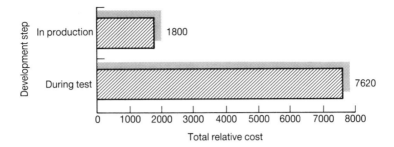

Figure 12.8 Total cost without inspection. This chart shows that when no inspections are applied, then the entire error correction burden falls on test and on the corrections to the system installed in the field. The total burden of cost correction is high because the much cheaper correction cost which is available at the inspection stage is not being exploited.

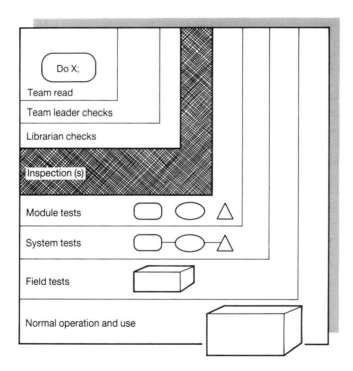

Figure 12.9 Inspection is only one kind of quality control. Inspection replaces all corresponding reviews and walkthrough processes. It does not replace testing, even though it reduces dependency on testing. Inspection does not preclude earlier, less formal testing. In fact, it may motivate a clean-up process within a team before they will submit to inspection.

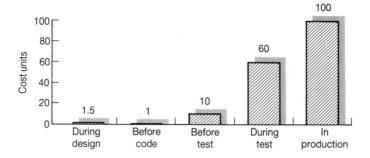

Figure 12.10 Relative costs to fix defects when they are caught at different development stages. These are illustrative figures only. Actual figures will vary with place and time. For example, IBM Santa Teresa Laboratories have reported at various times that errors caught at test were either 67 or 82 (as opposed to 60 in this chart) times more costly to fix than at inspection time.

- Testing is a maximum of 50 to 55% effective at defect identification and removal for a single test process.
- Inspection is about 80% (± 20%) effective in removing existing defects.
- Inspection can operate on specifications which computers cannot examine (like high-level prose, as opposed to process languages). It can operate in the area where the defects occur. It can operate at much earlier stages where the defects are one or two orders of magnitude cheaper to correct, when found.
- Although correction and finding of defects at inspection phases uses scarce qualified technologists, it is these same level (and pay-rate) of people who must carry out the defect finding and correction at later stages. The average is five hours saved for every hour invested in inspection.

Figures 12.10 and 12.11 provide further illustration of the economics of inspection.

> **Practical hint:** *Make sure you measure and predict savings in manpower, money and time to your management in order to justify your investment in starting and continuing an inspection effort. One client of mine neglected to do this, and dropped inspection. One year later they discovered that 400 inspected programs were ten times cheaper to maintain than 400 similar non-inspected programs. (ICI, UK.)*

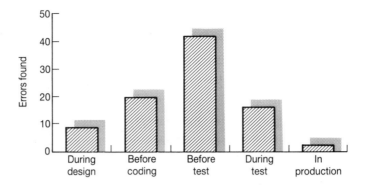

Figure 12.11 Errors found when inspection is used on design stages, Standard Chartered Bank data. The main point is that inspection is capable of catching most errors before testing, and that few real errors remain in production.

■ 12.11 Case study

The IBC case study itself did not use inspection in any immediate or major way. Inspection was included as a solution (see DBO.INSPECT, Table 10.5) primarily in order to reduce maintenance effort for new projects.

In order to provide some practical background for the reader on the use of the inspection method to contrast with the 'how to' description of the method given here, one of my clients has given a detailed practical account of the introduction and use of inspection in a large software engineering environment. This will be found as the Omega project in Chapter 21.

■ 12.12 Inspection is not merely for computer projects

Although inspection is particularly applicable to computer projects, it is by no means limited to them. Experience shows that it can be applied to any written documentation which is a part of the process of planning solutions to management goals.

The only criteria for its use are that management really care about getting things right the first time. Our experience is that in most organizations there are all kinds of documentation concerning such things as new products, new organizational plans, new services, long term strategies, contracts, sales proposals, just to name a few, which badly need some kind of quality control – especially consistency control – which they are *not* getting. The result is wasted management and organizational time.

> **The universal inspection principle:**
> Inspection can be used effectively on any technology or management documentation. It is not limited to software.

Inspection is really a kind of proofreading process, a comparison of a recently generated document with earlier documents and with standards within the organization for production of that class of documents. Inspection provides management with a clean-up process before they waste their valuable resources acting on the basis of inconsistent and incomplete documents. The only reason we do not easily recognize this fact is that we do not keep a measure of how much time we are wasting because of the defects in the documents which we are presently producing.

■ 12.13 Applications of inspection

Applications of inspection include:

- quality control of business documents (contracts, re-organization proposals, sales proposals (before you deliver them)),
- quality control of technical documents (goals, design strategies, detailed design specs, test plans documentation, programs)
- motivating people to raise the quality of their work,
- increasing group participation,
- training people in the work procedures and content.

> **Practical hint:** *You can demonstrate the power of inspection to your management by inspecting marketing and management documents. This device can be used to get understanding and goodwill from management. Remember, your own projects should be integrated with both the highest company planning and marketing strategy documents.*

> **The principle of highest level inspection:**
> If you fail to inspect the higher levels of planning and goal-setting, then inspection at the lower levels will only serve to confirm errors made earlier!
> or
> What is put into a design-or-planning process should always have exited successfully from inspection beforehand.

■ 12.14 The quality of documentation being inspected

A major effort at IBM development laboratories has been to improve the quality of planning documentation at the highest possible levels, so that inspection could succeed at those levels. One of the tools which they have studied and used in that effort is the set of ideas in this book, particularly the concepts surrounding quantified testable quality objectives (see Chapters 9 and 19).

Inspection is not only the quality control procedure described above. You have to have clear intelligible documentation on which to do your 'proofreading.' What happens in proofreading, for instance, if the proofreader cannot interpret someone's handwritten correction? Much of the material management is faced with today is not clear in meaning. It may be printed by a good word processor, but nobody may understand what the writer intended. In fact, often we suspect the writer did not know what he was saying, and hides this fact in obscure language.

Practical hint: *You must be prepared to raise the clarity of planning, requirements specification, and design documentation substantially in order to exploit inspection. Inspection will in itself stimulate this improvement by making poor practices more publicly embarrassing.*

The invisible-defects-don't-count principle:
If you don't understand exactly what someone says, you cannot be sure if they are wrong.
or
There is a good reason why politicians make vague promises.

■ 12.15 Summary

If you really want to improve your quality to cost ratio, you have to consider inspections seriously at several points in your organization the earlier the better.

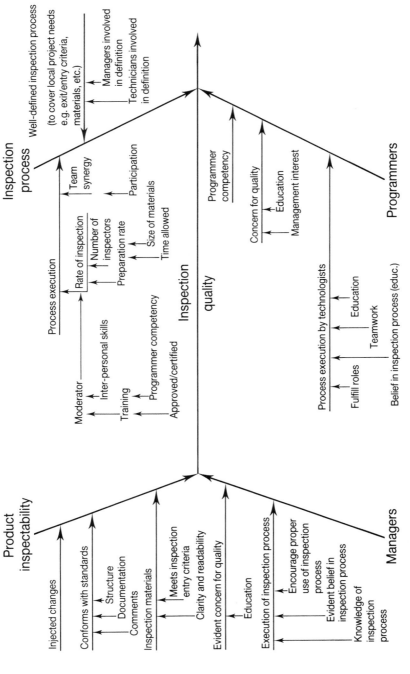

Figure 12.12 Contributors to inspection quality. This chart shows the large number of items that define an inspection process. Notice the strong lower half, with the emphasis on people, managers, training and motivation. Source: Fagan, M.E., *IEEE Trans. on Software Engineering*, July 1986. (© 1986 IEEE)

13

Evolutionary delivery planning and implementation

■ Introduction

This chapter is an introduction to the nuts and bolts of evolutionary planning, including an illustration using the IBC case study. For a more philosophical introductory view, and for a broader range of experience data, see Chapter 7.

Traditional *phased* planning is based on 'trying to do it all at once.' It starts by asking the questions: 'How *much* can we deliver within our recognized constraints?' For example: 'How much of the marketing director's dream project can we complete, by the deadline he has demanded and with the budget he (optimistically) thinks he can give us, when no headcount increase is possible?'

This question 'how much?' is dangerous. It invites us to try to estimate resource requirements for large and therefore quite complex systems. Perhaps it is about time we admitted that we cannot do this with the necessary accuracy. Perhaps it is about time that we admitted that we create more problems than we solve when we try to estimate the costs, plan for and implement such large units. There are, of course, considerable pressures to make such commitments. And there is always someone (either a fool or a weak manager) who will do so. But there is an alternative which has a proven track record of producing good results, and one which is far more appealing to management: evolutionary delivery.

Evolutionary delivery planning concentrates on short-term results. There is a short-term budgeting and project-time estimation process for the steps which we plan to deliver in the immediate future.

For example, we may have a budget for something to be delivered in one month, using five work-months of effort. This short-term budget approval process is the only really firm commitment and the only real risk that management takes. If we fail to deliver the promised and planned results for those estimated resources, management is in a position to stop further development, or to give us more resources to get there if necessary. If we show that we know what we are doing, by delivering these short-term results to estimated budgets, then we have earned the confidence of management for the next step.

We do make long range plans too, although only at a high level, or as a rough overview level. We can and do give very rough long-range estimates of costs and time. But we always do so with a clear warning that it is very rough, and cannot be relied upon until it is confirmed by the experience which we get in the implementation of the short-term steps. We also make the point that both the users and management will, based on their short-term experience with the partial deliveries of the system, be able to make considerable changes in the plan.

Evolutionary delivery does not ask 'how much?' Evolutionary delivery asks: 'how little?'

How little can we expend to produce a useful result for the ultimate user of the system. In particular it asks: 'What is the smallest development effort for us, with the largest payoff for the user, that we can make now?'

In even more complete wording, evolutionary delivery planning asks: 'What is the series of steps which will lead to complete long-term goal satisfaction, which has the largest value to cost ratio in the earliest steps?'

Although we shall sketch such a series of steps, there is only one that we are really committed to: the next one. This is not unlike selecting chess moves. You can have an idea of the strategy you will use to win, but you really only have a possibility for full control over the next move. The rest depends on the opponent, chance, or your improved perception of the position and possibilities once you actually make that next move.

Many people wrongly assume that the first step cannot be delivered until a rather large, critical minimum new system is designed and built. This is not true if you start by using the existing system – however much you dislike it.

It is possible to get to the system of your dreams by using the existing system as a starting point. In some years time, you may find little trace of the original system. But there are several concrete advantages in starting from whatever you have today:

- you improve the existing system for all present customers and users in a very short time frame;
- you do not have to take the risk of disturbing the present users and customers with a totally new (but bug-ridden) system;
- you save the direct expense of system creation;
- you have much less overhead in study of the old system;
- you can concentrate all energy and resources on solving the really pressing problems.

In spite of the inherent common sense of this approach. I find that software engineering projects, and organizational improvement projects for software engineers, constantly violate it. They are usually convinced that their new system creation approach is absolutely necessary.

I have found that we can always make an evolutionary plan, even when many 'experts' claim it is impossible. They are usually not thinking as broadly as they should. In particular, technologists get stuck by thinking too much about the system construction technicalities, and too little about results improvement.

■ 13.1 The technical process of evolutionary delivery planning

13.1.1 The major rules for creating evo plans

Here is an overview of the issues which will be detailed below.

Identify and organize delivery steps

Use lists of major functional requirements and major solution specifications for ideas of small-but-useful steps for meeting your objectives. Build up a list of step ideas which are then sorted in a sequence of delivery activities. These should be based on high-value steps coupled with low-cost and low-risk steps, placed early in the delivery schedule.

If you have built up a list of functional requirements (Chapter 8) and solution ideas (Chapter 10) then you should use these in some combination, distributed along a series of implementation steps.

Their value-to-cost ratio is the same as you might have estimated in an impact estimation table (Chapter 11). But a simple subjective zero-to-nine scale of value and then cost is sufficient. The value-to-cost ratio is in any case the value of step components in contributing towards your formal planned levels of attributes (Chapter 9).

Top-down plan until the smallest feasible steps are identified

Having got a set of major delivery steps, take each one of these in turn and break it down into a series of smaller, but useful, delivery steps. Continue this process until it is impossible or uninteresting to 'explode' into any more detail. Each implementable step should be somewhere between 1% and 5% of the total project effort. You may have to plan 20 to 100 individual implementation steps. I usually list the top ten step ideas on a single page using a ladder or step graphic notation. I usually find space for one or two levels of explosion of the initial step on that same page.

Make sure the solution is built on an 'open-ended' structure

Every living system has to adapt easily to change in order to survive. Software is no exception. But we do not, in my opinion, devote enough attention as to exactly how we are going to engineer adaptable software systems. The basic structure of the solution must be easy to build on, in a number of relatively unforeseen directions. It must, to use an analogy, have 'sliding internal walls' rather than internal 'brick walls' for room partitioning.

Open-endedness is a product design technique. (Inspection and evolutionary delivery methods are development process tools.)

13.1.2 The management responsibility for open-ended design

As a manager you can provoke these measures by making sure the 'adaptability' objectives are clearly and demandingly set (see Sections 19.2.3 and 19.3.3).

You must also make it clear that system adaptability is a high priority. If you only give signals about immediate delivery, immediate performance and reliability, then the people you are managing will not be motivated to give you open-ended designs for the long-term performance of the system. See more on open-ended architecture in Section 13.4.

■ 13.2 A more formal process for evolutionary delivery planning

13.2.1 A more formal process description

Set functional goals

Explode functional goals according to the major rule of 'division into groups of functions that must be delivered earlier, and groups of functions which can be delivered later.' The smaller the resolution of the steps, the smaller your evolutionary steps can be.

Set measurable attribute goals

Each evolutionary step must be measurable both as to its contribution to function, and its contribution to, or upholding of, the quality and resource goals. It is from the attribute goals such as early delivery and low risk that the pressure comes in favor of making use of an evolutionary delivery method.

Explode into detail

The technical and managerial solutions, which are directly derived from the attributes, must also be exploded into detail according to the

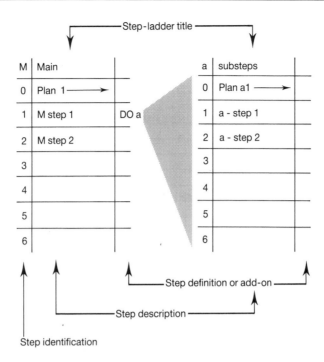

Figure 13.1 The ladder notation. This notation was developed to allow the analysis of evo-planning steps. The notation is due to a suggestion by David Parry of ICL, Reading, UK.

principle of necessary early delivery and possible later deliveries of those solution areas. The better this is done, the better the evolutionary plan.

Inspect evo plans

Make the effort to control the quality of all levels of planning documents with a strong method, such as Fagan's inspection method (Chapters 12 and 21). This will repay itself richly.

Create an open architecture

Before you get into the detailed implementation of the first steps, make sure that you have a robust and open architecture on which to build successive evolutionary additions. This may be the most difficult thing to do for conventional planners.

If they do not understand what this is all about, they will have to

Table 13.1 The top level of the IBC case evolutionary plan.

Step	Name
0.	Overall IBC new organization architecture policy plan and approval
1.	Measurable, testable project objectives for all qualities and resources. (IBC.DBO.SAS) see Table 13.2.
2.	Evolutionary delivery planning for all projects and developments (IBC.DBO.EVO) see Table 13.2.
3.	Infotecture, softecture, software and systems engineering using DBO (IBC.DBO.INFOTECT) see Table 13.2.
4.	PERSON, implement work planning, work reporting, team, DEVELOP
5.	Quality control, inspection, external DP audit, user valuation
6.	BUSINESS ANALYST, hire, train and integrate into organization
7.	AUTOMATE, develop and provide automated tools for productivity

learn the hard way by experiencing difficulty in the initial steps. Then, as a result, they will have to change the basic architecture of the solution to one which more easily tolerates constant unpredictable change.

Plan evolutionary steps in a top-down hierarchical explosion

It is only necessary to plan the immediately forthcoming steps in detail, since we want to learn from experience and modify plans to fit realities, as we progress. Do not do too much detailed planning before you have started deliveries of actual results.

You would be wasting your time, and binding planning resources unnecessarily. If your basic architecture is change-tolerant, then you can safely get on with delivering results and avoid 'planning yourself to death in an ivory tower,' without contact with realities of the future and the user environment. See Section 13.2.5 for the next step of the evolutionary planning process. We want to digress from the theory with practical examples first.

13.2.2 An evolutionary example

Let us look at our case study evolutionary plan as an example (Table 13.1).

13.2.3 A comment on the IBC case evo plan

This plan was originally written in a hurry – to have some plan rather than none when we presented our ideas to the Director. The main points of the plan are that the attribute specification is the first order of business, and the other things we have suggested as solutions (Table 10.2 and Figure 10.2 are part of the solutions we presented) will be done sometime, and not all at once. We will make a firm decision as to which of these steps to do after we have some experience of doing the first one.

The attribute specification (IBC.DBO.SAS in Table 13.2) was selected as the first step, not only because it is a logical first step (it would not be logical for projects which are well under way, and have already been working to agreed objectives!). It was chosen because of the recognition that the Director had experienced it the previous day in setting objectives for his organization with us (this project, the IBC case study). He had seen the value (he discovered that his team had not understood the objectives) and the cost (two hours for us and 20 minutes for him).

In practice, the client IBC did this first step in considerable depth for the entire first year of the organizational improvement project.

13.2.4 The detailed explosions of the IBC initial steps of change

Table 13.2 is an 'explosion of the main IBC steps listed in Table 13.1. These are illustrations of the only level of detail we created and presented to the Director. I have edited them to fit the context of this book, but they were exactly those steps that were suggested at the time.

I have included in capital letters a cross-reference to the proposed solutions listed in Chapter 10. The point is that an evolutionary plan is merely a sequencing of previously made solution decisions. This also provides a means of cross-checking that all solutions ideas are planned to be carried out sometime.

> **Practical hint:** *Use cross-reference tags in your evolutionary plan specification to systematically check that all solution and function specifications are to be found in some step of your plan. You can refer to a large set of the ideas by means of a single high level tag, at rough step planning stages.*

We often find that we are creating steps and sub-divisions as we make an evolutionary plan. This is a sign that the initial planning work

Table 13.2 An evolutionary plan example from the IBC case study.

Step No.	Description and reference tag
	1. IBC.DBO.SAS (System Attribute Specification)
1.1	Do measurable goals for all projects (DBO.SAS)
1.2	Implement a goals standard to be followed (SAS.STANDARD)
1.3	Inspect measurable goals against the standard (SAS.INSP)
1.4	Train managers and analyze in measurable goals (SAS.TRAIN)
	2. IBC.DBO.EVO (Evolutionary Delivery Design)
2.1	1-day evolutionary design course for 5 to 10 planners (CLASSIC)
2.2	Make standards for EVO plans (STANDARDS) and checklists (INSPECT)
2.3	Create and approve EVO plans for biggest projects (DBO.EVO.big)
2.4	Get all other projects to do EVO planning (DBO.EVO.rest)
2.5	Do inspections of EVO plans (IBC.DBO.INSPECT.evoplans)
	3. IBC.INFOTECT
3.1	Create job of infotect (hire, train, staff, authorize): (IBC.INFOTECT)
3.2	Implement remaining design by objectives (impact est. for example) (DBO)
3.3	Design by objectives standards and checklists complete (STANDARDS)

was not detailed and complete enough. You might consider putting such spur-of-the-moment ideas into the plan officially, with their written identity tags later. If you don't, you can begin to lose control over results and costs.

13.2.5 Function steps

There are no functional specification steps in the case study because, as is so often the case, we are not changing any functions, and the function in this case (building new systems for the bank) is already there. We are merely improving it by adding solution ideas in order to impact attributes.

We must now choose a step sequence.

All sets of functional ideas, and/or 'solution' techniques can potentially be evaluated for separate delivery from all others.

Some steps must come before others, because the later steps make direct use of them. But after that you have a choice of sequence. You should try to pick the steps with the highest value to cost ratio to go in first. Always ask the user (even if you have to do so via 'marketing' or

Table 13.3 The value/cost ratio flip-chart method for IBC case step sequencing in the evolutionary plan.

Value	Cost	(see Chapter 10 for definitions)	Step sequence
8	4	PERSON	4
8	3	INFOTECTURE	3
9	0	ATTRIBUTE SPECIFICATION	1
6	5	BUSINESS ANALYST	6
7	4	QUALITY CONTROL	5
5	8	AUTOMATE	7
9	1	EVOLUTIONARY	2

other representatives) what they would prefer. You can calculate the cost, but the end users are the only ones who can say with authority what the real value is.

13.2.6 The value to cost ratio flip-chart planning method

Sometimes we solve this part of the planning using a flip chart with 6 to 10 steps at the same level on a page. Then we estimate, as a group, the value (scale 0 to 9 where 9 is the highest value) and cost (also scale 0 to 9, where 9 is highest cost). Steps with the highest value to cost ratio are selected for earliest implementation. If we had done this formally in the IBC case, it would have looked like Table 13.3.

Zero cost is a symbol for trivial cost and does not necessarily imply absolutely no cost.

It is not difficult to use a more sophisticated way of developing the value/cost ratio numbers. It is given in Chapter 11 on impact estimation. However, the flip-chart method is a useful practical tool for getting a group of people to think about evolutionary planning together, without the burden of too much formality.

The group dynamics stimulate better ideas, and such ideas can be absolutely critical to successful completion of the project. They might well be missed in a bureaucracy where everything is writing and there is only one person doing the planning.

The ultimate system users know their own system or environment better than software engineers. They must therefore be deliberately brought in as consultants in the evolutionary design process. They can give insights on possible practical steps, and warn of impractical steps. They can help you get your values straight.

It is important that the user-group is consulted, and understands the basis for the selection of that first step. This leads to acceptance and commitment. Potential strife and quibbling can be stopped by pointing out that:

- all steps beyond the first are subject to replanning based on actual experience, and
- the *exact* sequence of steps is not as important as getting the rough step sequence producing high values early, and avoiding high overhead costs from building up before value and political goodwill are created. The most important thing is that most 'juicy bits' get done before all the 'whistles and bells.'

■ 13.3 The delivery cycle process

The above sections describe the initial planning process. There follows a description of the delivery cycle itself.

1. Attempt formal measurement of the results you achieve and the cost you have had at each step. Your attributes should be measurable economically in practice, and measurable at each step. If not, then you may have selected a too-costly measuring technique.
2. If the results are not what you expected, take action. Change your immediate plan for the next steps, or change your higher level plans, or change your budget and user expectations. You may have to change your technical design, in order to keep on track towards your most critical objectives. You may have to modify previous attribute commitments of the low priority type, in order to meet your users' higher priority commitments. See Figure 7.10.

Don't be disappointed when results do not meet plans. Deviation is normal. That is the very reason you are evolving the system in small steps. It is so you can discover these differences early, before they become a real danger to your project, and do something effective about them.

In the last resort, admit defeat, early.

■ 13.4 Open-ended architecture

Evolutionary development will be smoother if the system architecture contains 'open-ended' design solutions. Open-ended design solutions for software, hardware and organizational aspects have seemingly never been explored systematically in the literature. The open-ended techniques are very many. They are quite simply any solution idea which displays strong attributes of adaptability, hereunder extendability, portability and improvability (defined in Chapter 19). I often feel that the most important design work we can do in the short term is to make sure that there are many open-ended solutions utilized. This will for example solve problems of performance degradation during growth of volume, and problems of reliability degradation.

Does open-endedness cost more? If cost is important, then of course we will select those solutions which cost the least, rather than expensive devices for open-endedness.

Open-endedness is usually some kind of interface, in the broadest sense of that concept. It need be no more costly in principle than the electrical socket in the household wall, even though that type of open-endedness is designed to cope with a wide variety of devices – some of which have not yet been invented.

The following is a summary of the basic principles of open-ended design, which I hope the reader will realize is merely a specialized set of the more general principles stated throughout this book.

The principles of open-ended architecture:
All solution ideas will to some degree allow change in a measurable way.

Each solution idea has multiple ease-of-change attributes.

The expected range of each solution idea's ease-of-change attributes can be noted and used to select them for new designs.

The need for open-endedness is relative to a particular project's requirements.

Each open-ended solution idea has side-effects which must ultimately be the basis for judging the ideas for possible use.

You cannot maximize the use of open-endedness – but must always consider the balance of all solution attributes against all requirements.

You cannot finally select one particular open-ended design idea without knowing which other design ideas are also going to be included.

There is no final set of open-ended design ideas for a system; dynamic change is required and inevitable because of the external environment change.

Open-endedness will, by definition, cost less in the long term, but not necessarily more in the short term.

If you don't consciously choose an open architecture initially, your system's evolution will teach you about it the hard way.

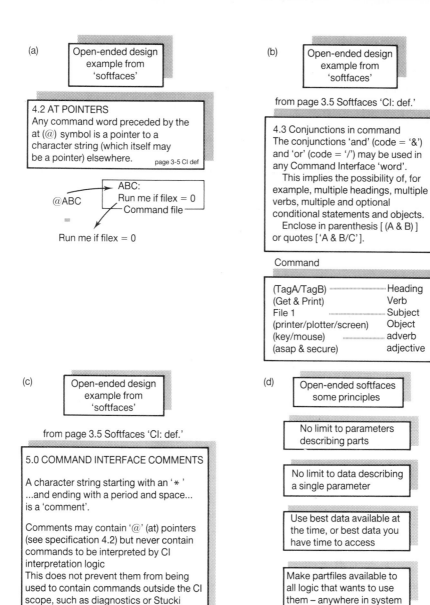

(a)

Open-ended design
example from
'softfaces'

4.2 AT POINTERS
Any command word preceded by the
at (@) symbol is a pointer to a
character string (which itself may
be a pointer) elsewhere.   page 3-5 CI def

ABC:
Run me if filex = 0
@ABC   Command file
=
Run me if filex = 0

(b)

Open-ended design
example from
'softfaces'

from page 3.5 Softfaces 'CI: def.'

4.3 Conjunctions in command
The conjunctions 'and' (code = '&')
and 'or' (code = '/') may be used in
any Command Interface 'word'.
  This implies the possibility of, for
example, multiple headings, multiple
verbs, multiple and optional
conditional statements and objects.
  Enclose in parenthesis [(A & B)]
or quotes ['A & B/C'].

Command

(TagA/TagB) ·············· Heading
(Get & Print)   Verb
File 1   ·············· Subject
(printer/plotter/screen) Object
(key/mouse) ·············· adverb
(asap & secure)   adjective

(c)

Open-ended design
example from
'softfaces'

from page 3.5 Softfaces 'CI: def.'

5.0 COMMAND INTERFACE COMMENTS

A character string starting with an ' * '
...and ending with a period and space...
is a 'comment'.

Comments may contain '@' (at) pointers
(see specification 4.2) but never contain
commands to be interpreted by CI
interpretation logic
This does not prevent them from being
used to contain commands outside the CI
scope, such as diagnostics or Stucki
Assertions. In fact the signal is our
device for 'other purpose commands'.

·············· * Version 3.5 5 aug ··············
·············· * Assert Verb = GET/PUT. ··············

(d)

Open-ended softfaces
some principles

No limit to parameters
describing parts

No limit to data describing
a single parameter

Use best data available at
the time, or best data you
have time to access

Make partfiles available to
all logic that wants to use
them – anywhere in system

Don't worry about storage
space or execution speed.
Open-endedness has higher
priority, and hardware is
its price

Figure 13.2 Some open-ended design details (a–c) and principles (d) from an actual design. The three designs were among about one hundred open-ended design ideas proposed in the design.

General Principle: Everything, without exception, which contributes to the completeness, usefulness and planned quality or resource attributes of the product at that stage

1. All functional configuration items planned for that cycle

2. All quality levels planned for that cycle, at the planned level

3. All resource objectives must be met at the planned level

4. Unpatched source code for all logic

5. Compiled code in runable form (linked together)

6. Input test cases for all modules. Complete set; meeting test standards. All non-computer-readable cases (flipping switches etc.) to be recorded and included

7. Module test output, for the above test cases, in magnetic form (for automatic compare when regression testing)

8. Cross-reference listing to all configuration items (ci's, tags) which are exercised by the test cases. See test standards for cross-referencing

9. Complete system specification, in detail, with ci tags attached, in text processor format

10. Complete set of user documentation, in text processor format, cross-referenced with tags of test cases which purport to test particular statements

11. Complete set of integration testing test cases, outputs, cross-references; as indicated above for module testing. Anything necessary to repeat the testing process easily and safely, after modifications are made

12. Hardware configuration presumptions. A list of the exact hardware configuration for which this testing is applicable.

13. A signed statement that the testing for this cycle is *complete and correct*: by the quality control officer, the technical controller and the project leader

14. A list of customer or field trial sites for whom this cycle is intended.

Figure 13.3 A list of things which must be delivered at every evolutionary delivery cycle.

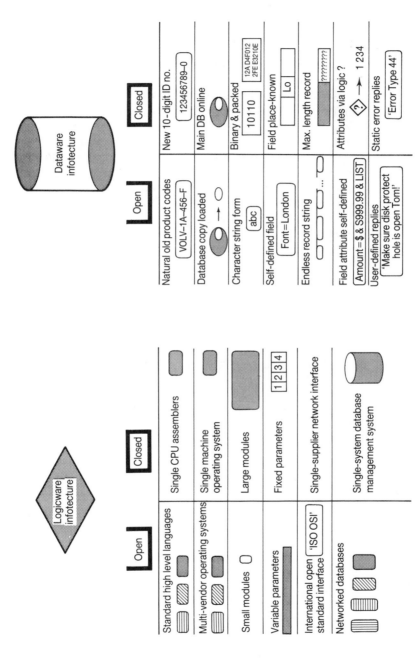

Figure 13.4 Two examples of policies for evolutionary planning. The first (left) is for a large (1000 people) telecommunications software developer. The second (right) is for a small (35 people) applications package software house which is part of a large computer corporation.

■ 13.5 Management actions for evolutionary delivery

1. Make it a matter of basic top management required planning philosophy. Make it known that management expects good evolutionary delivery plans unless otherwise stated.
2. Participate actively in the initial explosions of the evolutionary delivery plan, namely the long term high-level plan and the explosion of the first major step. You have time. We are talking about a maximum of 20 steps on two pieces of paper, but this will give you control over the process, and make your determination and interest in evolutionary delivery known to the planning group.
3. Make the training and theory of evolutionary delivery available to the responsible planners. Be patient. Nobody becomes good at this instantly or by intuition alone. It will take time and hard experience, as does any worthwhile management discipline. But you can still expect to see some of the rewards of the evolutionary delivery method early in your first conscious attempt to use it.
4. Free the planners from the chains of conventional thinking and planning by making it clear to them that they are at liberty to use any, even quite unconventional, approaches to meeting the attribute and functional goals for the long term.

You will have 'quantified attribute goals' to give them, so that they can measure their progress toward these goals. Make sure that your team understands that the success of evolutionary delivery is only defined and evaluated in terms of meeting the formally defined attribute and functional goals.

■ 13.6 The principles of evolutionary delivery

The principles of evolutionary delivery:
All large projects are capable of being divided into many useful partial result steps.

The only critical step is the next one.

Evolutionary steps should be delivered on the principle of 'the juiciest one next.'

Result delivery (not the construction activity) is the only point.

The principles of evolutionary delivery (cont.):

Open-ended architecture should be at the base, otherwise the step transition cost will be unnecessarily high.

Any step sequence you plan will be changed by the facts you learn as you deliver the early steps.

Maximizing your real progress towards your specified goals is the only measure of successful evolutionary delivery.

The evolutionary process can lead to change of your technical design solutions, or change of your lower-priority requirements so that you can reach your higher-priority goals instead.

You don't need to recreate a minimum working system before making your first improvements, if you use an already existing system to make a start with.

If the evolutionary delivery method doesn't work, then you haven't been doing it properly.

■ 13.7 Implementation

One student and colleague, when reviewing the manuscript, asked 'Have you asked a real manager what they want to see in the book?'

I put the question to a product planning manager who had already spent several months implementing these methods in his organization. He replied, 'When I read the manuscript, I keep on saying to myself that 95% of it is just good common sense, and that I ought to implement it immediately. But of course it cannot all be implemented at once. It needs to be implemented evolutionarily, at a pace my own people can absorb and feel comfortable with, even though I personally would want to put it in at a much higher pace. So I would like to see some more direct advice on the implementation process.'

13.7.1 Implementation advice

1. The implementation of the principles of software engineering management must be evolutionary.
2. The willing enthusiasm of the people in the organization being changed is the surest indicator that the pace of change is right.
3. Full implementation of all the ideas will actually take several years in any large organization.

4. The ideas must be tailored to local taste, and must contain a local contribution so that the ideas become their own.
5. The ideas must be sold and accepted as ordinary common sense, packaged so as to encourage consumption by the group.
6. The ideas must be seen by every individual involved as contributing to their ability to do good work.
7. Difficulties must be expected while the individuals become familiar with the new culture. Patient and helpful teachers must be provided while they learn.
8. Managers must create enthusiasm for dealing with problems earlier than the team is accustomed to. This will uncover numerous problems which previously would not have been identified until later.
9. The ideas must be fully led and supported at all times at the top of the organization. Lack of support is deadly – irrespective of the correctness of the ideas.
10. Don't give up just because the methods don't work initially. You have probably failed to implement them correctly, and the cause of that failure may well be something we have not treated in the book. You must be the diagnostician; find the problem, correct it and continue.

13.7.2 Where to start

Different clients will need to start with different methods. There is no single, correct starting point. It doesn't really matter where you start, because you will eventually need and want all the other ideas to improve your final result. They all fit together. It is important that the starting point be one which has interest, enthusiasm and support from the people involved. The best starting point is to tackle problems which everyone is aware of and irritated by.

13.7.3 Case one: inspection first

One software group in the Thames Valley, UK, started with Fagan's inspection because they were under high pressure to improve the reliability of the products they made. They quickly discovered that the only way they could get the time and energy to do inspection properly within the tight delivery deadlines and fixed headcounts which were imposed, was to adopt evolutionary delivery. When they got into inspection, they soon realized that high level inspections (requirements and design specification) were the most powerful things they could do.

But the early attempts to do high level inspections convinced them of the need for substantial improvement in the clarity and rigor of the requirement and design specification. This led to adoption of measurable attribute specification, tagging, and cross-referencing.

13.7.4 Case two: evolutionary planning first

A super-large German software development group was worried about the survival of their project, and of the project managers. They had planned a many thousand work-year 'big-bang' software component delivery. Their extremely detailed PERT charts warned them of delays of at least two years if they continued as they were doing. They solved their problem by starting off with the use of the evolutionary delivery method. Critical short-term delivery steps were inserted into the big-bang plan in order to allow delivery of something within a year, rather than delaying everything for two to three more years.

Almost at the same time, they discovered that they had a major fault in their previous quality metrics thinking, which was causing too much testing effort to be put into the software. Their problem was that they had fallen for the temptation to use an easy-to-measure objective, rather than the one which was really critical. They had chosen one highly ambitious level of 'reported bug rates' as a measure across all the software. This was now changed to 'system availability.' They applied the new measure selectively, so that the most critical real time components had high availability. The majority of components were allowed to have a lower level of availability. This change saved them from overtesting the software in 95% of the modules. Using these strategies, they managed to deliver well within the year, with no failures at all in the first customer installations.

About 15 months after I had originally worked with the group, they reached the stage of deciding they needed to do inspection. As a result of our work to solve the short-term crisis, the Director of the unit involved realized that they needed to work out a longer-term organizational improvement scheme. A three-day managers' conference was held where a larger selection of the methods and concepts were debated and adopted.

13.7.5 Case three: written metric objectives first

A third organization, in the City of London, asked me to examine their current projects. I found that rather large projects had no unambiguous goals in writing. I had a meeting with the source of project requirements, 'marketing'. The Director there was immediately receptive to a radical and immediate change in his team's language for specifying system requirements.

He said later, 'We were certainly guilty of woolly thinking.' He himself made frequent informal use of impact estimation to view his own plans, and to present them to his top executives, while his people were concentrating on quality metrics specifications, separation of functional requirements and attribute requirements. His team moved quickly to making evolutionary plans, and recognized that individual functional components might need differentiation of attribute specification.

Inspection of requirements is viewed as a probable evolutionary improvement to their process, but was intentionally not implemented at the early stages. In parallel with the development in the product planning group, the company's development team (ten times larger in people) is going through the initial stages of learning about the methods. The product planning manager is leaving them free to go about their business, while cleaning his own house up first. But he is showing discreet interest in the development group's parallel intake of the new methods, so that his products get reliably developed.

13.7.6 Case four: solution comparison first

Another client in Reading (UK) had used solution comparison (a variant of impact estimation used to select the product or method which impacts your quantified multiple objectives best) for a few months after attending a course. They needed to make decisions regarding the software support tools and programming languages appropriate to their new development environment.

Once they got going with their product development itself they tried to quantify their attribute objectives. They went through many versions of this and never seemed to pin it down officially. Finally, the project manager did sign a simplified top-ten, one-page version of it. They then did some inspections of design documentation. This had become company policy.

The Director of the project manager was shocked that 18 months into the project it wasn't being planned and delivered evolutionarily, as he thought it perfectly good practice. He had some words about this with the project manager who promised to take steps, and did. But they wasted at least another year before they even got close to it.

It turned out that this was because the project manager did not understand what was meant by 'evolutionary planning'. He remarked when finally presented with a very detailed evolutionary plan, with weekly increments, combined with a weekly impact estimation table, 'Now I finally understand what was meant all this time by evolutionary delivery!'

The fact that they were wasting their time without evolutionary planning became apparent after the first attempt to deliver something to a real user, about 28 months into the project. Almost all design was discovered to be worthless and they had to make a fresh start. This was something they could have discovered two years earlier. They had been living in their ivory tower too long.

13.7.7 Summary

The point of these cases is that every organization has different immediate needs and will therefore choose to pick up different tools initially. But they will be led gradually into picking up all the tools in the toolkit in time. Sometimes they will misuse those tools and fail in their endeavor. Sometimes they will blame the tools themselves for their failure too!

PART THREE

Advanced insights and practical experiences

14

The management of software productivity

■ Introduction

Productivity should be measured in terms of net real effects on high-level management goals of a business or institution. Any attempt to quantify productivity by many common, but more partial measures, such as 'volume of work produced' is a great deal less useful. These partial measures do, however, have a place. They can provide some insight and control over productivity in the early stages or at a low measurement cost.

Productivity should be measured as the net effect of a solution on results. This means that we have to account for the cost of developing and operating the solution in both the short and long terms, as well as the cost of all the side-effects of the solution.

Productivity planning must be carried out at a high management level in order to guarantee the relevance of the solutions to management objectives. Productivity goals are usually multi-dimensional and complex, but they can be written down, agreed upon, and expressed in clear and measurable ways.

The tools for improving software productivity are many. They can be implemented immediately with interesting results, and then strengthened by a long-term series of evolutionary changes and improvements. Each of these changes is based on continual monitoring of productivity results up to that point.

■ 14.1 What is software?

Most professionals interpret the term 'software' itself in a dangerously narrow way. Behind most uses of the term 'software' we find the concept of what I prefer to call 'logicware,' or what we call 'programs.'

Websters Unabridged Dictionary defines software as 'the programs, data, routines, etc. for use in a digital computer, as distinguished from the physical components (hardware).'

Since the production of software today involves many more additional non-hardware components than were formally recognized in the early days of digital computers, it is only natural that we update our concept of software by including these new items in our consideration of software productivity. We cannot discuss 'software productivity' adequately, if we do not have a complete definition of the term 'software' itself.

Software can be divided into the following main categories: logicware (computer program logic); dataware (computer-readable files and databases); peopleware (plans and methods for organizing people to make use of the system or to develop it or test it); userware (user documentation in paper or display screen versions, and user command languages).

■ 14.2 Evaluating the software product

Productivity is, as mentioned earlier, measured in terms of the planned attributes of the product. It is these attributes which will enable us to determine whether, and to what degree, the user has attained his objectives (user productivity). One 'user' of the product can be the producer himself, and the use can be to sell the product or to sell related products (such as hardware).

There are a large number of attributes which together determine the total short-term and long-term usefulness of software. They have been discussed extensively in this book, and are catalogued in Chapter 19.

There are some software product attributes which are of immediate everyday value; for example reliability, usability, and work-capacity. It is *productive work* which is necessary to achieve the needed levels of these attributes. It is a very common failing to ignore these qualities, and to think that productivity is in 'coding' the bare functional logic only. The result is an illusion of productivity, but not the reality.

It is a very dangerous illusion, since high quality attribute levels can cost the largest part of the entire development effort. This is easily illustrated by observing the huge effort needed to build extreme ease of use (usability) into software. The Apple Macintosh design effort is an example of this. A series of articles relating to the effort to design ease-of-use into the Macintosh, can be found in *Byte*, February 1984, August 1984, and December 1984.

■ 14.3 The long-term productivity considerations

Developer (producer) productivity produces good software effectively. User productivity is enhanced by the use of good software. The quality attributes of software impinge on user productivity.

The particular quality attributes which impact the productivity of both user and producer in the long run can be difficult to see. The primary ones are maintainability, extendability and portability (see Chapter 19 for definitions) which are all related to the ease of change of the product in order to meet long-term future needs.

If these attributes are poorly engineered in the software product, then there is a great danger that the product will die or become poorer in use. The investment needed to design and build these long-term qualities into the system will determine whether it is really productive in the future.

Many a software project has suffered from insufficient effort in the engineering of these areas, due to poor management leadership. They have created the illusion of software productivity (in the short term), at the expense of the long-term productivity.

Somebody (it is not likely to be a programmer) who cares about the true long-term productivity of the software effort, must ensure that these long-range factors are engineered into the software product.

You should not wait to be asked, because the marketing people and end users may not be wise or mature enough to explicitly ask for these properties. A responsible professional will raise the issue, and force the people requesting the software to include high quality long term attributes, or at least to take full responsibility for not having done so.

The user as judge principle:
The end users themselves, not the producers, should be the final judge of productivity in the sense of software quality.

The intention of such a principle is to ensure that we can measure the true user productivity given by the software product, in all important areas, throughout its lifetime. Here is a more detailed background for these principles.

■ 14.4 Users should judge software: the BHP and Volvo cases

For software producers selling to a free market, there is adequate public judgement of the software quality in the trade press, by the sales statistics, or at user group meetings. For more captive users of software, such as those from a company producing software for internal consumption, a more drastic remedy is needed.

Volvo of Sweden provided this by making it mandatory for internal Volvo computer users to ask for a bid from their internal Data Processing development facility, while at the same time encouraging those users to ask for and accept alternative bids for better software products from outside suppliers.

Example: Broken Hill Pty

One of the most interesting examples of a powerful internal control by the user of application software was at BHP (Broken Hill Pty), the largest Australian industrial corporation (steel, mining, oil, finance) from 1972.

The users were given total power over the software producers. After nine previous years of unprofitable and unresponsive data processing development, top management stepped in and introduced a user-controlled profitability measure of the software value. This applied to internal developments, as well as any support software required from outside. The result was that the 'academics' fled, and the survivors became dramatically more responsive to the users' needs.

The basic mechanism was a continuous (monthly) application-lifetime budgeting and accounting system which compared a user-determined application 'value' (in terms of real money savings or productivity increases – no 'intangibles') to the real current costs of running the application. Projects which fell below a minimum set level of profitability were initially given a chance to improve the ratio. If this failed, they were quickly killed.

The net result, even in the first year, was that in spite of a budgeted loss of several hundreds of thousands of dollars, the actual result was a clear profit of several hundred thousand dollars for the surviving software applications.

Nobody in BHP was worried about producing 'lines of code.' The entire surviving data processing staff (six hundred people) had only two questions in their minds about all projects, at all times: how can we keep the costs down as low as possible?; how can we make the software so useful in terms of user cost saving and user productivity (more steel plant productive capacity for example) that the user management profit centers will give our product a high dollar rating (part of which is charged back to them), and thus keep it alive?

■ 14.5 Continuous monitoring

> **The never ending judgement principle:**
> Software systems need to be judged on a continuous basis throughout their lifetime – not just by the first user, the first month.

Software applications cannot simply be judged once, in a post-implementation return-on-investment-analysis (though in my experience, even this is not done often enough).

Here are some of the reasons why the evaluation of software applications should be reviewed regularly:

- hardware costs change dramatically year by year;
- maintenance changes might degrade performance and other qualities;
- the user-environment changes – yesterday's winner may be tomorrow's loser;
- management employees change jobs, and with that goes a style of management which may have been key to the value of the product.

■ 14.6 Formal testing of productivity-related software attributes

> **The multiple test principle:**
> Software systems should have formally defined acceptance test criteria which are applicable at all times for all critical qualities.

Several software qualities (for example maintainability, portability, and usability) are keys for allowing the product to be really productive. All of them are measurable and testable in practice (see Chapter 19). There are unfortunately far too few software professionals who know anything about measuring and testing these properties of software.

Software engineering management must institute a rigid requirement for testing these qualities and other critical attributes of the software system. If they fall below critical levels, as determined by yourselves and your users, it could kill the entire software effort or product.

■ 14.7 Productivity is managerial not technical

> **The principle of software productivity:**
> It is not the software itself which is productive. The interesting results are created by people who make use of the software.

Most of the productivity improvement techniques with really significant impact are managerial, not technical in nature. This was the conclusion drawn by Horst Remus of IBM after years of monitoring productivity figures at IBM at their California Santa Teresa Laboratories

(Remus, 1980). My own observation, based on measures of software project productivity, is the same.

Many software technologists seem totally ignorant of the existence of the managerial and organizational methods which lead to highly improved human productivity. The technologists seem to believe that productivity is to be had through technical means, such as ever more sophisticated programming languages, or more sophisticated software support for their working environment. There is some truth in this viewpoint, but it is not where the really big improvements have been found.

This point is brought out in a number of management texts such as Peters and Austin (1985). It is clearly motivation and organization that increases human productivity in relevant directions. Technical devices may increase productivity 'in the wrong direction.' (We can always increase 'lines of code', even where the software being produced for the market is the wrong design!)

■ 14.8 Management productivity

Productivity of management at all levels above the software tech-nologist can be improved by:

- concentrating on determining user requirements;
- particularly noting those fluctuating or uncertain user require-ments which will require a suitable flexible softecture (software architecture);
- creating an organization which is totally user-result-oriented, even at the most technical level;
- implementing measurement systems which relate all technical work to corresponding user-value and user-cost concepts;
- filtering user needs through competent business analysts, infotects, softects and software engineers (do not allow things to go directly to the softcrafters);
- provide users with the means to do a maximum of 'software development' themselves; either by building such devices into the product, or by supplying user-oriented development languages (like spreadsheet software) to the users.

■ 14.9 Professional productivity

The *business analyst* function can increase productivity of the user by avoiding computerization when other options are better or more cost effective, and by worrying about the 'non-software' aspects of making your software productive for the user (like whether people are still motivated to use it at all). The business analyst operates at a higher level than most present day system analysts. Too many analysts are primarily concerned with analyzing the function to be automated. The business analyst does not even presume that software is to be written, or even that there is an information system problem.

The *infotect* can contribute to professional productivity by making sure that the information system problem is channelled to the best solution area. Too many analysts are trained and working in an environment where they really see only one technical solution; for example, the company standard computer, the prevalent languages and database support system. Sometimes using a computer is not the most cost-effective way of doing things, and some alternative computerized solutions are far better than the conventional ones. The infotect is charged with finding the most productive 'results' solution, irrespective of the devices needed to accomplish it.

The *softect* is a necessary function in a large software engineering environment, in which there are many specialist software engineers. The softect is the necessary synchronization and co-ordination function for the many specialized engineers and builders. The softect presumes that software must be designed, and is only concerned with finding a technical solution set which will satisfy the multiple conflicting objectives of the user as well as possible.

The *software engineer* is also a productivity professional. We speak of software engineering as though it were a single speciality. But the history of other professions makes it clear that specialization is the norm for large projects. We can certainly identify the specialists even today in this area, even though they do not always call themselves software engineers.

The softect is also a specialist software engineer, the speciality being overall control of a complex engineering process. Other software-engineering specialists are, for example, concerned with work-capacity, availability, usability and security.

Software engineers can be expected to increase productivity in their special area of competence. That is exactly what their training should enable them to do. One measure of their competence is how much they can improve their specialty attributes; another is the degree to which they can correctly predict or estimate what they will in fact achieve when all side-effects are considered.

■ 14.10 Productivity tools

Most all of the highly-touted productivity tools (programming languages, software support environments, database support systems, operating systems) offered by traditional industry, have failed to deliver substantial net user-productivity in a well-documented way. This has not prevented them from claiming impressive productivity increases, forgetting that the real end-product is user productivity. My experience in years of trying to substantiate such claims is that:

- they are based on isolated cases and may well be due to uncontrolled factors (the super-programmer on one project, for example);
- they do not note, or even consider, undesirable side-effects (such as performance destruction, or portability reduction) which need to be considered in any fair evaluation of real productivity;
- almost none of them meets the conditions of scientific verification via controlled experiments, and statistically valid assertions;
- most of them are concerned with producing only one area of productivity, namely 'logic for functions.' Few of them address any of the critical attribute dimensions of technical software quality and cost; even fewer address user benefits or results.

I do not deny that some of these productivity tools have a beneficial effect. But I have not yet found evidence for impressive net benefits in software productivity which are as impressive as those I have found for methods such as Fagan's inspection, for evolutionary delivery and even the simple act of formal specification of objectives.

■ 14.11 Fagan's inspection method

Fagan's inspection method (Fagan, 1976) has regularly measured net productivity increases of about 25% to 35% in software project time to delivery. Exceptionally high savings have been reported in the test planning area (Larson, 1975). Larson reported, with Fagan later confirming the long term consistency of the effect, 85% of test effort was saved as a result of using inspection to check the quality of test design and planning. Crossman (1979) has reported 18 to 1 and 30 to 1 improvements in maintenance effort needed for software which has been inspected. ICI in the UK has privately reported on one project that the 400 out of a total of 800 production planning programs which had been inspected during their development were ten times cheaper to maintain.

These are the once-off productivity effects of inspection. The really significant news about inspection is that the statistical feedback it gives on defects and costs provides the manager with a software engineering management accounting system. This can be used to identify a wide range of productivity problems in a software development process, and then to measure and see if the suggested solutions are working as expected.

Both IBM in the US, AT&T and ICL (International Computers) have regularly used inspection for monitoring and improving their software development processes, in order to improve productivity.

The real productivity benefit is greater than is indicated by a productivity curve alone. At the same time, a quality indicator (lower defects) is improving, and this saves productive effort in error repair (maintenance cost), as well as enhancing the desirability of the supplier's products to customers. It is highly probable, because of the nature of inspection, that other quality indicators are also increasing the net productivity of the use of inspection, as a management accounting system, at the same time.

■ 14.12 The productivity of evolutionary delivery

The most impressive practical method for ensuring dramatic productivity in software projects, is still the least understood of all the methods, evolutionary system delivery.

IBM Federal Systems Division is a long-time leader (since about 1970) in the use of this method in the software engineering arena. (Mills, 1980). Mills reports that all projects using the method for the last four years have been completed 'on time and under budget.' Surely that is a form of productivity in itself which few software engineering managers can claim (Gilb, 1985). See also Chapter 15 for an extensive literature and experience survey.

■ 14.13 Project data collection and analysis

Another under-utilized method for productivity through management analysis of facts is the use of systematic project data collection and analysis.

The only really good example, in terms of an ongoing collection process, that I have found in the public literature is at IBM Federal Systems Division (Walston and Felix, 1977). An interesting collection of data, but not so clearly ongoing, is published in *Software engineering economics* by Barry Boehm of TRW Systems (Boehm, 1981). Many pages of project data are collected at the end of each project and analyzed in an APL database at IBM FSD, Bethesda, Maryland.

IBM FSD is able to compare systematically a large number of projects on a number of factors regarding cost, delays and methods used. This enables them to spot methods or environments which are more or less productive, and to take management action to weed out the bad and to nurture the good.

Most software engineering environments are not able to do this anywhere nearly as well. Most rely on the faulty memories of old warriors. The objective of software engineering management is to increase the predictability in meeting our objectives, whatever those objectives may be. We can therefore measure our ability by measuring the deviation from our plans in high priority areas.

We must probably do this statistically, by collecting the kind of data which IBM FSD has been collecting, or which Barry Boehm has collected. For example, Boehm (in *Software engineering economics*) says that in his selection of past projects, 70% of the projects would be within 20% of the cost predicted by his COCOMO cost estimation model and 30% of the projects would be outside that.

Harlan Mills of IBM claims to have found a method, in the same class of systems that Barry Boehm is dealing with, which guarantees no significant negative deviation for two important attributes (delivery on schedule and cost). By the above principle, Mills' methods (evolutionary delivery) are better software engineering management principles than using the best-known cost estimation models, in terms of getting real management control over cost and delivery.

Both examples are based on comparable sets of statistics for comparable projects.

■ 14.14 Summary

We can sum up with a set of principles regarding people productivity as follows:

If you can't define it, you can't control it:
The more precisely you can specify and measure your particular concept of productivity, the more likely you are to get practical and economic control over it.

Productivity is a multi-dimensional matter:
Productivity must be defined in terms of a number of different and conflicting attributes which lead to the desired results.

Productivity is a management responsibility:
If productivity is too low, managers are always to blame – never the producers.

Productivity must be project-defined; there is no universal measure:
Real productivity is giving end users the results they need – and different users have different result priorities, so productivity must be user-defined.

Architecture change gives the greatest productivity change:
The most dramatic productivity changes result from radical change to the solution architecture, rather than just working harder or more effectively.

Design-to-cost is an alternative to productivity increases:
You can usually re-engineer the solution so that it will fit within your most limited resources. This may be easier than finding ways to improve the productivity of people working on the current solution.

A stitch in time saves nine:
Frequent and early result-measurements during development will prevent irrelevant production.

The ounce of prevention (which is worth a pound of cure):
Early design quality control is at least an order of magnitude more productive than later product testing. This is because repair costs explode cancerously.

Do the juicy bits first:
There will never be enough well-qualified professionals, so you must have efficient selection rules for sub-tasks, so that the most important ones get done first.

■ References and further reading

Boehm, B.W., 1981, *Software engineering economics*, Prentice-Hall, N.J.

Crossman, T., 1979, 'Some experiences in the use of inspection teams in application development,' IBM Guide/Share applications development symposium proceedings, Monterey, California

Fagan, M.E., 1976, 'Design and code inspection to reduce errors in program development,' *IBM Systems Journal*, **15**, (3)

Gilb, T., 1985, 'Evolutionary delivery vs. the waterfall model,' *ACM Software Eng. Notes*, July

Kitchenham, B., 1982–85. See frequent contributions to *ICL Technical Journal*. ICL, Bridge House, Putney, London SW6 3JH

Larson, R., 1975, 'Test plan and test case inspection,' *IBM Technical Report TR 21.586*, Kingston NY, April 4

Mills, Dyer and Quinnan articles in *IBM Systems Journal*, **19**, (4) 1980

Peters, T. and Austin, N., 1985, *A passion for excellence*, Random House (USA) and Collins (UK)

Remus, H., 1980, 'Planning and measuring program implementation', *IBM Technical Report TR 03095*, June

Walston, C.E. and Felix, C.P., 'A method of programming measurement and estimation,' *IBM Systems Journal*, **16**, 54–73

15

Some deeper and broader perspectives on evolutionary delivery and related technology

■ Introduction

The objective of this chapter is to show the extent of understanding of the idea of evolutionary delivery inside and outside of software engineering, to show that it is not a new or unappreciated idea.

■ 15.1 Software engineering sources

These follow in alphabetical order.

15.1.1 Allman and Stonebraker

Source: Eric Allman and Michael Stonebraker, UC Berkeley, 'Observations on the Evolution of a Software System', IEEE Computer, June 1982, pp. 27–32. (©1982 IEEE)

The authors led the development of a 75 000 line C database system, for over six years, in a research environment, but ultimately having over 150 user sites.

'It seems crucial to choose achievable short-term targets. This avoids the morale problem related to tasks that appear to go on forever. The decomposition of long-term goals into manageable short-term tasks continues to be the main job of the project directors.

Short-term goals were often set with the full knowledge that the longer-term problem was not fully understood, and were retraced later when the issues were better understood. The alternative is to refrain from development until the problem is well understood. We found that taking any step often helped us to correct the course of action. Also, moving in some direction usually resulted in a higher project morale than a period of inactivity. In short, it appears more useful to "do something now even if it is ultimately incorrect" than to only attempt things when success is assured.

As a consequence of this philosophy, we take a relaxed view towards discarding code . . . our philosophy has always been that "it is never too late to throw everything away."' (p. 28)

'Our largest mistake was probably in failing to clearly pinpoint the change from prototype to production system.' (p. 32)

15.1.2 Balzer

*Source: Robert Balzer, USC/Information Sciences Institute, 'Program
Enhancement', in* ACM Software Eng. Notes, *August 1986, Trabuco
Canyon Workshop position paper, pp. 66–67*

'There are two reasons for such enhancements. The first is that no-
one has enough insight to build a system correctly the first time
(even assuming no implementation bugs). The second is that the
mere existence of the system, and the insight gained from its
usage, create a demand for new or altered facilities.'

Dr Balzer comments on two of the main reasons that the waterfall
model cannot work well in most high-tech environments. Software is
different from hardware in at least one major respect. It can be more
cheaply reproduced (copied, ported, converted reused). The consequence of this is that, like music composition, each effort is
essentially an attempt to create something very new. This implies that
we are bound to be working with more unknown factors than the
bridge builder. So, we must have some processes for exploring the
unknown, like evolutionary delivery.

*Source: William Swartout and Robert Balzer, USC/Information Sciences
Institute, 'On the Inevitable Intertwining of Specification and Implementation',*
Comm. of ACM, *July 1982, pp. 438–440*

'For several years we and others have been carefully pointing out
how important it is to separate specification from implementation. . . . Unfortunately, this model is overly naive, and does not
match reality. Specification and implementation are, in fact,
intimately intertwined because they are, respectively, the already-
fixed and the yet-to-be-done portions of a multi-step development.
It is only because we have allowed this development process to
occur unobserved and unrecorded in people's heads that the
multi-step nature of this process was not more apparent
earlier.' . . . 'Every specification is an implementation of some
other higher level specification. . . many developments steps . . .
knowingly redefine the specification itself. Our central argument is
that these steps are a crucial mechanism for elaborating the
specification and are necessarily intertwined with the implementation. By their very nature they cannot precede the implementation.' (p. 438)
    'Concrete implementation . . . insight provides the basis for
refining the specification. Such improved insight may (and usually

does) also arise from actual usage of the implemented system. These changes reflect (also) changing needs generated by the existence of the implemented system.' (p. 439)

'These observations should not be misinterpreted. We still believe that it is important to keep unnecessary implementation decisions out of specifications and we believe that maintenance should be performed by modifying the specification and reoptimizing the altered definition. These observations indicate that the specification process is more complex and evolutionary than previously believed and they raise the question of the viability of the pervasive view of a specification as a fixed contract between a client and an implementer.' (p. 439)

15.1.3 Basili and Turner

Source: Victor R. Basili, University of Maryland, and Albert J. Turner, Clemson University South Carolina, 'Iterative Enhancement: A Practical Technique for Software Development', IEEE Trans. on Software Engineering, *December 1975, pp. 390–396. (©1975 IEEE)*

'Building a system using a well-modularized top-down approach requires that the problem and its solution be well understood. Even if the implementors have previously undertaken a similar project, it is still difficult to achieve a good design for a new system on the first try. Furthermore, the design flaws do not show up until the implementation is well under way so that correcting problems can require major effort.

One practical approach to this problem is to start with a simple initial implementation of a subset of the problem and iteratively enhance existing versions until the full system is implemented. At each step of the process, not only extensions but also design modifications can be made. In fact, each step can make use of stepwise refinement in a more effective way as the system becomes better understood through the iterative process. This paper discusses the heuristic iterative enhancement algorithm.' (p. 390)

They recognize that evolutionary progress is made by a combination of function ('extensions') and solution ('design modification') enhancement.

'A "project control list" is created that contains all the tasks that need to be performed in order to achieve the desired final documentation. At any given point in the process, the project control list acts as a measure of the "distance" between the current and final implementations.' (p. 390)

'The project control list is constantly being revised as a result of this analysis. This is how redesign and recoding work their way into the control list. Specific topics for analysis include such items as the structure, modularity, modifiability, usability, reliability and efficiency of the current implementation as well as an assessment of the goals of the project.' (p. 391)

From this it is clear there is a dynamic revision of the design based on a multi-dimensional quality goal analysis. This is therefore quite close to the method described in this book. It is worth noting that Basili cites Harlan Mills and Parnas, both at one time colleagues of his.

'A skeletal subset is one that contains a good sampling of the key aspects of the problem, that is simple enough to understand and implement easily, and whose implementation would make a usable and useful product available to the user.' (p. 391)

This last sentence is explicit recognition of the value-to-cost step selection heuristic we recommend.

'The implementation itself should be simple and straightforward in overall design and straightforward and modular at lower levels of design and coding so that it can be modified easily in the iterations leading to the final implementation.' (p. 391).

This sentence is recognition of the factor that we have called 'open-ended design'.

'It is important that each task be conceptually simple enough to minimize the chance of error in the design and implementation phases of the process.' (p. 391) 'The existing implementation should be analyzed frequently to determine how well it measures up to project goals.' (p. 391)

It is clear that Basili and Turner are of the 'small is beautiful' school.

'User reaction should always be solicited and analyzed for indications of deficiencies in the existing implementation.' (p. 391)

Thus user experience played a major role not only in the implementation of the software project (i.e. the compiler) but also in the specification of the project (i.e. the language design). No doubt that the process is designed to make use of real user feedback. The authors go into some detail about a case study and even present a full table of preliminary numbers regarding the effectiveness of the technique!

'The development of a final product which is easily modified is a by-product of the iterative way in which the product is developed.' (p. 395)

This is explicit recognition of the observation that the mere use of an evolutionary development process promotes frequent designer awareness of the practical need for open-ended and otherwise easily modifiable design.

'Thus, to some extent the efficient use of the iterative enhancement technique must be tailored to the implementation environment.' (p. 391)

15.1.4 Boehm: the spiral

Source: Barry W. Boehm (TRW Defense Systems Group), 'A Spiral Model of Development and Enhancement', ACM SIGSOFT Software Eng. Notes, Vol. 11, No. 4, August 1986, pp. 14–24 (Proceedings of International Workshop on the Software Process and Software Environments, Trabuco Canyon CA 27–29 March 1985, ACM Order 592861)

Barry Boehm has a simple 'incremental step' evolutionary delivery model included in his *Software Engineering Economics* book. In 1985 he presented his spiral model to give more detail to this idea. The spiral model is not, however, in any sense identical to the evolutionary delivery model explored in this book. It is, it seems, a framework for including just about any development model which seems appropriate to the risk levels in the project at hand, or in particular components at particular points in the development process. The spiral model could be viewed as a framework for choosing evolutionary delivery as a strategy, or deciding not to choose it and to choose a traditional waterfall model, or other alternative instead. The spiral model, as befits the author's industrial background in military and space contracting in the US, shows due consideration to current political considerations and traditions or standards to which a large contractor might be subjected. The spiral model might also offer a politically viable way to convert from a waterfall model dominated environment into a more evolutionary environment, without having to make a major formal shift of direction. Here are Dr Boehm's own words on the subject:

'The spiral model['s] . . . major distinguishing feature . . . is that it creates a risk-driven approach for guiding the software process, rather than a strictly specification-driven or prototype-driven process.' (p. 14)

'One of the earliest software process models is the stagewise model (H. D. Benington, 'Production of Large Computer Programs,' *Proc. ONR Symposium on Adv. Prog. Meth. for Dig. Comp.*, June 1956, pp. 15–27, also available in *Annals of the History of Computing*, October 1983, pp. 350–361). This model recommends that software be developed in successive stages (operational plan, operational specifications, coding specifications, coding, parameter testing, assembly testing, shakedown, system evaluation).' (p. 14)

'The original treatment of the waterfall model given in Royce (W.W. Royce, 'Managing the Development of Large Software Systems: Concepts and Techniques', *Proc. WESCON*, August 1970. Reprinted in *Proc. 9th International Software Engineering Conf.*, 1987, Monterey, Calif., IEEE) provided two primary enhancements to the stagewise model:

- Recognition of the feedback loops between stages, and a guideline to confine the feedback loops to successive stages, in order to minimize the expensive rework involved in feedback across many stages.
- An initial incorporation of prototyping in the software life cycle, via a 'build it twice' step running in parallel with requirements analysis and design.'

The waterfall approach was largely consistent with the top-down structured programming model introduced by Mills (H.D. Mills, 'Top-Down Programming in Large Systems', in *Debugging Techniques in Large Systems*, R. Ruskin (ed.), Prentice-Hall, 1971, pp. 128–137). However some attempts to apply these versions of the waterfall model ran into the following kinds of difficulties: the 'build it twice' step was unnecessary in some situations . . . ; The pure top-down approach needed to be tempered with a 'look ahead' step to cover such issues as high-risk, low-level elements and reusable or common software modules.

These considerations resulted in the risk-management variant of the waterfall model discussed in B.W. Boehm, 'Software Design and Structuring', (1975) in *Practical Strategies for Developing Large Software Systems*, E. Horowitz (ed.), Addison-Wesley, pp. 103–128 and elaborated in B.W. Boehm, 'Software Engineering', *IEEE Trans. Computers*, December 1976, pp. 1226–1241. In this variant each step was expanded to include a validation and verification activity to cover high-risk elements, reuse considerations, and prototyping. Further elaborations of the waterfall model covered such practices as incremental development in J.R. Distaso, 'Software Management: a Survey of the Practice in 1980', *IEEE Proc.* September 1980, pp. 1103–1119.

Boehm continues to note further alternatives to the waterfall model developed to cope with its weaknesses, but he finds weaknesses with each of these approaches, which he tries to resolve using the spiral model.

How does the spiral model relate to this book?

Note that Boehm is suggesting doing the kinds of activities which in this book we would call impact estimation and impact analysis, high-level inspection of design, as well as what we would also try to discover by means of actually delivering small evolutionary steps, to see how things worked in practice, and to identify possible risk elements. Boehm suggests that any appropriate techniques can be used for this risk analysis phase. His model is open to all useful tools. His basic advice is to choose the appropriate next step based on 'the relative magnitude of the program risks, and the relative effectiveness of the various techniques in resolving the risks.'

I would argue that the evolutionary delivery process together with the set of software development and software project management tools and principles in this book is a complete set of tools for making the decisions about risk which the spiral model attempts to tackle. I cannot see that the spiral model adds anything necessary to the development process. This is not to say it is not useful, especially in the environmental context which Boehm is in where a large bureaucracy is emerging from the waterfall model situation. Boehm seems to be trying to 'patch' the existing culture and to be diplomatic with our professional peers. There is necessary virtue in this, of course, but it is a subject with which only some of our readers must contend.

What does the spiral model not specifically incorporate?

Of course the spiral model, in admitting the use of any ideas, past, present, or future, doesn't need to specifically incorporate anything, yet can claim that anything necessary is acceptable. However I find that the following elements of evolutionary delivery, as preached in this book are missing from the spiral model:

- The concept of producing the high-value-to-low-cost increments first. Cumulation of user value. (The spiral model is so dominated by risk consideration that value concepts are not directly mentioned, except in the form of objectives and constraints, yet risk is risk of not getting value for money.)

- The concept of actually handling over to users usable increments, at 1% to 5% of project total budget.
- The concept of intentionally limiting step size to some maximum
  cycle of a week, month or quarter of a year.
- The concept of constantly being prepared to learn from any and
  all of the frequent step deliveries, and in so doing, being
  prepared to change any requirement or any technical design
  solution necessary in order to satisfy the users' current real
  needs.
- The concept that productivity is measured by incremental
  progress towards and planned increment of either function,
  quality or resource reduction.
- The concept of open-ended architecture as a desirable base for
  evolution.

15.1.5 Brooks

Source: F.P. Brooks, The Mythical Man-Month, *Addison-Wesley, 1975*

'Fred Brooks presented some thoughts on the traditional life cycle,
arguing for "growing," rather than building software: making a
skeleton run (attributed to Harlan Mills), and the progressive
refinement of design (Wirth). He suggested that software projects
must be nursed and nurtured, and that you should plan to throw
one version away, even if you do so part by part. The traditional
life cycle was useful primarily for building batch applications.
Today most systems are interactive and they require changes in the
life cycle. The life cycle should be divided into three segments,
with iterations occurring within each of the segments. The first
segment is a requirements segment, design specification, and user
manual. The next segment is the design, coding of a "minimal
driver," and debugging of this initial skeleton of the application.
In the next segment, functional sub-routines are coded, debugged,
and integrated with the main system.

Benefits of this approach: it supports a progressive refinement
of specifications which is better suited to interactive systems. It
facilitates the concept of rapid prototyping and much greater
interaction with users. It is better suited to the idea of "throw-
away" code since you can deal in smaller functional elements and
can redo them more easily if some problem becomes apparent.
This approach improves the morale of the developers since they
can see results more quickly and more directly related to their
efforts.' (from *Data Processing Digest*, 8/84 p. 11 and *System
Development*, **4**, May 84)

15.1.6 Currit, Dyer and Mills IBM FSD

Source: P. Allen Currit, Michael Dyer and Harlan D. Mills, 'Certifying the Reliability of Software', IEEE Trans. on Software Engineering, Vol. SE–12, No. 1, January 1986, pp. 3–11. (©1986 IEEE).

This work needs to be looked at in light of the work of Mills, Dyer, and other IBM Federal Systems Division authors in *IBM Systems Journal*, (4) 1980, reported earlier in this book, on evolutionary delivery. Their work here shows the slow but predictable exploitation of the evolutionary delivery method (they prefer the term 'incremental development' as they are not releasing software to their real users at each increment) to control other aspects (in this case reliability) than the time and cost factors which dominated their earlier work.

'This paper describes a procedure for certifying the reliability of software before its release to users. The ingredients of this procedure are a life cycle of executable product increments, representative statistical testing, and a standard estimate of the MTTF (mean time to failure) of the product at the time of its release.

The traditional life cycle of software development uses several defect removal stages of requirements, design, implementation, and testing but is inconclusive in establishing product reliability. No matter how many errors are removed during this process, no one knows how many remain. In fact, the number of remaining errors tends to be academic to product users who are more interested in knowing how reliable the software will be in operation, in particular how long it runs before it fails, and what are the operational impacts (e.g. downtime) when it fails.

On the other hand, the times between successive failures of the software as measured with user representative testing are numbers of direct management significance. The higher these inter-fail times are, the more user satisfaction can be expected. In fact, increasing inter-fail times represents progress towards a reliable product, whereas increasing defect discovery may be a symptom of an unreliable product.

To remove the gamble from software product release, a different life cycle for software development is suggested in which the formal certification of the software's reliability is a critical objective. Rather than considering product design, implementation, and testing as sequential elements in the life cycle, product development is considered as a sequence of executable product increments. . . . A life cycle organized about the incremental development of the product is proposed as follows: . . . increments (and product releases) accumulate over the life cycle into the final product.'

They suggest the use of an 'independent test group' who will be 'responsible for certifying the reliability of the increments . . .' This independent test group has the character of a user group, and indeed could be a real user of some friendly nature. They then go on to point out that they recommend testing from the standpoint of user frequency of operations.

They are aware of the narrow scope of their activity: 'There will be other properties – such as modularity or portability – that are not considered.' By modularity they probably intend to refer to modifiability and with typical current confusion of ends and means, mention one solution to it, modularity.

The article deserves to be read in its entirety by any serious manager of software engineering. My main point in quoting it here is to point out how the evolutionary delivery cycle can be combined with reliability management.

It seems obvious that any attribute of the system can be similarly controlled. It also is clear that the reader may choose to deliver increments directly to some real users at each increment, rather than to an independent in-house certification test team.

15.1.7 Dahle and Magnusson

Source: Swedish language article in Nordisk Datanytt 17/86 pp. 40–43, 'Programmeringsomgivninger' (Software Environments), by Hans Petter Dahle (Inst. for Informatikk, University of Oslo), and Boris Magnusson (Lund's Engineering University)

Resources: an English report Mjølner – 'A Highly Efficient Programming Environment for Industrial Use,' edited by H.P. Dahle et al., Mjølner Report No. 1, available from Norsk Regnesentral, Forskningsveien 1b, Blindern, Oslo 3, Norway

Here is my translation of their remarks concerning evolutionary delivery:

'In traditional development environments we have created methods based on a "batch" mentality. These use names like "life cycle model" and "the waterfall model".

In each step one or more documents are produced which are then

REQUIREMENTS ANALYSIS
  REQUIREMENTS SPECIFICATION
    SYSTEM DESIGN
      IMPLEMENTATION
        TESTING
          MAINTENANCE
            TERMINATION
The traditional software development model

used as the input to the next step. This model is coupled at times with more or less formal methods being used at each individual step. The model has been shown to bear fruit for problems which admit formalization, which can be specified in a formal language, which – in other words – can be fully understood in all its components.

The method is less useful for situations where the requirements are less clearly specified, for example by an inexperienced customer, or by vague specifications such as "the response time shall be satisfactory." The non-formalized requirements get discovered late in the development process. A completely different problem is that a change involves updating of a number of documents – which is often a time-waster and an unpleasant job which doesn't always get done.

The first integrated software development environments were developed at research centers. The environments usually supported a particular programming language. Smalltalk and Interlisp were among the first complete program development environments, both developed at Xerox Palo Alto Research Center.

These and similar systems are coupled to a software development model which aims to get an early "prototype" of the object system operational with limited function. On the basis of experience from using the prototype, one can incrementally improve and finally deliver a product which satisfies the (ultimately) clarified requirements. This method is occasionally called "explorative programming."

The fact that the software can have bugs is considered of less importance than the ability to try out changes.

This working environment is very fruitful when solving problems which are not perfectly defined, and where all requirements can not be formally specified.

Of course the methods can be combined. A prototype can be made initially to map the requirements, and the traditional development model can be used to produce a final version.'

This quotation is from a fairly narrow context of advanced programming environments. It is included because it recognizes explicitly the need for an evolutionary delivery model of some kind.

15.1.8 Dyer

Source: Michael Dyer, IBM Federal Systems Division, 'Software Development Processes', IBM Systems Journal, *Vol. 19, No. 4, 1980, pp. 451–465*

Michael Dyer is one of the core team led by Harlan Mills which implemented evolutionary delivery, and reported it in public literature, on a larger industrial scale than any other group. Here are some quotations from his article which shed additional light on the exact process used.

'Each increment is a subset of the planned product.' (p. 458)

'The software for each increment is instrumented for measurement of such system resources as primary and secondary storage utilization.' (p. 459)

'As these actual performance measurements become available, software simulations that may have been initialized with estimates should be continually calibrated to enhance their fidelity.' (p. 459)

This recommendation is a direct reference to the ability of evolutionary delivery to improve our estimating and prediction capability. It was also used in reliability estimation in later years (see Currit, in this chapter).

'Software integration plans are recorded in controlled documents containing the following minimum information:

- scheduled phasing of the integration increments;
- system functions included in each increment;
- test plans to be executed for each increment . . . ;
- support requirements for each increment in terms of system hardware simulation, tools and project resources;
- criteria for demonstrating that the increment is ready for integration . . . the exit condition from the unit test;
- quality assurance plans for the tracking and follow-up of errors discovered during the integration process.' (p. 462)

'A group separate from the software developers should have responsibility for planning the software integration process, for developing the integration procedures, and for integrating the software according to these procedures.' (p. 463)

'Control is achieved by careful system partitioning, incremental product construction, and constant product evaluation.' (p. 465)

15.1.9 Eason

Source: Ken Eason, HUSAT, Loughborough, UK, 'Methodological Issues in the Study of Human Factors in Teleinformatic Systems', Behaviour and Information Technology, *Taylor & Francis, UK, 1983, Vol. 2, No. 1, pp. 357–364*

'One of the best ways of achieving action research and active collaboration between technical and social scientists is to follow an evolutionary process of design . . . In this process early versions of the system are implemented, user responses assessed, the system revised, enhanced, etc. the new version implemented. . . . If this iterative process is not present in design the result will probably be that technical staff dominate design and, subsequently, evaluations are conducted by human and social scientists. The latter will consequently have no impact on the former.' (p. 363)

15.1.10 Gilb

Source: T. Gilb, Software Metrics, *October 1976, (Winthrop).*

'Evolution is a designed characteristic of a system development which involves gradual stepwise change.' (p. 214)

On step results measurement and retreat possibility

'A complex system will be most successful if it is implemented in small steps and if each step has a clear measure of successful achievement as well as a "retreat" possibility to a previous successful step upon failure.' (p. 214)

On minimizing failure risk, using feedback, correcting design errors

'The advantage is that you cannot have large failures. You have the opportunity of receiving some feedback from the real world before throwing in all resources intended for a system, and you can correct possible design errors before they become costly live systems.' (p. 214)

On total project time

'The disadvantage is that you may sometimes have to wait longer
before the whole system is functioning. This is offset by the fact
that some results are produced much earlier than they would be if
you had to wait for total system completion. It is also important to
distinguish between a date for total system operation and a date
for total "successful" system operation.' (p. 215)

On the general applicability

'Many people claim that their system cannot be put into operation
gradually. It is all or nothing. This may conceivably be true in a
few cases . . . I think we shall find that virtually all systems can be
fruitfully put-in in more than one step, even though some must
inevitably take larger steps than others.' (p. 215)

A measure of degree of evolution

'A metric for evolution is degree of change to system "s" during
any time interval "t".' (p. 214)

On risk and predicting requirements

'Risk estimates plus/minus worst case are key to selection of step
size', and 'Saving of analysis of future real world'. (p. 217)

The first remark is recognition that step sizing is determined by the
need to control risk of failure. It is not small steps in themselves which
are important. A large step may be taken if the risk is under control; for
example by using contract guarantees or known technology. The
second remark is recognition that the evolutionary method avoids the
need to predict requirements and environments in the future; it allows
us to wait until the future has arrived, to see the current requirements
and the current environment.

On the scientific experiment analogy

'The concept of stability (where evolution is a technique for
achieving stability) at individual levels of a system has the same
usefulness as the concept of keeping all-factors-except-one constant
in a scientific experiment. It allows systematic and orderly change
of systems where the cause and effect may be more accurately
measured without interfering factors, which may cause doubt as to
the reason for good or bad results.' (p. 217)

'Systems may be specifically designed to go through a revolution in several phases, where only one level of the system is changed significantly at a time.' (pp. 217–8)

Evolutionary modularity design: conflict and priority

On p. 187 I raised the issue of 'Modularity division criteria', and gave six examples of rules for dividing software modules. Rule six was 'By calendar schedule of need of module' and the explanation for this rule was: 'Early implementation; evolutionary project develop.'

'Each rule can conflict with other modularization rules and with other design criteria. Resolution of the conflict can be achieved by a clearly stated set of priorities'.

This is a forerunner to the present perception of step design and selection being based on those elements of the total system which will contribute the greatest value towards stated objectives at the least development resource cost.

Later writings on the subject

The evolutionary idea was developed by articles in the trade press: 'Evolutionary Planning and Delivery: an Alternative', *Computer Weekly*, 2 August 1979; 'Evolutionary Planning can prevent Failures', *Computer Data*, Canada, April 1979, p. 13; 'Realistic Time/Cost Data', *Computer Weekly*, 16 August 1979; 'Eleven Guidelines for Evolutionary Design and Implementation', *Computer Weekly*, 12 March 1981; and 'The Seventh Principle of Technology Projects: Small Steps will Result in Earlier Success', *Computer Weekly*, 30 July 1981. In all there were about 122 Gilb's Mythodology Columns in *Computer Weekly*, which developed many of the ideas in this book.

15.1.11 Glass

Source: Robert L. Glass, 'An Elementary Discussion of Compiler/Interpreter Writing', ACM Computing Surveys, Vol. 1, No. 1, March 1969, pp. 55–77

'Chronological Development
In the case of the SPLINTER interpreter, two facts dominated the chronology:

1. The processor was to be developed incrementally.

2. Some of the building blocks were available from other, previously developed processors.

The first fact meant that the initial development goal was to reach a minimally usable level of implementation in a minimal amount of time. The assumption was that with a well-modularized system design, the clutter which often comes with systems development conducted in this add-on fashion could be avoided.' (p. 65)

'It is the opinion of this author that incremental development is worthwhile. Reaching system usability early in development leads to a more thorough shakedown, avoids implementer and management discouragement and/or disinterest, and allows the user to get "on the air" in minimum time. . . . However, incremental development demands careful planning of the basics, especially table and list formats and modular construction, if it is to avoid resembling a house made of a packing case with rooms tacked on helter-skelter as they become needed.' (p. 68)

Open-endedness and the original 'stub'

'The SPLINTER processor has been built incrementally via an open-ended design process. Because of this there are always loose ends in the system that have not been implemented. IMPDEL, a general purpose subroutine, magically handles all these problems. (IMPDEL merely prints IMPLEMENTATION DELAYED as a diagnostic and returns control to the normal logic stream).' (p. 73)

This paper is particularly interesting because of its early date, beating even Basili and Turner by six years. It must be one of the earliest clear published recognitions of evolutionary delivery methods in the computer business.

15.1.12 Jackson and McCracken

Source: Michael A. Jackson and Daniel D. McCracken, 'Life Cycle Concept Considered Harmful', ACM Software Eng. Notes, Vol. 7, No. 2, April 1982, pp. 29–32

At a conference in September 1980 (at Georgia State University), these two well-known authors developed a 'minority dissenting position,' which eventually became this paper.

'To contend that any life cycle scheme, even with variations, can be applied to all system development is either to fly in the face of reality or to assume a life cycle so rudimentary as to be vacuous.' (p. 30)

'The life cycle concept perpetuates our failure so far, as an industry, to build an effective bridge across the communications gap between end-user and systems analyst. In many ways it constrains future thinking to fit the mold created in response to failures of the past.' (p. 30)

'It ignores . . . an increasing awareness that systems requirements cannot ever be stated fully in advance, not even in principle, because the user doesn't even know them in advance – not even in principle.' (p. 31)

'We suggest an analogy with the Heisenberg Uncertainty Principle: any system development activity inevitably changes the environment out of which the need for the system arose.' (p. 31)

The authors eloquently point out that the life cycle is obsolete. They do so at a time when most others are starting to adopt the idea. They do not suggest a particular remedy.

15.1.13 Jahnichen and Goos

Source: Stefan Jahnichen and G. Goos. GMD Research Center. Karlsruhe, 'Towards an Alternative Model for Software Developments', ACM Software Eng. Notes, August 1986, pp. 36–38

This paper proposes a novel idea.

'We therefore propose to view the process of software construction as a network in which each node represents the product in a certain state and each edge is an action (transition) to transform one state into another. Alternative actions are modelled by multiple edges originating from the same node. Whenever a state is inconsistent [with objectives] a backtracking takes place which leads to the previous state where alternative paths are possible, which have not been tried. As the information on alternatives is part of a node's properties, the node cannot be disconnected from any previous node and the full development history remains stable and consistent.' (p. 37)

15.1.14 Krzanik

Source: Lech Krzanik, 'Dynamic Optimization of Delivery Step Structure in Evolutionary Project Delivery Planning', Proc. Cybernetics in

Organization and Management, *7th European Meeting, Vienna 24–27 April 1984, R. Trappl (ed.), North-Holland, 1984*

Dr Krzanik has since 1980 worked on the automation of our Design by Objectives methods on personal computers. The objective of that research effort is to see how far the software engineering design process can be automated. The current implementation of the tool, the 'Aspect Engine,' operates in Pascal on the Macintosh and is shared with suitable research colleagues. Krzanik, in writing this paper, is in fact preparing for his own implementation of fully automated evolutionary step size selection. The author's conclusion includes:

> 'An approach to delivery step structure optimization in evolutionary project delivery has been presented. A model and two simple and easy-to-use optimal algorithms MI and VMI for controlling the contents of the project transient set have been given. Elsewhere ('On-line tuning of the smallest useful deliverable policy in evolutionary delivery planning,' 1983) we have given alternative methods for simultaneous optimization of delivery schedule, step range and structure.'

For the management reader, this means that one day you may be offered personal computer tools for dealing with evolutionary planning. For the academic reader, it implies that there is a fairly unexplored mathematical area out there and that evolutionary delivery is capable of formal treatment.

15.1.15 Lehman and Belady

Source: M.M. Lehman and L.A. Belady, Program Evolution: Processes of Software Change, *Academic Press, 1985; originally published in* Journal of Systems and Software, *Vol. 1, No. 3, 1980 (© 1980 Elsevier Science Publishing Co, Inc.)*

This text and the research of the authors cannot be ignored in any overview of software engineering evolution. In one sense it is outside of the scope of our text because it takes an anthropological study view of program evolution, while this book's main subject matter is in management of the development process. The exploitation of specific evolutionary delivery mechanisms in order to achieve specific management targets is our subject. However, the reader is bound to find much of the material rich in ideas and insights. The authors primarily depart from their own well-known studies of the evolution of the IBM 360 Operating System (1969, IBM Research Report RC 2722, *The Programming Process*, M.M. Lehman).

Since this book is fond of trying to state principles, it is fitting that we introduce this work to the reader by citing some they have derived from their studies. These were apparently first formulated in 1974.

Continuing change

'A program that is used and that, as an implementation of its specification, reflects some other reality, undergoes continuing change or becomes progressively less useful. The change or decay process continues until it is judged more cost effective to replace the program with a recreated version.' (p. 381)

This can be compared with Gilb's Fourth 'Law':

'A system tends to grow in steps of complexity rather than of simplification; this continues until the resulting unreliability becomes intolerable.'

This Law was first published in Gilb, *Reliable Data Systems*, 1971, Universitetsforlaget, Oslo, and in *Datamation*, March 1975, and in Gilb, *Reliable EDP Application Design*, 1973, Petrocelli. It was later used in Gilb and Weinberg, *Humanized Input*, 1984, QED Inc., Waltham, Mass.

Increasing complexity

'As an evolving program is continuously changed, its complexity, reflecting deteriorating structure, increases unless work is done to maintain it or reduce it.' (p. 381)

The fundamental law (of program evolution)

'Program evolution is subject to a dynamics which makes the programming process, and hence measures of global project and system attributes, self-regulating with statistically determinable trends and invariances.' (p. 381)

Conservation of organization stability (invariant work rated)

'The global activity rate in a project supporting an evolving program is statistically invariant.' (p. 381)

Conservation of familiarity (perceived complexity)

'The release content (changes, additions, deletions) of successive releases of an evolving program is statistically invariant.' (p. 381)

The authors provide comment and data to support their Laws.

A current source of Lehman's work more in line with our interest in the development process itself will be found in *ACM Software Engineering Notes*, Aug. 1986, 'Approach to a Disciplined Development Process – the ISTAR Integrated Project Support Environment,' pp. 28–33. A co-operative project with British Telecom, it stresses a 'contractural model of system development.'

15.1.16 Melichar

Source: Paul R. Melichar, IBM Information Systems Management Institute, Chicago, 'Management Strategies for High-risk Projects', Class Handout, approx. 1983

Melichar identifies three project strategies, monolithic, incremental, and evolutionary, which are 'different in their ability to cope with risks that undermine manageability, because they reflect different attitudes towards: productivity . . . responsiveness . . . adaptability and . . . control.'

'Projects get into trouble precisely because managers treat them as if they were all alike, disregarding three vital factors that impact manageability: duration . . . expectations and . . . volatility.'

Using an IBM study his organization carried out, Melichar goes into depth on optimum project length before delivering meaningful results to the user.

'This testimony strongly suggests that there is a narrow six to twelve month "time window" for optimum manageability. A good rule of the thumb is nine months.'

His distinction between monolithic, incremental and evolutionary system development strategies is argued with case studies and comparative tables, in favor of the latter two options. His incremental strategy is what we have defined as an evolutionary delivery strategy. What he calls evolutionary is what most people would call 'usable prototypes, made by the users themselves', as opposed to professional developers. I would personally not make the distinction, since both options are valid strategies under the evolutionary umbrella. Indeed there is nothing to inhibit us from mixing such strategies within a project. Terminology, is a minor issue. He is bringing the non-monolithic development options to the attention of his students in a lively and deeply analytical manner.

15.1.17 Parnas

Source: David L. Parnas, 'Designing Software for Ease of Extension and Contraction', IEEE Trans. on Software Engineering, Vol. SE–5, No. 2, March 1979. (© 1979 IEEE)

'Software engineers have not been trained to design for change.' (p. 129)

'In my experience identification of the potentially desirable subsets is a demanding intellectual exercise in which one first searches for the minimal subset that might conceivably perform a useful service and then searches for a set of minimal increments to the system. Each increment is small – sometimes so small that it seems trivial. The emphasis on minimality stems from our desire to avoid components that perform more than one function. Identifying the minimal subset is difficult because the minimal system is not usually one that anyone would ask for. If we are going to build the software family, the minimal subset is useful; it is not usually worth building by itself. Similarly the maximum flexibility ("easily changed") is obtained by looking for the smallest possible increments in capability . . .' (p. 130)

'There is no reason to accomplish the transformation . . . (to) all of the desired features in a single leap. Instead we will use the machine at hand to implement a few new instructions. At each step we take advantage of the newly introduced features. Such a step-by-step approach turns a large problem into a set of small ones and . . . eases the problem of finding the appropriate subsets. Each element in this series . . . is a useful subset of the system.' (p. 131)

'Subsetability is needed, not just to meet a variety of customers' needs, but to provide a fail-safe way of handling schedule slippage.' (p. 136)

Parnas has also said in a private communication:

'There are lots of people preaching evolutionary delivery. For a few of those whose content is more than mere exhortation, see Habermann (*Modularization and Hierarchy*, CACM, Vol. 5, 1976), Liskov (*The Design of the Venus Operating System*, CACM, July 1975), Dijkstra (*The Structure of T.H.E. -multiprogramming system*, CACM, May 1968, and CACM, August 1975), Per Brinch-Hansen (*The Nucleus of a Multiprogramming System*, CACM, April 1970), P.A. Janson (*Using Type Extension to Organize Virtual Memory*, MIT-LTS-TR167, September 1976).'

15.1.18 Quinnan

Source: Robert E. Quinnan, 'Software Engineering Management Practices',
IBM Systems Journal, *Vol. 19, No. 4, 1980, pp. 466–477*

Quinnan describes the process control loop used by IBM FSD to ensure
that cost targets are met.

> 'Cost management . . . yields valid cost plans linked to technical
> performance. Our practice carries cost management farther by
> introducing design-to-cost guidance. Design, development, and
> managerial practices are applied in an integrated way to ensure
> that software technical management is consistent with cost
> management. The method [illustrated in this book by Figure 7.10]
> consists of developing a design, estimating its cost, and ensuring
> that the design is cost-effective.' (p. 473)

He goes on to describe a design iteration process trying to meet
cost targets by either redesign or by sacrificing 'planned capability.'
When a satisfactory design at cost target is achieved for a single
increment, the 'development of each increment can proceed con-
currently with the program design of the others.'

> 'Design is an iterative process in which each design level is a
> refinement of the previous level.' (p. 474)

It is clear from this that they avoid the big bang cost estimation
approach. Not only do they iterate in seeking the appropriate balance
between cost and design for a single increment, but they iterate
through a series of increments, thus reducing the complexity of the
task, and increasing the probability of learning from experience, won
as each increment develops, and as the true cost of the increment
becomes a fact.

> 'When the development and test of an increment are complete, an
> estimate to complete the remaining increments is computed.'
> (p. 474)

This article is far richer than our few selected quotations can tell in
concepts of cost estimation and control.

15.1.19 Radice

Source: Ron A. Radice et al., A Programming Process Architecture, IBM
Systems Journal, *Vol. 24, No. 2, 1985, pp. 79–90*

Radice and his team have developed a model of software engineering management which has been voluntarily adopted as a basis by many IBM development laboratories. It is partly based on the best practices of several laboratories in the past. The central idea of the method is that IBM should not establish the particular programming languages and software tools to be used corporate-wide at all. They should rather give the laboratories a framework for making their own decisions on the particular tools to be applied to particular product developments at particular times.

The idea is that software engineering should be based on a 'process control idea.' Subsidiary support ideas are that Fagan's inspection method should be used to collect basic data about the development process. In addition, the driving force should be measurable multi-dimensional objectives (using Gilb's method).

> 'An underlying theme of the architecture process is a focus on process control through process management activities. Each stage of the process includes explicit process management activities that emphasize product and process data capture, analysis and feedback.' (p. 83)
>
> 'Indeed, to achieve consistently improving quality, the management practices of goal setting, measurement, evaluation, and feedback are an absolutely essential part of the process.' (p. 82)

The actual selection of particular software development languages and tools is thus evolutionary. IBM is using a very conscious application of evolutionary delivery to deliver improvement to their individual laboratories' development process.

Some further quotations from that article follow:

> 'Just as timely data are needed to manage the quality of the developing product, historical data are required to evaluate and correct weaknesses in the process over a succession of projects.' (p. 88)
>
> 'The (IBM) Process Architecture emphasizes quality over productivity, with the understanding that as quality improves, productivity will follow.' (p. 88)
>
> 'Early quality goal setting and evaluations can lead to an earlier focus on areas of initial high difficulty. As a result, better initial allocation of key personnel and other resources can follow.' (p. 88)

It is my personal opinion that the work of the IBM team is a very important set of ideas for other people trying to organize their software engineering process for the long term. Earlier efforts in our field concentrated on the product development itself, or upon the tools for making that product. Radice and his team have given us a framework for *making* those more short term decisions, based on a rich process control architecture for the entire development process. The paper is so rich in ideas that the serious reader should read the complete paper.

15.1.20 Robertson and Secor

Source: Leonard B. Robertson and Glenn A. Secor, AT&T, 'Effective Management of Software Development', AT&T Technical Journal, March/ April 1986, Vol. 65, Issue 2, pp. 94–101. (©1986 AT&T)

'Large projects usually have more success by spreading releases over time. Development strategy addresses the same issue internally: one delivery to the test organization or several incremental deliveries. Projects in which the interval from design through unit test is longer than four to six weeks should use incremental development.' (p. 96)

'In addition, quality goals and quality improvement goals should be stated.' (p. 96)

'Testing should start during the requirements phase and should use an independent system test group, test inspections, and frequent demonstrations.' (p. 97)

'To provide for the unexpected, the development plan should include a contingency plan, which may involve having increments only partially full, or an extra increment following a risky increment.' (p. 96)

'At the end of each project review meeting, supervision should see a demonstration of completed increments. Demonstrations, more than any other approach, make mileposts visible.' (p. 100)

15.1.21 Rzevski

Source: Leonard B. Robertson and Glenn A. Secor, AT&T, 'Effective Management of Software Development', AT&T Technical Journal, March/April 1986, Vol. 65, Issue 2, pp. 94–101. (©1986 AT&T)

The evolutionary design methodology

'The evolutionary design methodology (EDM) is a body of knowledge aimed to help designers to:

1. identify and formulate design problems,
2. establish design goals,

3. understand the design process,
4. select and apply methods for design and management.

The word "evolutionary" in the title indicates that EDM gives prominence to design methods that allow systems to grow in an incremental fashion and thus enable both user and designers to learn as they take part in the design process. It also indicates that EDM evolves and changes with time.'

Rzevski's detailed picture of the EDM method, which he uses primarily as a teaching vehicle, not as a publicly marketed methodology, emerges as essentially similar in objectives and nature – though not exact detail – to the methods in this book (which I collectively call design by objectives [DBO]). He simply chooses to view the set of sub-methods he teaches from the evolutionary point of view, while I prefer to think of my methods primarily in terms of the design objectives to be attained, and evolutionary delivery is but one tool for reaching those objectives.

'There are two major objectives of EDM; firstly to increase productivity of the design process, and secondly to achieve the desired quality of the design product.'

In his detailed treatment of quality it is clear that Rzevski has a very broad multidimensional and quantitative view of quality – including for example 'social acceptability.'

'EDM can cope with a variety of types of design problems including those characterized by fuzziness and complexity.'

This specific willingness to deal with fuzziness is a clear sign that Rzevski is of the real word. Indeed he is also an active industrial consultant. He is closer in his thinking to my ideas than perhaps any other author cited here.

'Systems whose requirements are rather complex or fuzzy should not be designed and implemented in one step. It is wiser to allow them to evolve and thus enable both users and designers to learn as design progresses.'

This gives explicit recognition of the necessary learning process.

'It is advisable to produce solutions that are easy to modify or replace.'

I take this as recognition of the necessity for open-ended design solutions discussed earlier in this book.

Additional Source: G. Rzevski, 'Prototypes versus Pilot Systems: Strategies for Evolutionary Information System Development', in Approaches to Prototyping, *Budde et al. (eds.), Springer-Verlag, 1984*

Rzevski on Popper and evolutionary knowledge growth

'According to Popper (K.R. Popper, *Objective Knowledge, an Evolutionary Approach,* Oxford University Press, 1972) human knowledge grows by means of never-ending evolution. The vehicle for this growth is the process of problem solving: we create theories (i.e. knowledge) in order to solve problems; however, every solution to a problem creates new problems which arise from our own creative activity . . . they emerge autonomously from the field of new relationships which we cannot help bringing into existence with every action, however little we intend to do so.

The inevitable growth of knowledge which takes place during systems development should not be suppressed by imposing linear life-cycle discipline upon the development process. On the contrary, every effort should be made to take advantage of the human propensity to learn. . .'

Kuhn's paradigm theory

T.S. Kuhn (*The Structure of Scientific Revolutions,* University of Chicago Press, 1970) has a theory of revolutionary growth of knowledge – which needs to be balanced against Popper's ideas. It can be summarized as follows:

'Knowledge grows through the work of scientists who organize themselves into different disciplines . . . solving problems within the framework of a dominant paradigm. . . . Over a period of time problems emerge which cannot be solved within the established paradigm . . . new paradigms are proposed . . . one . . . emerges as the main challenge to the established order . . . transfer to a new paradigm occurs . . . only after considerable resistance . . . from . . . established . . . members . . . who do not accept that there is a need for change. . . . Scientific argument and feuds are typical for those periods preceding the revolutionary change of the dominant scientific world view. . . . The evolutionary approach . . . offers . . . a new paradigm. . . .'

15.1.22 Sachs

Source: Susan Lammers, Programmers at Work, *Microsoft Press (USA and Canada), Penguin Books elsewhere, 1986 (© 1986 by Microsoft Press. All rights reserved)*

Jonathan Sachs wrote the best-selling Lotus 1-2-3 software. In his interview in *Programmers at Work*, he cites several evolutionary viewpoints:

> 'The spreadsheet was already done, and within a month I had converted it over to C. Then it started evolving from that point on, a little at a time. In fact, the original idea was very different from from what ended up as the final version of 1-2-3.' (p. 166)
>
> 'The methodology we used to develop 1-2-3 began with a working program, and it continued to be a working program throughout its development. I had an office in Hopkinton where I lived at the time, and I came to the office about once a week and brought in a new version. I fixed any bugs immediately in the next version. Also, people at Lotus were using the program continuously. This was the exact opposite of the standard method for developing a big program, where you spend a lot of time and work up a functional spec., do a modular decomposition, give each piece to a bunch of people, and integrate the pieces when they're all done. The problem with that method is that you don't get a working program until the very end. If you know exactly what you want to do, that method is fine. But when you're doing something new, all kinds of problems crop up that you just don't anticipate. In any case our method meant that once we had reached a certain point in development, we could ship if we wanted to. The program may not have had all the features, but we knew it would work.' (p. 167).

Sachs then goes on to remark that this method 'doesn't work very well' with more than one to three people! A conclusion that must be based on the wrong experiences or none at all, as the documented large-scale cases in this book evidence.

Sachs continues:

> 'Success comes from doing the same thing over and over again; each time you learn a little bit and you do it a little better the next time.' (p. 170)

Sachs even touches on open-endedness when asked to describe his basic approach to programming.

> 'First, I start out with a basic program framework, which I keep adding to. Also I try not to use many fancy features in a language or a program. . . . As a rule I like to keep programs simple.'

15.1.23 Shneiderman

Source: Ben Shneiderman, Designing the User Interface: Strategies for Effective Human-Computer Interaction, *Addison-Wesley, 1987*

'Designs must be validated through pilot and acceptance tests that can also provide a finer understanding of user skills and capabilities.' (p. 390)

Iterative design during development

Design is inherently creative and unpredictable. Interactive system designers must blend a thorough knowledge of technical feasibility with a mystical esthetic sense of what will be attractive to users. Carroll and Rosson ('Usability specifications as a tool in iterative develop-ment', in H. Rex (ed.), *Advances in Human-Computer Interaction* 1, Ablex Publishing, Norwood NJ, 1985) characterize design this way:

- 'Design is a process: it is not a state and cannot adequately be represented statically.
- The design process is non-hierarchical; it is neither strictly bottom-up nor strictly top-down.
- The process is radically transformational; it involves the development of partial and interim solutions that may ultimately play no role in the final design.
- Design intrinsically involves the discovery of new goals.

These characterizations of design convey the dynamic nature of the process.' (p. 391)

■ 15.2 Management sources

15.2.1 Garfield

Source: Charles Garfield, Peak Performers, *William Morrow & Co., Inc., NY, 1986*

'Many of the major changes in history have come about through successive small innovations, most of them anonymous. Our dramatic sense (or superficiality) leads us to seek out "the man who started it all" and to heap upon his shoulders the whole credit for a prolonged, diffuse and infinitely complex process. It is essential that we outgrow this immature conception. Some of our most difficult problems today . . . defy correction by any single

dramatic solution. They will yield, if at all, only to a whole series of innovations.'
(Quoting John Gardner, founder of 'Common Cause' p. 128

'Again and again, we see results emerging from the many jobs that take meaning from – and give form to – a few strategies. Lawrence Gilson, a former vice-president of Amtrak, is one of a group that worked to build a high-speed "bullet train" railroad in the United States. The odds, as it turned out, proved too great even for peak performers. But it was a near thing: the Japanese government cooperated; Wall Street gave it a serious look; builders invested $1 million of their own money. Investors were not putting their money into a fuzzy R&D project. Gilson knew that "you have to know what the three or four steps out in front of you are. You have to set milestones that are achievable. You can't expect someone to come in on the basis of being sold the big picture. You have to sell each incremental step. What you bring to them at each phase is not just conceptual, it is work completed."

Visionaries who were less than peak performers in handling incremental steps might have failed to get the project out of the dream stage, or might have deluded themselves that they could continue when the fact was they could not. Gilson and his partners raised $10 million toward the $3.1 billion project. They knew they would need another $50 million in risk capital to keep operating until the planned beginning of construction in 1985. They had done their detail work. When they saw that the $50 million was not going to come in by the time they had to have it, they knew it was time to quit, and sold their engineering plans to Amtrak. The peak performer's perspective not only lets you know when to continue. It also lets you know when to stop.' (p. 129)

'Through repeated educated risks, the peak performers learn as they go along, and over time their confidence in their own judgement gains strength. It is not fear of failure that drives them along, but a strong desire for achievement.

Remember Warren Bennis's finding that the ninety leaders he interviewed would use almost any word – "glitch", "false start", "bug" – rather than "failure". The reason goes beyond semantics. It has to do with learning. When high achievers get less than the results they plan for and work toward, they allow the normal human feelings of disappointment, or anger, or fatigue, to pass; then they start analyzing. They search for information in the situation: Where are we now? Where are we headed? How do we get there? They operate as both innovator and consolidator, and resume moving towards completion of their mission and goals.

Even when circumstances are totally beyond their control,

peak performers learn what they can from an experience so as not to knock their heads against the wall again. They keep their eyes open so that they do not, as mythologist Joseph Campell once put it, "get to the top of the ladder and find it's the wrong wall."'
(p. 138)

This activity is clearly identical to the evolutionary delivery pattern of working towards well defined objectives.

15.2.2 Grove

Source: Andrew S. Grove, Intel Chairman and Founder, High Output Management, *Souvenir Press (UK), Random House (USA), 1983*

'How far ahead should the planners look? At Intel, we put ourselves through an annual long-range planning effort in which we examine our future five years off. But what is really being influenced here? It is the next year – and only the next year. We will have another chance to replan the second of the five years in the next year's long-range planning meeting, when that year will become the first year of the five.

So, keep in mind that you implement only a portion of a plan that lies within the time window between now and the next time you go through the exercise. Everything else you can look at again.

We should also be careful not to plan too frequently, allowing ourselves time to judge the impact of the decisions we made and to determine whether our decisions were on the right track or not. In other words, we need the feedback that will be indispensible to our planning the next time around.'

This statement is similar to the evolutionary delivery philosophy of keeping the steps beyond the next one as fluid planning elements, to be finally decided on in the light of real experience.

15.2.3 Moss Kanter and Quinn

Source: Rosabeth Moss Kanter, The Changemasters, *copyright © 1983. Reprinted by permission of Simon & Schuster, Inc.*

'The most saleable projects are likely to be trial-able (can be demonstrated in a pilot basis); reversible (allowing the organization to go back to pre-project status if it doesn't work); divisible (can be done in steps or phases); consistent with sunk costs (builds on prior resource commitments); concrete (tangible, discrete); familiar (consistent with a successful past experience); congruent (fits the organization's direction); and with publicity value (visibility potential if it works).' (p. 221)

This is a fairly complete description of the main parameters of the evolutionary delivery process.

' "Too much talk, too little action" is a common complaint about participative vehicles that do not have concrete tasks to carry out. For this reason, a Hewlett-Packard facility uses its MBO (management by objectives) process to prioritize a team's activities; they are encouraged to work on a succession of easy problems before tackling tough ones.' (p. 254)

This philosophy is consistent with the evolutionary delivery rule of prioritizing the high value and low development cost steps first.

' "Breakthrough" changes that help a company attain a higher level of performance are likely to reflect the interplay of a number of smaller changes that together provide the building blocks for the new construction. Even when attributed to a single dramatic event or a single dramatic decision, major changes in large organizations are more likely to represent the accumulation of accomplishments and tendencies built up slowly over time and implemented cautiously. "Logical incrementalism," to use Quinn's term, may be a better term for describing the way major corporations change their strategy:

The most effective strategies of major enterprises tend to emerge step-by-step from an iterative process in which the organization probes the future, experiments, and learns from a series of partial (incremental) commitments rather than through global formulations of total strategies. Good managers are aware of this process, and they consciously intervene in it. They use it to improve the information available for decisions and to build the psychological identification essential to successful strategies. . . . Such logical incrementalism is not "muddling" as most people understand that word . . . . [It] honors and utilizes the global analyses inherent in formal strategy formulation models [and] embraces the central tenets of the political power-behavioural approaches to such decision-making.' (pp. 289–90 quoted from James Brian Quinn, *Strategies for Change: Logical Incrementalism*, Homewood, Illinois: Richard D. Irwin, 1980)

15.2.4 Peters and Austin

Source: Tom Peters and Nancy Austin, A Passion for Excellence, *Collins (UK), Random House (USA), 1985 (© 1985 Thomas J. Peters and Nancy K. Austin)*

'It is precisely when the buyer has become less dependent on the technical help or brand support of the originating buyer, that greater attention may be beneficially focussed on a systematic program of finding customer-benefiting and therefore customer-keeping augmentation.' (pp. 69–70)

This point simply reminds us of the evolutionary nature of all product development which needs to compete for customers.

'And yet we go wrong time and again because we do rely on numbers and transparencies alone, and lose our "feel". The only way to enhance feel is to be there.' (p. 94)

This point is central to evolutionary delivery which is among many things a way to regain realistic touch with a complex software development, and to avoid relying too much on paper specifications for understanding and control.

'The course of innovation – from the generation of the idea through prototype development and contact with the initial user to breakthrough and then to final market – is highly uncertain. Moreover it is always messy, unpredictable and very much affected by the determined ("irrational"?) champions, and that is the important point. It's important, because we must learn to design organizations – those that are public as well as private, banks as well as software developers – that take into account, explicity, the irreducible sloppiness of the process and take advantage of it, rather than systems and organizations that attempt to fight it. Unfortunately, most innovation management seems to be pre-dicated on the implicit assumption that we can beat the sloppiness out of the process if only we can make the plans tidier and the teams better organized. . . in that single phrase "Let's get organized for the next round" lie the seeds of subsequent disaster.' (pp. 115–6)

Evolutionary delivery is a specific example of a process for coping with the inherent messiness of user requirements and our poor understanding of new untried technology.

'*Myth:* Complete technical specs. and a thoroughly researched market plan are invariant first steps to success.
Counterpoint: You must move as rapidly as possible to real tests of real products (albeit incomplete) with real customers. That is, you must experiment and learn your way toward perfection/completion.

Myth: Time for reflection and thought built into the development process are essential to creative results.

Counterpoint: "Winners" – e.g. successful champions/skunks – are above all, pragmatic non-blue sky dreamers who live by one dictum: "Try it, now!"

Related Myth: Big projects are inherently different from small projects – or, an airplane is not a calculator.
Counterpoint: Some projects are indeed much bigger than others. Yet the most successful big-project management comes from small within big mindset, in which purposeful "suboptimization" is encouraged.'

The above comments are directly aimed at the heart of the debate between waterfall model planning and evolutionary delivery.

'Develop a prototype, or a big hunk of it in 60 to 90 days. Whether your product or service is a digital switch, a new aircraft or a computer – or a new health service or financial instrument or a store format – our evidence suggests that something can always be whacked together in that time.

Then evaluate the prototype: that takes another 60 days . . . You're already playing with something tangible, or, say, a large hunk of primitive software code. Now you take the next little step. Maybe it costs a little more, for a more fully developed prototype . . . But again you build it fast . . . And this time you can probably get it, or part of it, onto the premises of a user (customer) – not an average user (that is a bit away, but a "lead user" who's willing to experiment with you, or at least an in-house lead user (a forward thinking department). And the process goes: slightly larger investments, timeframes that never run more than 60 to 90 days. It's the "learning organization" or the "experimenting organization."

At each step you learn a little more, but you have harsh reality tests – with hard product/service and live users/customers – very early. If it doesn't work you weed it out quickly, before you have career lock-in and irreversible psychological addiction to the "one best design." (This approach) can cut the time it takes to complete the development cycle by 50% or more.' (pp. 129–130)

This quotation is an excellent explanation of the reasoning behind evolutionary software delivery methods. Needless to say the entire book is rich with practical examples and detail to support this theory.

'Multiple passes usually take much less time, and result ultimately in the development of simpler (more reliable), more practical (if less "beautiful") systems than the single "Get it exactly right the first time" blitz.' (p. 150)

This comment applies directly to the big-bang theory of software development compared to the 'multiple pass' evolutionary development model. Maybe the interfacing isn't beautiful, but it is more practical.

> 'A "learning system" is vital. . . . And make sure the learning "system" or process encompasses (and generates) many small wins. Get people to make daily assessments; then act on those assessments. (Incidentally the small-win quick-feedback process actually generates practicality.' (p. 298)

Evolutionary delivery is a learning process with many small wins on the way which generates practical action.

> 'For heaven's sake, go after the easy stuff first! What's the thrill of beating your head against a brick wall?' (p. 301)

This is one of our evolutionary delivery methods central principles: the highest user-value to development-cost steps ('easy stuff') shall be identified and done first. I have never been able to understand why some software people plan as though they enjoy waiting years to see any results handed to their users and customers. My theory is that the problem is caused by the fact that they get paid monthly regardless.

> 'With respect to individuals, psychology (theory) focuses on the overriding importance of commitment, if motivation is to be sustained, and of the quick feedback associated with human-scale, tangible achievements. The literature on resistance to change (in both individuals and groups) suggests that the best way to overcome it is taking tiny steps, and, moreover working on the positive ("we can do something right"), rather than trying to confront negative feelings directly. . . . The small win is exactly about the creation of plausible, positive role models.' (p. 304)

15.2.5 Peters and Waterman

Source: Peters and Waterman, In Search of Excellence, *Harper and Row, New York, 1982*

> 'The essence of excellence is the thousand concrete minute-to-minute actions performed by everyone in an organization to keep a company on its course.'
>
> 'P&G (Procter and Gamble) is apparently not afraid of testing and therefore telegraphing its move. Why? Because, we suspect, the value added from learning before the nationwide launch so far exceeds the costs of lost surprise.' (p. 136)

. . . TI's (Texas Instruments) ability to learn quickly, to get something (almost anything) out in the field. They surprised themselves: as a very small company, $20 million, with very limited resources, they found they could outmaneuver large laboratories like Bell Labs; RCA and GE in the semiconductor area, because they'd just go out and try to do something, rather than keep it in the lab.' (Charles Phipps, of TI) (p. 136)

'At Activision the watchword for video-game design is "build a game as quickly as you can." Get something to play with. Get your peers fooling with it right away. Good ideas don't count around here. We've got to do something.' (p. 136)

'At HP (Hewlett-Packard), it's a tradition that product-design engineers leave whatever they are working on out on top of their desk so that anyone can play with it. . . . You are told probably on the first day that the fellow walking around playing with your gadget is likely to be a corporate executive, maybe even Hewlett or Packard.' (p. 137)

■ 15.3 Engineering sources

15.3.1 Deming

Source: W. Edwards Deming, Out of the Crisis, *MIT CAES, 1986 and Cambridge University Press*

Deming cites the 'Shewhart Cycle', known in Japan as the Deming Cycle. It is an example of an evolutionary product development method under competitive conditions.

'At every stage there will be . . . continual improvement of methods and procedures aimed at better satisfaction of the customer (user) at the next stage. Each stage works with the next stage and with the preceding stage toward optimum accommodation, all stages working together toward quality that the ultimate customer will boast about.' (p. 87)

In addition to this direct mention of the cycle, it is worth noting that the statistical quality control charts, which are the primary tool of Dr Deming, are one way of viewing the evolutionary progress results. They can also be viewed by readers of this book as another kind of measurement process for critical system attributes. Indeed, Deming is cited by Michael E. Fagan, as one of his sources on quality control ideas which led him to develop software inspections.

15.3.2 Koen

Source: Billy V. Koen, 'Toward a Definition of the Engineering Method', in Spring 1985 THE BENT of Beta Pi, ©IEEE reprinted there with permission from Proceedings; Frontiers in Education, 14th Annual Conference, Philadelphia, PA, 3–5 October 1984. It also appeared in Engineering Education, *December 1984.*

Koen is at University of Texas, Austin, E.T.C. Building, Room 5.134B, Austin TX, USA 78712. He solicits engineering heuristics. Koen is a professor of mechanical engineering. In his article he defines as one of several heuristics, the Engineering Method:

> 'The Engineering Method is the use of heuristics to cause the best change in a poorly understood situation within the available resources.'

He defines heuristics as hints or rules of thumb in seeking a solution to a problem. The principles in this book are 'heuristics' in this sense. Professor Koen manages to comment on several points central to this book, including evolutionary delivery.

> 'Engineering is a risk-taking activity. To control these risks, engineers have many heuristics.
>
> 1. They make only small changes in what has worked in the past, but they also
> 2. try to arrange matters so that if they are wrong they can retreat, and
> 3. they feed back past results in order to improve future performance.
>
> Any description of engineering that does not acknowledge the importance of these three heuristics and others like them in stabilizing engineering design and, in effect, making engineering possible, is hopelessly inadequate as a definition of engineering method.'

Later in discussing the structure of engineering methods he says:

> '. . . engineers cannot simply work their way down a list of steps, but . . . they must circulate freely within the proposed plan – iterating, backtracking, and skipping stages almost at random. Soon structure degenerates into a set of heuristics badly in need of other heuristics to tell what to do when.'

15.3.3 Shewhart

In W.E. Deming, 'Tribues to Walter A. Shewhart', Industrial Quality Control, *Vol. 24, No. 2, August 1967, cited in* AT&T Technical Journal *March/April 1986, pp. 11–12, Deming emphasizes the grand old man of industrial quality control had a very wide view of the process:*

> 'Quality control meant to him use of statistical methods all the way from raw material to consumer and back again, through redesign of product, re-working of specifications, in a continuous cycle, as results come in from consumer research and from other tests.'

In the version of evolutionary delivery recommended in this book, this is exactly the view. The evolutionary cycle must encompass all elements of system design and construction. It must deliver results to consumers. And, it must learn both from data collected from real consumers and other tests.

■ 15.4 Architectural sources

15.4.1 Alexander

Source: Christopher Alexander, Murray Silverstein, Sara Ishikawa et al., The Oregon Experiment, copyright © 1975 by The Center for Environmental Structure. Reprinted by permission of Oxford University Press, Inc.

Alexander and his group developed and practiced a number of relevant and interesting ideas within architecture. They practiced them in connection with the long-term architectural planning at the University of Oregon, thus the name of the book.

The major idea is that long-term developments should not be constrained by a static master plan. They should be allowed to grow incrementally, by user-participation, within certain overall guiding principles called 'patterns.'

There are six fundamental principles of implementation:

> '1. *The principle of organic order.*
>   Planning and construction will be guided by a process which allows the whole to emerge gradually from local acts.
> 2. *The principle of participation.*
>   All decisions about what to build, and how to build it, will be in the hands of the users.
> 3. *The principle of piecemeal growth.*
>   The construction undertaken in each budgetary period will be weighed overwhelmingly towards small projects.

4. *The principle of patterns.*
   All design and construction will be guided by a collection of communally adopted planning principles called patterns.
5. *The principle of diagnosis.*
   The well being of the whole will be protected by an annual diagnosis which explains, in detail, which spaces are alive and which ones dead, at any given moment in the history of the community.
6. *The principle of coordination.*
   Finally, the slow emergence of organic order in the whole will be assured by a funding process which regulates the stream of individual projects put forward by the users.' (pp. 5–6)

Each principle is further exploded into more detailed principles and explained and illustrated in the book. For example:

'The principle of participation:
All decisions about what to build, and how to build it, will be in the hands of the users.
To this end:

- there shall be a users' design team for every proposed building project;
- any group of users may initiate a project, and only those projects initiated by users shall be considered for funding;
- the planning staff shall give the members of the design team whatever patterns, diagnosis and additional help they need for their design;
- the time that users need to do a project, shall be treated as a legitimate and essential part of their activities;
- the design team shall complete their schematic designs before any architect or builder begins to play a major role.' (p. 58)

The 'patterns' can be compared with our notion in this book of 'open-ended solutions.' They are design rules which do not merely limit themselves to ensuring ease of growth and change, but they ensure all manner of other objectives such as human convenience and economics.

The ideas here are quite exciting and revolutionary – we must wonder who will be the people to document that they have applied such rules in software development?

15.4.2 Frank Lloyd Wright

Source: Frank Lloyd Wright, An Autobiography, *Horizon Press, NY, 1977*

Admitting to being an evolutionist

'The revolutionary evolutionist is never exactly penitent.' (p. 447)

'Mastery is no mystery. Simple principles of nature apply with particular emphasis and force to all a true master does: . . .

Planned progressions, thematic evolution, the never-ending variety in differentiation of pattern, integral ornament always belonging naturally enough to the simplest statement of the prime idea upon which structure is based: Beethoven's rhythms are like that – integral like those of nature!

And likewise the work of the inspired Architect.' (p. 454)

Another Source: Patrick J. Meehan (ed.), The Master Architect – Conversations with Frank Lloyd Wright, *John Wiley & Sons, Inc., 1984*

On organic architecture versus military architecture

'Well, call organic architecture a natural architecture. It means building for and with the individual as distinguished from the pseudo-classical order of the American schools today, mainly derived from the survivals of ancient military and monarchic orders.' (p. 122)

Evolutionary delivery could well also be called something like organic systems development. It is distinguished by 'building for and with the user' as opposed to building for the technologist.

'. . . but "organic architecture" which is the architecture of nature, the architecture based on principle and not upon precedent. Precedent is all very well so long as precedent is very well but who knows when it is very bad? Now that's something to guard against in architecture – know when to leave your precedent and establish one.' (p. 80)

The major philosophy of this book is that design is based on principle, not precedent. We must not spend so much energy looking for the right languages, structures, and tools, as we should spend in finding the principles by which we can select our technologies for the task at hand and the environment of the present day.

'Organic architecture comes of nature.' (p. 112)

I find all too often that software people are too ready to throw away existing systems entirely, and replace them with a totally new design. In doing this they ignore the fact that the existing system is thrown away without adequate replacement. This includes not only code but also traditions of work, methods that have been learned, patterns that are now easily recognized (screens, forms and codes), are also – often inadvertently – the very glue and oils that make the system work well in the real world. We throw the baby out with the bath water.

Software people need to have much greater respect for existing 'natural' ideas and systems. They are too cock-sure that their traditions and methods are the right ones. This is explored in depth in our book *Humanized Input* (Gilb and Weinberg, 1984, QED Publishers). For example, computer people are so sure that a ten digit number is the only right way to refer uniquely to a customer or product, when the age old tradition of names and varying alphabetic names is usually clearly superior from a human point of view according to Bell Labs research (cited in *Humanized Input*), because it is easier to access, to remember and contains useful redundancy from which a computer can spot errors and automatically correct them.

> 'Organic architecture is the architecture from the inside out.' (p. 201)

Evolutionary systems (a synonym for organic architecture) evolve from an inner essential core of the system and they add layers of function and qualities – from the inside and outwards.

> 'Lao-Tse, of course, was the man which proclaimed modern organic architecture and that was 500 years before Jesus.' (p. 218)

The main point here being that we are not speaking of a new idea, but one which the ancients recognized. Indeed, how could they not observe nature?

On flexibility design for robustness

> (The Imperial Hotel in Tokyo survived the great earthquake there.) 'And it was built to do it. It was thought-built to stand against an earthquake. That was the thought from beginning to end, and when the earthquake came it got up against that thought, and sneaked off.
>
> Falkenburg (interviewer) "Was it the only building in Tokyo to stay standing?"
>
> Wright: "The only building, practically, that's ever been built on the principle of flexibility. . . . It is welded together on the principle of flexibility, and that was new in the building world.' (p. 280)

This is one famous example of Wright's design engineering. He carefully noted the earthquake-prone environment. He designed a building to be robust and withstand the disaster. He used a design principle of unified flexibility of parts of the system. He spoke here about 'the new architecture . . . is organic . . . making it all as one.'

On the definition of architecture

'I think architecture is the science of structure and the structure of whatever is, whether it is music, whether it is painting or building or city planning or statesmanship.' (p. 131)

Wright admits to a very broad interpretation of architecture. This perhaps admits 'softecture' (software architecture) and 'infotecture' (information systems architecture) as sub-specialities. Certainly one characteristic of information systems is that they must bend to serve their environment and real people, just like buildings. They must be composed of many disciplines of technology – just like building.

On the value to cost relationship

'Student: " . . . aren't most of your buildings relatively expensive as far as the common man is concerned?"
Wright: "I wouldn't say so, although the profession has slapped me with that. I don't think that my buildings, wherever they stand, for the space they enclose and the accommodation you'll find in them cost as much as those standing around them and I'm prepared to demonstrate.
    What I'm anxious to do is the best that can be done no matter what. Now you don't sell houses, you don't sell buildings, you sell your services to help the man get the best thing that can be had according to his idea of the thing – you're working for him. . . . Ask them, lots of them will say: 'Well it cost more, Mr Wright, than we wanted it to cost but we're glad to get it.' None of them are sorry. Now isn't that the real thing . . . ? . . . I don't believe that one building that I've built . . . per square foot . . . costs any more than those standing around it and often times very much less." ' (pp. 220–1)

Wright is concentrating on providing the best possible value to the customer. But, he takes pride in the fact that he does it in a competitively economical way. Evolutionary delivery has the basic planning principle built into it that we should build in evolutionary steps which create the highest value for the user in relation to the cost as we can, and we should do it as soon as we can in the evolutionary process.

15.4.3 Victor Papanek

Source: Victor Papanek, Design for the Real World, *Granada, 1974*

Victor Papanek studied with Frank Lloyd Wright. He champions meaningful and socially responsible design. He describes his design method in terms which have elements of the evolutionary delivery method. He describes a series of steps:

- Assembling a design team representing all relevant disciplines, as well as members of the 'client group'.
- Research and fact-finding phase
- Design and development of ideas.
- Checking of these designs against goals established . . , and correcting the designs in the light of these design experiences
- Building of models, prototypes, test models, and working models.
- Testing of these by the relevant user-groups.
- The results of these tests are now fed back into master plans.
- Redesign, retesting and completion of the design job together with whatever documentation is necessary.
- The master plan is to be preserved and used as a follow-up guide in checking actual in-use performance characteristics of the designed objects. It can then also be used as a template for future design jobs that are similar in nature.

'It should be obvious that in reality the design process can never follow a path quite as linear and sequential as suggested by this example. (For one thing new research data emerge continuously.)' (pp. 256–7)

While we are on to Papanek, there are some other quotations which are relevant to this book:

'The wrong kind of problem statement . . . can effectively stop problem solving.' (p. 133)
'The most important ability that a designer can bring to his work is the ability to recognize, isolate, define and solve problems.' (p. 132)
'. . . design as a problem-solving activity can never, by definition, yield the one right answer: it will always produce an infinite number of answers, some "righter" and some "wronger". The rightness of any design solution will depend on the meaning with which we invest the arrangement.
Design must be meaningful.'

He then proceeds to examine system function and related

attributes of use, method, aesthetics, need, telesis (the deliberate, purposeful utilization of the process of nature and society to obtain particular goals), and association (the psychological conditioning . . . which pre-disposes us, or provides us with antipathy against a given value). The main point in this context being that he goes far beyond mere functional (what is the design supposed to do?) thinking into the other attributes of the product.

■ 15.5 Other sources

15.5.1 Davies

Source: A. Morley Davies, Evolution and its modern critics, Thomas Murby & Co., London, 1937. Reproduced by kind permission of Unwin Hyman Ltd

Cuvier's principle of correlation

He translates Cuvier's principle of correlation:

'Every organized being forms a whole, a unique and closed system, of which all parts mutually correspond and cooperate by reciprocal reaction for the same definite end. None of these parts can change without the others changing also; consequently each of them, taken separately, indicates and gives all the others.' (p. 133)

This sounds very much like a software (and hardware and human) system. As we evolve we are forced to consider the effect on all parts of the system. This reminds us also that we need configuration management, so that we can account for all related parts during the evolutionary change process, and so that we can define the exact status of a particular evolutionary step.

The fundamental necessity principle

'The one fundamental necessity of a developing animal is that at every stage of its growth it should be able to live in its particular surroundings.' (p. 138)

Evolutionarily developing systems must also live in a real world of some form of usage, not mere testing of individual modules – in order that the 'test' reflects realistic conditions. We want the data provided to be as near to the truth of the future as possible.

Dohrn's principle of change of function

'Anton Dohrn was, the founder of the Naples Zoological
station, (who) enunciated the "principle of change of function"
(Princip des Funtionwechels) in 1875. The principle is that an organ
may have, in addition to its primary function, one or more
subsidiary functions, and when changed conditions render the
original function unnecessary one of the minor functions may
assume primary importance and lead to new developments in the
organ. The value of this principle lay in the clearing away of those
formidable obstacles to the acceptance of evolution presented by
organs or systems of organs which would apparently be quite
useless until fully developed.' (p. 149)

This principle reminds us that in an evolving system we must
design some technologies which have only a short-term function at
early steps; or even no initial use at all. Yet, we are wise if we can find
and apply technologies (solutions) which have additional attributes to
those initially necessary, and perhaps not useful in the long term. We
should want solutions which display versatility in helping us fulfill our
objectives even when the exact sequence of content of the evolutionary
steps is unknown. I have called these technologies 'open-ended
architectures' in this book.

For example, a simple facility for enabling a text comment, which
can be inserted in the midst of a programming language can initially
serve as a means of documentation of the language usage. But, as Leon
Stucki has shown us it can also later be adapted to extend the language
system by means of allowing for comments in a formal language which
can be interpreted by a computer. For example: 'Comment: all global
variables are positive or zero now.' See Figure 13.2c.

Dollo's law, or the principle of irreversibility

'The past is indestructible.' (Louis Dollo, Belgian palæontologist,
1857–1931.)
'It was never intended as a denial of the possibility of reversing
its direction, but of the possibility of such reversal being exact.'
(p. 164)

We can decide that an evolutionary step is a failure and we can
revert to the status immediately previous to that step. But, we cannot
eliminate the user and developer experience of the failed step. Indeed,
we want to learn from the mistake and change the future for the better.

The user experience however must never be so bitter as to reduce
their willingness to use the system we are developing. This means that

the developer must exercise caution when designing a step so that it cannot at worst be destructive (for example lead to long down-time or destroyed databases). It means that new steps should be introduced cautiously and spread further only after being proven in a limited environment. It means not merely that a step be small – this is not even in itself important. It does mean that the maximum risk of negative experience at one single delivery step must be kept to a planned maximum, to a level fully acceptable to the users involved.

The principle of vestigal organs

'The existence in many animals of structures to which no use can be assigned, but which are obviously identical with structures that are useful in other animals, has always been a fact easier to reconcile with evolution than with creation.' (p. 166)

Software system evolution has analogies to this. We are often forced to keep data codes, report formats, programming language artifacts and other structures which have long since lost their present and future meaning, but which were necessary at some time in the past of the evolution of the system. They remain when the damage they do is less than the cost and potential damage done if we get rid of them, or if they are invisible and not the cause of serious problems.

A book such as this which takes the entire concept of evolution up to lengthy debate is rich in concepts which could be of interest to systems engineers. But, I hope that the above samples show some of the thinking around the conventional biological evolutionary world which might give us some insights about the software evolutionary world.

15.5.2 Franklin via Tuchman

Source: in Barbara Tuchman, The March of Folly, *Abacus, 1984, p. 248*

'Benjamin Franklin, a wise man and one of the few who derived principles from political experience and were able to state them, wrote during the Stamp Act crisis that it should not be supposed that honor and dignity are better served "by persisting in a wrong measure once entered into than by rectifying an error as soon as it is discovered."'

16

Ten principles for estimating software attributes

■ Introduction

There is a great deal of interest in software cost estimation models (Boehm, 1981) and in the prediction of software project cost or reliability through models (such as those of Halstead, McCabe and Putnam, referred to in Boehm's book *Software engineering economics*).

I want, here, to give an alternative point of view. My view is that for software management in practice, there already exist more powerful ways of getting control over quality and cost parameters than the above-mentioned prediction models. The important question is, do you want prediction, or do you want control?

At an IEEE conference in Chicago, a New York computer science professor asked me to give my opinion regarding three models for predicting software reliability. I asked him to tell me what his real objectives were. Initially he said 'to predict accurately.' I then asked whether he wanted to know which of the models was most accurate, even if none of them gave him control over the final results. I then suggested that what he really wanted was control over the final result, even if it involved none of the prediction models he mentioned.

He readily admitted that what he really wanted was control over the final results. 'In that case,' I said, 'let us discuss how to get control over the results, and I think you will find that there are more powerful ways to get what you really want than any of these particular modelling techniques.'

I shall summarize the discussion that followed in the form of Ten Principles of Estimation.

■ 16.1 The dependency principle

> **The dependency principle:**
> All system attributes are affected by all others.

Boehm (1981) shows that cost is the result of a large number of parameters; about 50 are dealt with in his COCOMO model. (COCOMO is an acronym for COnstructive COst MOdel.) However, most of these parameters reflect attributes of the production environment (software tools, language experience, applications experience).

Only a few of the critical product attributes themselves are represented (required reliability, timing constraint, database size), and they are represented with a highly generalized definition. Some of those product attributes which could have a significant impact on costs are not included in the cost estimation model at all, such as usability, ease of international usage, marketability, availability.

I want to state clearly that I have no wish to attack Boehm or his excellent book. In fact he is his own book's best critic. But it could be dangerous for readers who decide to adopt it as their only method for cost estimation and cost control, an assertion Boehm would be unlikely to disagree with.

The problem lies in the fact that such general models will be inadequate for giving us the answers we need for project management, though they may give us a much-needed 'jolt', and some insights, before we are ready to get into the detailed work of our projects.

Static cost prediction models cannot replace the need for other forms of control over costs and product attributes. In order to predict a resource usage (money, time, people, space) during a project, we would need to know the exact levels of the other quality and resource attributes which we want. For, if any of them is highly ambitious, it can have a strong effect on the one we are seeking to estimate. In particular, if we specify attributes at levels near the state of the art (or near to perfection), then we can expect great uncertainty in our estimates.

Even when we have some kind of a specification of all critical and ambitious attributes, we have no formula for predicting the exact result in terms of cost. All experience clearly shows that we must be prepared to specify priorities, and allow attribute trade-offs as we get a more realistic view of the system through a design or development process.

If all other initially required attributes are held at some constant level of ambition, we must accept the resulting cost. But if this cost is considered an unacceptable cost, but we are willing to modify our demands for some of the other qualities or resource attributes, then we will probably be able to modify the final cost to an acceptable one.

In addition, if we are willing to modify the development environment or the product's technical design (by 'value engineering') then we may also achieve a reduction of the final cost to an acceptable level. This can be done if the design and development process is evolutionary (Gilb, 1985).

■ 16.2 The sensitivity principle

> **The sensitivity principle:**
> Even the slightest change in one attribute can cause uncertainly large changes in any other attribute.

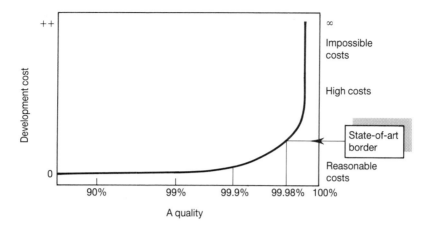

Figure 16.1 In any system, including logicware or dataware systems, perfection is infinitely expensive. The diagram is based partly on data from the Bell Laboratories switching software, which in the 1970s was rated at 99.9% availability. Eight years of improvement later, the software availability was 99.98% (0.08% better). In 1985 the British Ministry of Defence was reputed to require 99.9999999% software availability. When do you estimate their projects will pass acceptance tests?

You can observe in all areas of engineering and management that there are certain levels of ambition for attributes which cost much more than they are really worth. Economists speak about the 'diminishing returns on investment.' Managers speak of 'marginal benefits.'

Further, when we attempt to cross the 'state of the art' borderline for any quality (or benefit or return) we must expect to pay a penalty of costs which cannot be calculated in advance. There is, by definition, no experience to tell us what it really costs. We have to find out by trying. Yet we are constantly being pushed into crossing that borderline in order to beat our competitors.

We must have a language for expressing the vital difference between the known cost of qualities, and the unknown cost area. The COCOMO types of cost estimation models do not allow us to express our ambitions in these quality areas. They can never, therefore, be a guide to the costs of ambitious levels of quality or required resource usage to obtain those levels. In fact, these models may give us the illusion that we have some idea of the cost, when a single over-ambitious, high-priority quality requirement may give us more than an order-of-magnitude of cost estimation error.

■ 16.3 The zeroth law of reliability generalized

> **The zeroth law of reliability generalized:**
> You can reach almost any ambitious level if you are willing to sacrifice all the other attributes.

It is all a matter of your priorities. If your first-priority product attribute is ambitious but achievable, you can usually find a way to get it. But as you increase the number of the second-priority attributes you wish to achieve, you will find it increasingly difficult to meet all of them as well.

One famous computer designer, Seymour Cray, is described (Casale, 1985) thus: 'He intends not to attempt to exceed engineering limits in more than two areas at the same time because the risk of failure is quite high when you do that.'

Gene Amdahl, another famous computer designer said (Amdahl, 1985), 'What happened with Triology' (a company he ran that failed) 'was that the company overevaluated its ability and underevaluated the technical difficulties. It is not impossible to make chips the size Triology wanted, but they wanted in addition to make complicated logic (VLSI) on them. That's when we got both design and production problems.'

■ 16.4 The design-to-price principle

> **The design-to-price principle:**
> You can get more control over costs by designing to stay within interesting limits, than you can by passively trying to estimate the costs resulting from a design which gives priority to other objectives.

Estimation is a passive reaction to a problem. There is a well known active response to the problem of desired resource-constraints on projects. Engineers have always called it 'design to cost.' I call it 'design by objectives' to stress the fact that you can design towards *any* set of objectives, cost being only one. (Other examples are calendar deadlines and ease of use.)

If you are really concerned with estimating things like costs, delivery dates or reliability, then perhaps this is an indicator that these items are high priority attributes for you. If they are, then the 'design to cost' approach must be considered as a means of getting control over these critical attributes.

■ 16.5 The iterative estimation principle

> **The iterative estimation principle:**
> You get more control over estimation by learning from evolutionary early-and-frequent result deliveries, than you will if you try to estimate in advance for a whole large project.

You can try to calculate what the cost will be. If you are wrong, you will probably only begin to see how inaccurate you really are when you are well into the project. Your option is either to complete the project, with cost and time over budget, or to cancel the project after a substantial investment has been made.

There is a better option. Insist on a plan to deliver the development in small (1% to 5% of total budget) organic incremental steps. As each incremental delivery step is completed, and ready for some sort of practical use, you can measure the resources actually expended, and the benefits (qualities) obtained.

You can compare these against your short-term estimates for each step. You can use these short-term data to make a far more realistic long-term predictions for any quality area, or for any particular resource limitation. In cases of negative deviation from long-term plans, you can take management action to correct the situation. Your options might be to:

- improve the design engineering (value engineering),
- modify the benefit estimates to be more realistic,
- modify the resource estimates to be more realistic,
- cancel the project development early, because it is an inevitable loser.

The evolutionary method is different from the conventional software engineering model. The conventional software development model presumes that once development (actual building of the new system) is in progress, the requirements and the design are 'frozen' untouchables. In fact they should be dynamically adjustable at each evolutionary step. The evolutionary model reflects this real world situation.

The evolutionary method has a consistent record of accomplishment in industry (Peters and Austin, 1985). The evolutionary approach presumes that we are dealing with things which are too unique and too complex for us to make accurate estimates at the initial stages for the long term. It admits our human limitations in a complex world.

Evolutionary delivery seeks to find a reasonable and practical way to get control over the critical elements of what we are doing at the earliest possible moment. It seeks to calibrate our estimation apparatus, based on present reality, with all its particular complexities – rather than on a general model of the past. It allows us to deal with rapid change in the state of the art – both in the development environment, and in our product environment.

It allows us to see the combined effects of a large number of factors in the most simple and direct manner – by observing the final costs and benefits in practice as each step emerges.

■ 16.6 The 'quality determines cost' principle

> **The quality determines cost principle:**
> You cannot accurately estimate the costs of anything when cost determining quality attributes are unclearly defined.

It is simply not possible to determine the final development cost for a high quality product without knowing the quality ambition level. How much will it cost to build an automobile? How much will it cost to build a house? How much will it cost to educate a child? We can give answers. We can even prove that those answers match the question. But, we have left out the question of the quality of the auto, the house and the education. (You risk getting only what you pay for.)

Every estimate I have ever seen for a budget or a deadline ignores this vital question to some critical degree. This would be of no consequence if whatever quality that emerged (by chance) were acceptable. But, it isn't. On the contrary, the result is that either much-needed quality is compromised, in order to meet deadlines and budgets, or budgets and deadlines are exceeded to achieve the essential quality.

In either case there is a disappointment, one which we could have reduced or even avoided if we had made a bigger effort to be more explicit about the qualities or benefits we required.

There are many barriers to doing this properly. First we must identify those qualities which might impact other attributes substantially. To do so, we also usually need to learn a language for expressing those qualities in an unambiguous and testable way (see Chapter 19).

Estimating cost based on design objectives

Even with clearly stated quality objectives we cannot expect to immediately deduce the cost of achieving those levels of quality desired. But, we can expect to begin a process of determining if they are within the bounds of possibility, and what we will have to trade off to get them.

It is my frequent observation in large-scale high-technology projects in several countries and different types of businesses, that many of the critical quality parameters are not stated in unambiguous and testable ways. When the budget is used up, or the deadline rolls around, it is tempting to declare the project finished, and deliver it without any proof that a particular ambitious quality level has been achieved.

I am highly sceptical of the real meaning of any claim to 'finish large scale software projects on time and under budget' until there is clear evidence that the initial estimates and deadlines are based on a clear and complete statement of all critical quality and resource attributes. I often suspect that measures of deviation from estimates are really measures of our ability to slam on the project brakes when we see the 'red light' (deadline or budget) approaching us.

Yet, most of us fail to specify our quality objectives in such unambiguous and measurable terms. Indeed, most software engineering professionals have not yet learned or practiced the art of specifying their most common critical quality attributes (such as 'usability' (Gilb, 1984a) or 'maintainability' (Gilb, 1984b)) on measurable, testable scales. It is as if we were electronics engineers with no knowledge of volts, watts or ohms.

■ 16.7 The natural variation principle

> **The natural variation principle:**
> All system attributes can be expected to vary to some degree throughout their lifetime.

There is a myth about attributes of development. The myth is that there is some particular constant level of 'cost to be estimated' or even of 'quality to be reached.' It would be convenient if the world would hold still while we tried to understand it better. So far, it has refused to do so. We need to come to terms with this dynamic world of ours by recognizing its true nature:

- all attributes are changing through time,
- our perception of what is desirable is changing constantly,
- our ability to measure many attributes is not exact,
- we don't know how to exercise control over many attributes exactly.

We must therefore resign ourselves to a 'fuzzy,' out-of-focus, multi-dimensional and dynamically changing world. We have to find realistic ways of coping with the uncertainty involved. No invention is necessary; people have had to deal with this problem for a long time. What is important is that we must not hide our heads in the sand and pretend that things are less dynamic than they really are.

I do not here propose to list the many mechanisms (Deming, 1986) which exist for dealing with dynamic uncertainty but merely to recognize that we must take these uncertainties into account when making estimates. We must continually, during development, revise our estimates, based on the dynamic change and the latest events which impact our situation.

Those who seek a clean simple static formula for predicting the future may find this disturbing. But realistic managers and engineers have always lived with the need to control a dynamic situation.

■ 16.8 The early bird principle

> **The early bird principle:**
> Any method which gives you early feedback and correction of reality is more likely to give you control over the final result than big-bang methods.

Software problems are like cancer. It pays to get control early.

We must recognize the limitations in our ability to predict the long-term future for complex and large state of the art systems.

The real point of any estimate is to serve as a step in the process of getting what we finally decide we want, or what we are prepared to put up with. We need to emphasize methods and strategies which give us early feedback on the realities of our project, while we still have time and money to change course if necessary. In software development there are two basic techniques for helping us here, and they are still widely unknown and unused by the industry.

The first is evolutionary delivery – of which we have written earlier (see Gilb, 1985 and Chapters 13 and 15 of this book for more detail). This gives us the chance to 'sample reality,' and change our future, while we still have the credibility and the resources to do so.

For example, suppose in a 45-month project, which is planned as a series of 45 monthly delivery steps, that the first three steps each take three months, instead of the estimated one month. Your long term estimation for the remaining 42 steps will have to be modified to 42×3 months.

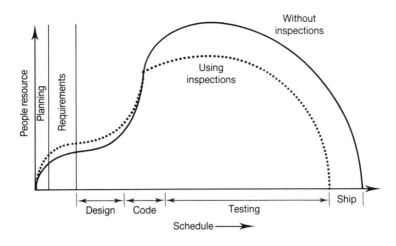

Figure 16.2 Resources with inspection. Fagan's inspection method uses a maximum of 15% of total development resources. However it uses them more heavily in the early stages. Towards the end of the delivery cycle, there is a net saving of resources, in the 25–35% range. Derived from Fagan, M., Advances in Software Inspections, IEEE Trans. on Software Engineering, July 1986. (© 1986 IEEE)

This is unless you change something, such as the technical design or the development environment, or the quality requirements (which may be set unnecessarily high). This course-correction process is described in detail by Quinnan of IBM Federal Systems Division (Quinnan, 1980).

The second is Fagan's inspection method (Fagan, 1976). (See also Chapters 12 and 21.) This method provides discovery of the errors in design documentation at the earliest stages of design, before the corresponding system is actually constructed.

There is also evidence that the inspection process is dependent on the creation and use of a far more unambiguous design specification language than most people are currently using. IBM, for example, has recognized this and taken appropriate steps. International Computers (ICL) has too. Most others are so far behind that they don't even recognize the price being paid for fuzzy specification languages, and the opportunity to change to less ambiguous ones.

Work done at IBM by Jones (1977), Remus and Zilles (1979) and IBM Federal Systems Division (Walston and Felix, 1977) serves as admirable examples of data collection and analysis for software engineering estimation and control which most of the world has yet to act on.

■ 16.9 The activist principle

> **The activist principle:**
> Estimation methods alone will not change a result which is off the track. Active correction must be a part of your methodology. (Action, not estimation, produces results.)

Estimating costs is a passive exercise. So is the estimation of reliability. If you care about something enough, go after it more directly.

This point has been discussed in terms of design to cost (Principle 16.4 above). It has also been illustrated in our earlier discussion of the evolutionary development method, where after every step of delivery you have a chance to take action to create the results you want.

Estimation, even when used in the context of evolutionary delivery cycle feedback ('this one month cycle took three months') is of no use if you cannot act on the information and change your design or your development process. A rapid-cycle change process is necessary for meeting difficult development targets and coping in the real world today.

■ 16.10 The 'future shock' principle

> **The 'future shock' principle:**
> Data from past projects might be useful, but it can never be as useful to you as current data from your present project.

Most estimating techniques rely on historical evidence in past projects, on how well certain design or development process techniques correlate with other parameters such as cost or deviation from expected costs. We must try to learn from our history, or paraphrasing Santayana, we are doomed to repeat it.

However, such facts from the past must not blind us to the fact that our particular project will be using a great many new elements in combination with the old ones, and the only interesting truth for us is what is going to happen in *this* particular project. It is nevertheless important to document our experiences of where estimates went wrong, for future use.

We can use the past as a guide to some things we might reasonably expect in the future: but we are fools if we do not test these presumptions every step of the way! (Glegg, 1973)

■ 16.11 Summary

Estimation, while admirable, is no replacement for action to change things to be the way we really want them today, regardless of what we thought we wanted yesterday!

Any estimation or control technique must reflect a large number of complex and dynamic factors. No static model can meet this requirement. A diversity of approaches will be necessary throughout the development and maintenance process, and throughout the system lifetime, to ensure that you keep on getting what you really need.

The principles in this chapter are more universal in their application than to software alone. I hope to have led the reader to a more flexible point of view regarding the estimation of software attributes and system attributes as well.

■ References and further reading

Amdahl, G., 1985, Polyteknisk Review, February, p. 11

Boehm, B.W., 1981, *Software engineering economics*, Prentice-Hall, N.J.

Casale, C., 1985, *Computer Weekly*, 17 January, p. 16

Deming, W.E., 1986, *Out of the crisis*, MIT Press and Cambridge University Press

Fagan, M.E., 1976, 'Design and code inspections,' *IBM Systems Journal*, **15**, (3), 182–211

Gilb, T., 1976, *Software metrics*, Studentlitteratur, Lund, Sweden (out of print)

Gilb, T., 1984a, 'The impact estimation table,' *Proc. of IFIP Interact. Conf.*, London, September

Gilb, T., 1984b, 'Maintaining software systems,' in *Data Processing*, June, pp. 19–23

Gilb, T., 1985, 'Evolutionary development vs the waterfall model,' *ACM Software Eng. Notes*, July, pp. 49–61

Glegg, J., 1973, *The science of design*, Cambridge University Press

Jones, C., 1977, 'Program quality and programmer productivity,' *IBM Technical Report*, TR 02.764 also 1986, *Programming productivity*, McGraw-Hill, N.Y.

Peters, T. and Austin, N., 1985, *A passion for excellence*, Random House (USA), Collins (UK)

Quinnan, R.E., 1980, 'Software engineering management practices,' *IBM Systems Journal*, **19**, (4), 466–477

Remus, H. and Zilles, S., 1979, 'Prediction and management of program quality,' *Proc. 4th Int. Conf. on Software Eng.*, Munich, pp. 341–350

Santayana, G., 1903, *The life of reason*, Vol. 1, Chapter 12

Walston, C.E. and Felix, C.P., 1977, 'A method of programming measurement and estimation,' *IBM Systems Journal*, **16**, (1), pp. 54–73

17

Deadline pressure: how to beat it

■ Introduction

Industrial software engineering environments are almost always under strong pressure to meet calendar deadlines. The pressure can be so intense as to tempt software professionals to follow primitive software practices, often resulting in poor product quality, and even more real delays in getting satisfactory products to the market. This chapter reviews a number of realistic strategies, with reference to practical experience, for dealing with this problem. The solutions are common sense, political and technical in nature. They involve software metrics to define the real problem, evolutionary delivery and Fagan's inspection method to correct process failures using early feedback. Ten guiding principles summarize the chapter.

■ 17.1 The problem

17.1.1 The problem as viewed by the project manager's manager

The big boss wants it. A deadline has been established. The pressure to deliver something, on time, is on. There may well be some reason given for the particular date chosen. It may be specified in a contract. It may be synchronized with other product developments. But, it could just be an arbitrary guesstimate. It could have simply been a rash promise by the project manager made to impress his boss.

It is probable that the big boss *really* would like to get even earlier delivery of something, has no clear unambiguous definition of *what* is to be delivered, thinks everybody knows, might accept later delivery of parts of the package, has been misunderstood as to what and when, hasn't told the project manager what he really wants (yet), is in the process of deciding differently about what and when. All of these represent potential opportunities for relief of deadline pressure.

17.1.2 The problem as viewed by the project manager

The project manager is caught between the pressures from above, and the finite productive capacity below him. You might wonder how intelligent people can voluntarily accept such lack of control over both their destiny and reputation.

The project manager feels that the demands from above are unreasonable. Further, that the resources, in terms of people, talent, budget, machinery and time for getting the job done, are inadequate. But the project manager is there to do as well as can be expected under the circumstances. And he will try to do so with the least pain to himself.

The project manager, either through ineptitude, or experience and cunning, usually has a situation where the exact nature of the project deliveries are entirely unclear. This has the effect of allowing him to deliver something, really anything, that is ready by the deadline, and claim on-time delivery. Who can prove otherwise?

17.1.3 The problem as viewed by the project professional

The people working for the project manager – the ones who do the real work – are perfectly prepared to let their boss worry about deadlines, as long as they can do whatever they most enjoy doing, the way they enjoy doing it. They realize that the project manager doesn't dare fire them or take similar drastic action (like training them) because that would destroy the project schedule.

As individuals each one of them would very much like to make a brilliant recognized contribution to the project. The problem is they are not sure what the project is all about, and they are pretty sure that somebody else will snatch the glory from them anyway. Better to save those brilliant efforts for when one starts one's own company.

17.1.4 The problem as viewed by the customer or user

The recipient of the project output probably needs the results 'yesterday'. Your deadline, as project manager, is probably viewed as the longest acceptable wait time until the product is ready.

The customer might very well be willing to wait longer for 90% of the project results, if only 10% were delivered on time. They might even be willing to let some of that 10% be delivered later if 1% were delivered much earlier. It is perfectly possible that they don't really need 99% of what has been asked for. There are a lot of people out there who have a vested interest in building new systems, rather than improving old ones.

■ 17.2 The solutions

17.2.1 Redefine the problem

I have never yet walked into a project of any kind, anywhere in the world, where I felt that the project deliveries were fully and completely defined. I'm not saying that all projects should be perfectly defined in advance. There are both good and bad reasons for incomplete requirements specification. But this lack of specification gives us a powerful tool for relieving deadline pressure, because it can put us in a position to clarify or detail the specifications in such a way as to make the delivery task easier.

Gerald M. Weinberg, in our book *Humanized Input* made use of this principle when he formulated his Zeroth Law of Unreliability: If a system doesn't have to be reliable, it can meet any other objective.

If a quality, like reliability, is not clearly specified you can deliver the project earlier, if you interpret the quality requirement as 'whatever it happens to be when the deadline arrives.' This, coupled with an innocent 'Oh! You wanted *more* than two minutes between failures!' after the first complaints arrive, will solve the deadline problem initially. You are of course prepared to discuss a new schedule and project for enhancing quality to the required levels, now clarified for the first time.

Whether or not 'reliability' is defined is irrelevant. There are a large number of quality attributes which probably have a dramatic influence on cost and schedule. You only need one of them to be unclearly specified to give you the opening you need.

The more quality requirement specifications that are added, the more uncertainty is introduced into the schedule estimation problem. In fact with ten or more demanding state-of-the-art quality requirements you can be certain that the project can never be delivered. The trick is to get the client to specify what they 'dream of,' rather than what they will want to pay for or wait for. They will always be tempted into this trap, and you will always have an excuse for non-delivery.

17.2.2 Don't work harder, work smarter

It is natural, when faced with deadline pressure, to consider various ways of working harder. More overtime, reducing employee vacations, working weekends. Such a response gives the impression of trying to meet the deadlines.

There is no certainty that hard work will help the deadline at all. The real problem is the individual who made a promise for a deadline, without considering whether it was realistic at all. Unfortunately, this person is often the Chief Executive of the company.

So, you have to work smarter. This involves doing things mentioned elsewhere in this paper, such as redesigning for evolutionary delivery, using inspection of requirements and high-level design to find problems while they are small ones, formally identifying the real goals measurably, and sub-contracting the work to someone else.

17.2.3 Refuse! Make counter-threats

Have you ever considered refusing to accept the deadline which someone is trying to impose upon you? You can do so under the guise of loyalty to your boss. But do it in writing. An oral refusal can too easily be misunderstood or misused. Here is an example of a diplomatic formulation:

> 'I must unfortunately decline, at the present moment, to accept full responsibility for meeting the suggested deadline. I sincerely believe that this would result in you (your boss!) getting blamed for non-delivery at a later date. The project is as yet not clearly defined (it never is) and it is by no means clear that we have the resources (you never will) to complete it on the suggested schedule to the quality expected by the customer. We must not be caught making promises we cannot keep, no matter how great the pressure. What we will promise is to do the very best we can to deliver as early as possible, with the resources we have or are later granted.'

(P.S. Remember to delete the parentheses in the above paragraph when you copy it!) If this diplomatic attempt to avoid responsibility doesn't work, don't worry. The project is sure to be late, or there will be some kind of a disaster. You can then prove that you were wise enough to disclaim responsibility in advance. If, by some miracle everything succeeds, you can safely assume that your disclaimer will be forgotten in the euphoria of success. If it is remembered, you can safely say that it was luck or that certain factors became clearer after it was written.

17.2.4 If necessary, use the counter-threat

A diplomatic disclaimer might not be enough to fool your boss. The counter-threat ploy may be necessary. The objective is to scare people into not imposing a really serious deadline. It might be along the following lines. (Do not copy this text exactly every time.)

> 'I cannot but note the deadline that you have felt it necessary to impose. We will naturally do our very best to meet it. However,

in your own interest please note the following problems which may occur as a result:

1. There is very little real chance of meeting this deadline. Can we afford the damage to our reputation?
2. If we do try to deliver something by this date it will certainly not have the quality level presently expected. Can we also afford *this* damage to our reputation?
3. The attempt to meet an impossible deadline, about which we have not been consulted, will result in severe stress to our staff. We risk our best people (who do all the real work) leaving us in frustration.

We do of course want to co-operate in any way we can to make a realistic plan, and to help estimate realistic resources for doing a job which will not threaten our standing as responsible professionals in the eyes of customers or the public.'

17.2.5 Redefine the solution

If these tactics fail, don't despair! There are still other avenues open to you. One is to redefine the solution so that it is easier to achieve than the one you were landed with. This can be a dangerous path because solutions are often 'holy cows' for somebody. However, just as often, the solutions are accidental and nobody really cares about the detailed solution type as long as they achieve their real objectives. Somebody (you, of course) has to take the initiative to change the solution so that the deadline can be met.

The steps are as follows:

1. Trap your boss or customer into **declaring** that the proposed deadline is extremely critical (if it is not, your problem dissolves anyway).
2. Entice them into agreeing that the results of the project are more critical than the means by which they are accomplished. Few managers will admit to anything else. Establish in formal measurable terms the results to be accomplished (savings of time and money, improved service or sales, etc.).
3. Show them that the presently suggested solution does not guarantee the achievement of these results. (No solution is ever guaranteed anyway.)
4. Then, find an alternative solution which at least looks far more safe in terms of getting the results. For example such a solution is likely to be based on existing and known products or

technologies, modified for your purposes. Possibly you can get some outside party to guarantee the deadline for the modifications in which case the monkey is off your back.

Naturally, you offer to manage the new effort. This gets you a reputation for sheer heroism in the face of impossible odds. (When it's all over, you can take the credit for the successful outcome.)

17.2.6 Define the solution yourself

Of course 'redefining' the solution might seem a bit too much for the cases where no clear solution has yet been defined. In this case you should make use of such an opportunity to get control over the solution definition before others do. They might suggest something which cannot be achieved within the deadline.

There is one cardinal rule when defining solutions. Make sure you have a clear idea of the objectives which top management has. This is often different from what your boss told you the goals were.

17.2.7 Get somebody else to do it

Next, you want to do what engineers call 'design to cost.' This simply means that you must find a solution architecture which ensures that you deliver the results as expected. It is vital that you are prepared to go outside your normal discipline to achieve this.

For example you may be a software engineer. The requirement may be for 'zero defects' software. You may not feel capable of producing that within the deadline. So, you must be prepared to swallow your pride, but deliver a solution.

You must for example find a ready-made solution with zero defects (or near to it, because perfection is mighty hard to find in practice). Or, you need to find a sub-supplier who will guarantee the result on time. They will not of course be able to do it, but you can blame them afterwards. Your job is to write a clear specification of what they will be attempting to deliver by the deadline. You should get them to guarantee this in a contract, or at least a letter or in writing.

You might feel more like a legal person than a technical person at this point, but remember legal people cannot write technical specifications and they don't care about your deadline pressure.

There is an important strategy of making sure it is someone else who is under the deadline pressure. Remember, management doesn't really care who does things, as long as they get done. If you can, make a strong case for letting somebody else do the job, then pressure is off your back.

It is important that you consider taking main contractor responsibility. That is, you find, then you control, the sub-contractor. This gives you something to do and to look busy with, but of course the sub-contractor does all the real work. You just sit there with a whip.

■ 17.3 The technologies of the solutions

17.3.1 Evolutionary delivery

The most powerful practical technique I have experienced for getting control over deadline pressure is evolutionary delivery. The evolutionary delivery method is based on the simple observation that not everything is needed all at one initial delivery or deadline.

An example

In the case of one national taxation on-line system, we had a deadline six months hence. The initial project plan was to use a staff of one hundred technical people (programmers) for probably (nobody knew) three years to complete delivery of a *totally new* design. I worked out an alternative design based on making use of all the *old* data and programs, with a few politically interesting frills thrown in.

This idea alone guarantees you will meet any deadline but it is not nearly as much fun for the technologists who want to play with new toys. In this case there were 98 programmers who wanted to learn a totally new programming language.

I made sure that I kept my eye on the essential deadline idea, that the Finance Minister was to see the new system in action personally in exactly six months. The new system was the old system, on a new computer mainly. Secondarily a 'while-you-wait' access to their base of taxation data was desired. We provided a way using a copy of their current data. The Finance Minister had to wait one full second to get the data, using binary search on disks, with my modified solution, as opposed to $\frac{1}{10}$th of a second with the previously committed 300 work-year solution.

They argued for a full three months about whether my simplistic solution could possibly work in such a large and complex environment. Then, using a mere handful of people, they actually delivered successfully within three months.

17.3.2 Using Fagan's inspection method

'A stitch in time saves nine' says the old folk wisdom. Many of the problems in meeting deadlines for large projects are caused by the tail end backlash. This is the penalty you pay for poor quality control in the early stages of design and planning. The small details that were overlooked come back to haunt you, as you desperately try to fix the problems that pop up when you try to meet required quality levels or performance levels for delivery.

Conventional quality control (Juran, 1974) methods insist that 'inspection' of product and process quality is a vital pre-requisite for being able to maintain the required cost and quality attributes of almost any development. Around 1972 Michael E. Fagan, of IBM in Kingston New York, began to transfer these methods to quality control of IBM software products. Nobody had tried to do this until then. In fact it was his training as a quality control hardware engineer which gave him the basic idea of applying inspection to software. It was an uphill battle at IBM, but very successful. Although the method is widely recognized internationally, it will still take many more years before it is widely used.

The aspect of inspection which is interesting in connection with deadline pressure is that it seems to have these repeatable general characteristics:

1. Delivery of major software projects is achieved in about 15% to 35% (Walston and Felix, 1977) less calendar time than otherwise. This saving can also be translated into cost or work-power savings if desired (Fagan, 1976).
2. The quality (in terms of defects removed) is measurably improved (by as much as one or two orders of magnitude) while this saving is made.
3. Improvements are cumulative, for several years. This is due to a process of management analysis of the time and defect statistics generated by inspection – combined with management taking change action to improve productivity.

Why does inspection save time and cost?

The details of inspection are described in Chapter 12 of this book. The reasons why inspection saves resources are simple.

1. It can be used at early stages of design and planning, before conventional product testing can be used. Sixty per cent of

software bugs exist already at this stage, according to a TRW study (Thayer *et al*, 1978). It identifies and cleans up defects which would cause much larger later repair costs. IBM data indicates as much as 82 times more to correct software errors found late at the customer site, as opposed to those found early at design stages.

2. The statistical data collected during the inspection process is carefully analyzed. This is much like Financial Directors who analyze accounting data to get insights into a company's operational weaknesses. It is then used to suggest, and confirm the results of, major changes to the entire development or production process.

If the changes are implemented early enough in a project, they can impact the deadline of that project. If the changes are implemented late, or even after the project is completed – they can at least improve your ability to perform better on the following project (Radice *et al.*, 1985).

17.3.3 Attribute specification

Another technique for getting some control over deadlines and other resource constraints is, as indicated above, setting objectives for quality and resources in a formal and measurable way. This process is described in Chapter 9.

The major reason why this impacts resources is that at the high levels of qualities desired by any user, even small improvements in a quality level, can cost disproportionate resources.

For example it took Bell Laboratories several years to move the best levels of availability they could report from 99.9% to 99.98% for computerized telephone switching systems. The difference 0.08% does not seem like a significant number in considering a project deadline. Both the above measures of system availability are 'extremely high state of the art levels', if described in mere words. But that little difference cost Bell Laboratories (or AT&T) about eight years of research and development.

It is obviously vital for management to know exactly what levels their projects are aiming for in relation to the state of the art limits. If they don't have full control over those factors, then they do not have control over meeting deadlines.

An example of the application of the ideas in this chapter on a large project

A company involved in a large (multi-thousand work-years, years of effort, $100 million dollars cost) software project asked me what they could do to avoid overrunning their deadline – a year from then – by more than two years.

Part of my advice was to break the project down, even at this late stage, into evolutionary deliveries. In this case the software critical to the initial and high-volume products to go before the very low volume product software which had been coupled to the same deadline.

Another part of my advice was to use Fagan's inspection method on their work.

A third component was to define the worst case quality levels and performance levels more precisely. They had to differentiate between those software components which needed high quality levels, and those that were not as critical. Most of the volume of the software was not as critical as the central 'real-time' components, and they had failed to make that distinction in their planning! They were quite simply committed to far too high a quality level, too early, for too much of their project product.

The results

After 11 months, in November 1985, one month before the 'impossible deadline,' this group reported to me that their first useful delivery had been operating for two continuous weeks without any problems. There were certainly many reasons for this, not all of which I have depth knowledge. But evolutionary extraction was certainly a key element.

■ 17.4 Summary

The guiding principles for resisting deadline pressure are as follows.

The deadline mirage principle:
Rethink the deadline given to you; it may not be real.

The solution mirage principle:
Rethink the solution handed to you; it may be in the way of on-time delivery.

The other viewpoint principle:
Rethink the problem from other people's point of view; it will help you simplify your problem and convince them to agree with you.

The expert trap principle:
Don't trust the experts blindly; they will cheerfully lead you to disaster. Be sceptical and insist on proof and guarantees.

The all-at-once trap principle:
Remember, nobody needs all of what they asked for by the deadline. They would simply like you to provide the miracle if possible.

The real needs principle:
Don't damage your credibility by bowing to pressure to make impossible promises. Increase your credibility by fighting for solutions which solve the real needs of your bosses and clients.

The ends dictate the means principle:
If the deadline is critical and seems impossible to reach, don't be afraid to change the solution.

The principle of conservation of energy:
If deadlines are critical, make maximum use of existing systems and 'known technology.' Avoid research-into-unknowns during your project.

The evolutionary delivery principle:
Any large project can be broken down into a series of earlier and smaller deliverables. Don't give up, even if you have to change the technical solution to make it happen. Keep your eye on results, not technologies.

The 'don't blame me' principle:
If you succeed using these principles, take the credit. Give your boss and these ideas some credit in a footnote. If you fail, you obviously didn't apply these principles correctly. If you must blame somebody, don't mention my name, mention your boss's. (Management is always at fault.)

■ References and further reading

Fagan, M.E., 1976, 'Design and code inspections to reduce errors in program development,' *IBM Systems Journal*, **15**, 182–211

Gilb, T. and Weinberg, G.M., 1984, *Humanized input: techniques for reliable keyed input*, QED Information Sciences Inc., Wellesley, Mass.

Juran, J.M., (ed.), 1974, *Quality control handbook*, 3rd edn, McGraw-Hill, New York

Radice, R.A. *et al.*, 1985, 'A programming process architecture,' *IBM Systems Journal*, **24**, (2) 79–90

Thayer, T.A. *et al.*, 1978, *Software reliability*, TRW series 2, p. 80, North-Holland, New York

Walston, C.E. and Felix, C.P., 1977, *IBM Systems Journal*, **16**, (1)

18

How to get reliable software systems

The Product

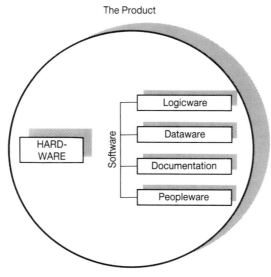

Software is more than logicware

Figure 18.1 Software is more than computer programs. It is all the non-hardware components of a system which need the attention of engineering and management.

■ Introduction

It is the purpose of this chapter to remind us of our sins, at least those I see professionals regularly committing in their workplace. I do not intend to repeat the conventional wisdoms of programming, such as structures, proofs, and high-level languages. Neither do I intend to repeat, at length, ideas which apply, but which I have covered elsewhere.

Briefly: software must be conceived of as something far broader than program code. It must at least include all design specifications, user documentation, data, test cases, codes and human interfaces. It must, in other words, include all 'non-hardware' aspects of the product. Figure 18.1 illustrates this.

Software reliability is not a simple metric such as 'bugs reported per thousand lines of code per month per field used.' It comprises a wide variety of concepts, such as bugs, breakdowns, difficulties in user understanding, unpredictability of result, and much more. Only if we take this broader view of design goals will we arrive at realistic answers on how to get full reliability.

■ 18.1 The architecture of a solution

'Software reliability' depends primarily on the architecture which we select in order to get that reliability. The key issue is to realize that the terms 'software' and 'reliability' have variable definitions. We cannot select an appropriate solution architecture until we have clearly defined our 'software reliability' objectives. But let us assume that we have done so already.

The 'architecture' is simply the high-level answer to the many quality and resource requirements of the system. Software reliability is but one of many such attribute requirements, and it must be satisfied in competition with all other requirements. So we cannot select an appropriate architecture until we have a fuller knowledge of all competing attribute objectives.

Let us ignore all the other objectives of a system and concentrate on the reliability objectives.

■ 18.2 The design process

Finding our way towards the appropriate software reliability solutions is not a simple process. The built-in complexity of large systems, many other conflicting objectives, and the fact that we are constantly moving towards the unknown, requires a well-designed and well-organized design process. Unfortunately it is usually the case that

1. The project objectives are not set clearly.
2. The experience base of design solutions is not well organized or available.
3. There seems to be very little professional knowledge of advanced reliability methods, even those which have been public for 10 years.
4. There is far too little quality control of any kind in the process, such as design inspections, thorough testing, correlation checking, and software configuration management.

These issues will now be explored in greater detail.

■ 18.3 Design by objectives: goal-directed reliability design

First we must establish what the attributes of our future system should be. This process has already been described at length earlier in this book, so let me explain the point by providing an example:

18.3.1 The European telecommunications system case

One of my clients recently illustrated the professional difficulties of this subject. It was in connection with a more than 1000 work-year telecommunications software project.

I asked the project manager if he could show me measurable availability objectives for the project, since another manager had told me that this was a critical objective of the project. He replied by quoting the company's official reliability objectives (no more than 0.5 bugs per 1000 lines of code per year reported).

In fact I had already had a discussion with his peers about this reliability measure. I had suggested that since they were producing a real-time system, they should have as their primary reliability measure something more like mean time to fail (MTTF).

They had agreed, in principle, but pointed out that 'bugs reported . . .' was easier to measure. I had reminded them that ease of measurement was less important than getting the product right for the customer environment. They had accepted this and had started to move in the MTTF direction. The project manager I was now meeting with had not been a party to those discussions! Now I had proof that even the senior project management was using this 'easy' measure!

The project manager then brought in to our meeting his specialist on setting project objectives. The specialist, when the question of reliability objectives was put, prompted his boss; 'you know, availability – like up-time'. The manager enthusiastically responded by grabbing a presentation page, with the list of features planned for the system, which were intended to influence up time. This included items like logging, automatic recovery, degraded-mode processing, i.e. it had the proposed solutions to the availability objective, but it did not mention any objective at all.

In fact, they then admitted they had no formal availability objective! The entire project had all been working on the assumption that the bug report rate covered the whole issue. But, of course it doesn't. There could be a million bugs reported without any customer systems failing to operate. There could be no bug reports, and customers' systems could be failing every second.

This case illustrates the professional problem. These people were mature professionals trying to do a serious job of software engineering. But, they suffered from the same problem that most software engineers suffer from today. They didn't know very much about software engineering.

■ 18.4 The problem with 'reliability'

The word 'reliability' can and does mean different things to different people. We can never use a mere word as an engineering objective. Yet our colleagues try to do it all the time.

We have to define the concept, or refer to a standard definition (of which there are too few in the software business). We have tried to build up reference handbooks like Gilb (1976a), Boehm (1978), Gilb (1983a), ICL (1985) from which software engineers could get some guidance in defining terms.

This is done at a general level. For example the basic breakdown for the software quality availability in Software Engineering Templates (see Chapter 19) is:

- reliability
- maintainability
- integrity

The quality 'availability' is a function of 'reliability', 'maintainability' and 'integrity.' This is based on the well-known systems engineering relationship (Ireson, 1966) of availability, reliability and maintainability. These concepts and their measures (% up time, MTTF or MTBF, and MTTR respectively) are classic, and all *software* engineers should get as firm an understanding of them as their hardware brethren are expected to have. See Figure 18.2.

From this relationship we learn that what many people loosely refer to as reliability is really only a function of reliability. They are really referring to availability. This was my client's problem in the case above.

The inability to distinguish between availability and reliability, for a software engineer, is roughly the same as the inability for an electronics engineer to distinguish between volts and amperes. If it is really system availability we want, then it is critical that we say so. Certainly for on-line and real-time systems, it is usually availability which is most critical.

If it is availability we are after, then the 'A = function (R,M,I)' law – shall we call it the availability law – gives us a clearer picture of our design options.

We can, for example, concentrate all our design effort on improving maintainability (Gilb, 1979) of the system (i.e. reduce the mean time to repair the reliability fault which has caused the system to fall from the available state). In other words, we can choose, as design engineers, to turn our attention away from the problem of preventing errors from occurring (the reliability syndrome). Instead, or in

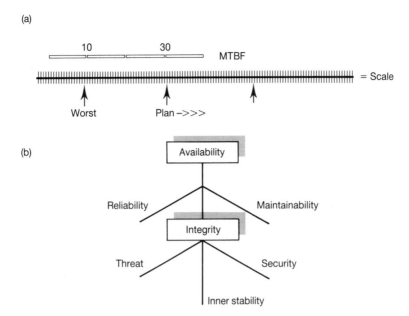

Figure 18.2 Setting the reliability levels: (a) software reliability can be measured like hardware reliability – for example, on a mean time between failure (MTBF) scale; (b) reliability, in the broadest sense, covers a wide range of terms associated with the proper operation of a system, such as those shown here in a related hierarchy.

addition, we can concentrate on the problem of fixing the result of the error, and perhaps the cause, so that the system is once more available.

If a system failed every second, but was repaired in one millionth of a second, we would consider it very 'reliable.' If a system failed every hour, but each such failure took at least six hours to be repaired, everybody would consider that a most unreliable system. We must seriously consider the possibility that our reliability problem is really a maintainability design problem.

Further, imagine a system which has failed in logicware, and perhaps destroyed part of a database as a result. Then, even when the faulty code has been logically corrected, the system is not yet fully available to the user. The trustworthiness of the database is changed. The integrity (wholeness) of the system is in question. Some data may be trustworthy, other parts of it are not. How are we to know what data and which results are to be trusted? If you know something is wrong somewhere, but you do not know where, then the safe course is to trust nothing. In such a case the system is unavailable to the user for practical purposes. This should remind us to recognise that mere technical availability of hardware and software is not sufficient. We must know something about the integrity (Gilb, 1976a) of the system. (See Chapter 19.) This last point shows how essential it is that the wider definition of software, explained earlier, is adopted.

■ 18.5 Tailoring the reliability objectives

Let me return to the same case study (a 1000 work-year tele-communications software project) described above. They were also facing problems of delivering on time. It was clear to me, and they later agreed, that they were making a fundamental mistake in having one set of overall reliability objectives for the entire gigantic software package. These objectives were set at the highest level needed for the most critical pieces of the software. It was clear that not everything being developed was so critical. For example the customer-site system-generation package would only be run once, in batch mode, on each customer site. I suggested that they review all their software and produce software metrics objectives. They should tailor objectives to the real needs of the individual components. This would save them the effort of building and testing components to levels of quality which were higher than they really needed. Even slightly higher levels can be extremely costly. Bell Laboratories reported that it took eight years to move software availability on one system from 99.9% (about 1972) to 99.98% (about 1980).

■ 18.6 How wide is the net? Human and data aspects

We have some strong thinking-habits about software reliability. For many of our fellow software professionals the center of the universe is the program. It has never entered their heads that the data storage aspects or the data input and output aspects at the human interface are also a vital sub-component of their system 'software reliability.' However they are certainly not hardware aspects either!

It is for this reason that I prefer to divide software into sub-classes of software like logicware, dataware, paperware and peopleware.

Clearly we must care about the end result in the hands of our customers. We must also specify the individual quality design requirements for each sub-system over which we can exercise some control in pursuit of the final result. There are too many narrowly-trained software engineers who mistakenly feel that their job is done when the logicware is acceptable. But in fact, somebody has to take care of the rest of the non-hardware part of the system. And nobody does! One part of the solution is to develop the 'softect' (the one who practices 'softecture', of course) to worry about these things. Under the softect will be a supporting cast of 'logicware engineer' (old title, software engineer), 'dataware engineer', 'peopleware engineer' (man-machine inteface specialist). Each no doubt supported by even more specialized engineers.

In the meantime, until we do train and organize our work like that, somebody has to make sure the design job is done properly. 'Improperly' means that the final detailed decision is left to the programmer – which seems to be the usual case in industry today.

The two things which may be more important to 'software reliability' (Thayer *et al.*, 1978) than logicware reliability, are dataware (Gilb, 1976b) and peopleware (Gilb and Weinberg, 1986, Damodaran *et al.*, 1980) reliability.

■ 18.7 Setting the levels

When you have decided on the quality concepts you want to deliver, you still have to go through a discipline of quantifying the quality levels you are going for. You have to decide on a measuring scale, and a practical test or tests for measuring your progress in these quality areas. You have to decide on worst-acceptable levels, at various points in time, and you have to decide on your planned ambition levels at various points in time (releases, usually). This discipline is described in Chapter 9 of this book and in Gilb (1981a, b).

■ 18.8 Finding reliability solutions

Let us assume you do learn to apply the discipline of setting your design objectives in a rich language of attribute specification, covering all your soft components, and all aspects of the broadest concept of reliability, as indicated above. You now know what the problem is. Now the really hard work begins: finding solutions.

The first principle of solutions:
There are usually a lot of them. You have to find an appropriate set of solutions to the total (not just for reliability) set of attribute-objectives which you have decided to aim for.

> **The second principle of solutions:**
> It is almost impossible to know exactly what the exact attributes of a specified solution are in advance. But you can know approximately.

One of the main reasons for not being able to calculate the effect of a solution specification in advance, is the fact that the real implementation of the solution specification might be different from what the softect (software architect) had in mind when the specification was made originally. One problem here may be lack of detail. But, another may be intentional or unintentional misinterpretation of the design solution specification by the actual builder.

> **The first defense principle:**
> The first defense is to not expect to get any particular level of attributes until you can measure that you have them.
>
> **The second defense principle:**
> Make it an integrated part of your design process to validate the solution ideas in practice before you promise them to anybody else.

There are many approaches to validating the effect of a design solution. My single favorite validation technique is by means of including such a solution in a very early evolutionary delivery step to the user (see Chapters 7, 13 and 15).

■ 18.9 Softecture

Instead of the term 'architecture' I personally prefer to use the more specialized term (attributed by *Computer Weekly* (UK) to the French) 'infotecture' to emphasize that we are not dealing with arches, but with software. Perhaps 'softecture' is even better. It describes a more specialized branch of infotecture.

Softecture is the design-engineering specification as to how the software quality and resource attribute requirements are to be met. It is the answer as to how we intend to 'get twice the current reliability at half the current cost', for example. I believe that this part of our profession, softecture, is underdeveloped. This is a major reason for our 'reliability problems.' Specifically, we do not train people in this level of design discipline.

■ 18.10 Tagging

Softecture is the set of solutions, perhaps no more than ten, expressed on perhaps a single page, which make or break a system design. They are the concepts which have the greatest influence on everything else. For example:

'L: The dominant programming language will be Smalltalk'

'H: The human interface will be based on Apple Macintosh principles'

'D: All logic and data modules will be delivered with functionally equivalent user-replacable distinct spare parts modules developed independently'

'T: The product will include a user-runnable test set proving all features'

The L,H,D and T prefixes above are 'tags' to help me keep track of these ideas at later stages of my design. A tag is simply a short identifier of an idea. We tag ideas in our design documentation all the time, when we feel the need for a short reference name.

As we move from broader softecture to more detailed software engineering we will begin to pin down the broad ideas into more specific ones. This detail reduces the scope for misinterpretation by the implementors. It also gives the engineer more control over the final results. For example:

T.USERUN: The user shall be able to run test sets, or selected parts of them, by simple on-line commands, at any point while they use that part of the system.

T.ALL-FEAT: Test cases for all features shall be included. They shall be updated at all times. The test cases shall be validated by inspection, including all features and facilities mentioned in any form of user-readable documentation, such as sales brochures, and the on-line help facility. The user shall be able to select, individually or by groups, those features to be tested.

T.TEST: the code shall be exercised on every line of code and data by test cases which cross-reference in the test case listing to those lines. All logical branches shall be exercised at least once. All loops at least twice.

T.PRODUCT: the 'product' to be tested is defined as everything delivered by the project to the customer, or used by anybody else to maintain the system. It includes all code, all documentation, all user instruction, all data, and all test cases (you must implement a way to test that a test-case set is complete: we suggest as a minimum, automated cross-referencing by 'tags').

T.XREF: all test cases must include systematic cross reference via tags or other devices to the parts of the specification they purport to test. This must be in such a format as to enable automated checking of completeness when changes are made by us, customers, or third parties.

This more detailed level of specification is necessary for making sure that you move systematically in the direction of a high level of reliability. At least it gives you something more concrete with which to estimate reliability impact.

■ 18.11 Evaluating the quality of the design

We need some way of telling us how well we are doing at meeting our design ambitions. Waiting until we test, or deliver the system, are two of the most-used approaches to validating a design. But they are both rather late in the process. Repairs to poor design at these stages cost 10 to 100 times as much as if we identify the design errors early. In fact 62% of all errors found in four large systems were later found to have originated before the program code was ever written (Thayer *et al.*, 1978, p. 80). The opportunity to find design errors early does exist.

In one English software requirement inspection effort (see Chapter 21) about 4000 defects were identified in documents which were normally handed over to programmers. We estimated that we were only 30% effective and that there were about 8000 more defects in the documentation which was handed over to coders.

The city bank case

At a London bank the very first trial use of inspection (1986), in a 30-page sample of design and requirements documentation, turned up 68 defects. One of these was classed as 'super-major' by the inspectors. It revealed a major sub-system which had been entirely forgotten. Using the bank's previous review procedures, these defects would have gone undiscovered until they delayed delivery or operation.

There are a variety of methods for finding design errors (not logical bugs, but specification errors which will prevent us from reaching our reliability objectives, and other objectives):

- Impact analysis and impact estimation tables (see Chapter 11)
- Evolutionary delivery (see Chapters 7, 13 and 15)
- Inspection (see Chapters 12 and 21)

■ 18.12 The engineering process

The software engineering process, and I stress that I am not here concerned with the program coding process, is really the softecture process described above, except we are now going to look at it at a more detailed level. The exact border between softecture and software engineering has not been drawn, and perhaps that is not essential.

The softecture process is the area stretching from the users', or marketing-specified, needs down to the software engineering area.

The software engineering area stretches from softecture to, but not including, the crafts area; i.e. it does not include the actual writing of code, test cases and user-documentation.

IBM calls this latter area coding and writing. Perhaps it is time we had a special generic term for the crafts area. I often refer to it as 'bricklaying.' It is the actual construction work of software, as opposed to the design, analysis and planning of that construction. 'Softbricking' springs to mind as a possible term. But I hereby invent 'softcrafting' to express the softcrafts, such as coding of logicware, coding test cases, and writing documentation.

Let me try to clarify the difference between the disciplines.

18.12.1 Softecture

Softecture is high level overall software architecture. It is the direct technical interface with the statement of the needs of the user; and it has the primary responsibility for meeting our priorities within our constraints.

Softects are entirely multi-disciplinary in their pursuit of solutions for meeting the users needs. They deal not only in 'software,' but in

(a) *The infotect*

1. Information systems architect
2. Responsible for all aspects of the system – manual procedures, people, training, documentation, motivation – and, if they are used at all, both hardware and software (including dataware)
3. Goal oriented: the infotect's job is to design a way to reach the stated objectives, measurably.
4. Discipline synchronizer: design and plan control for all speciality engineers and planners

(b) *The software engineer*

1. *Not* a programmer
2. A design engineer, with software as a major discipline and probably at least one speciality discipline
3. The software engineer can translate cost and quality requirements into a set of solutions to reach the planned levels
4. Specialities examples: reliability engineer, maintainability, portability, human factors, quality control, general architecture (infotect)

(c) *The specialist software engineer*

1. There is already a need for a trend towards specialist software engineers
2. The large amount of changing technical knowledge, combined with the competitive pressure to be best, leads to this specialization
3. Examples of specialization

   man-machine dialogue engineer
   reliability design
   portability
   database engineer
   quality control engineer
   maintenance engineering design
   the infotect function
   quantity surveyor (cost estimator)

Figure 18.3 Some new job function concepts: (a) the infotect, or information systems architect; (b) the multi-dimensional software engineer; (c) the specialist engineer (human factors, reliability, maintainability, for example).

things which impact the effect of the software like people, organization, contracts and hardware selection. Softects synchronize specialist software engineers.

18.12.2 Software engineering

This is a generic term for a set of specialized engineering disciplines. These are related to each other only by the fact that they are not traditional hardware engineering disciplines. They include, at their top level, logicware engineering, dataware engineering and peopleware engineering. Each of these has further areas of specialization. These specialities are sufficient to give any single individual a full-time field of expertise. The necessary degree of devotion to detail prevents the engineering specialist from getting time to perform the softecture task, which is that of overall overview of the ultimate user needs.

The specialized software engineer may be involved in designing a database structure, designing a human-interface structure, or designing the motivational aspects of a system. The specialist software engineers will be handed their objectives and constraints by the softect function. The softect will also evaluate and integrate the results of the specialist engineering effort, in terms of the overall design requirements specification.

The software engineers only have a responsibility for meeting the limited design objectives laid down for them by the softect. For example:

Requirement.DB.STRUCT: GIVE ME A DATABASE WHICH WILL ALLOW ME TO FIND ANY RECORD AT RANDOM IN A FILE OF OVER 20 MILLION RECORDS IN ABOUT ONE SECOND, AND WHERE THE ACCESS TIME IS NOT DEGRADED BY MORE THAN 20% EVEN IF THE FILE SIZE DOUBLES. THE SPACE FOR INDEXES, AND OVERHEAD OF CREATING AND MAINTAINING INDEXES, SHALL BE MINIMAL; PREFERABLY ZERO.

18.12.3 The softcrafter

The softcrafter works to the detailed design specifications laid down by the software engineering specialists. These specialist designs must be synchronized and checked by the softect. The response by the data engineer to the requirement above might be, for example:

Solution.DB.STRUCT:THE FILE SHALL BE SEQUENTIAL, ON A DIRECT ACCESS DEVICE. UPDATES MAY BE INSERTED INITIALLY BY PIGGY-BACK INDEPENDENT FILES ON-LINE, AND PERIODICALLY UPDATED BY MEANS OF A POINTER CHAIN TO NEW RECORDS OR RECORD DATA. ACTUAL FILE RE-ORGANIZATION WILL BE INITIATED WHEN A DAILY 100-RECORD SAMPLE OF ACCESS TIMINGS IS GREATER THAN 20% MORE THAN INITIAL SAMPLE TIMINGS AFTER THE LAST RE-ORGANIZATION. NORMAL ACCESS IS TO BE BY AN OPTIMIZED BINARY SEARCH, FOLLOWED BY SEQUENTIAL POINTER CHAIN SEARCH, FOLLOWED BY PIGGY-BACK FILE SEARCH. AVERAGE SEARCH TIME MAY NOT EXCEED ONE SECOND FOR A RANDOMLY CHOSEN RECORD.

Softcrafters will generate program code (logicware), generate test cases (based on a test plan written by a low-level-test-planning engineer), and they will write documentation for users, marketing and for system maintenance. All softcrafters are dependent on specifications provided by software engineers, or by the softect.

The softcrafters only have responsibility for their immediate product meeting the specifications laid down by the input documents given them by engineering.

18.12.4 From a reliability point of view

The softect will set the reliability metrics in co-operation with the user, perhaps according to a contract. For example:

AVAIL.RECORDS:

SCALE: % records available for reading, even when part of database is destroyed and even if parts (up to 50% of the fields) of the record are marked as unreliable after a deep quality-diagnosis, or as a result of earlier processing.

TEST: Deep database diagnosis of 1000 records at random from blocks updated 50% within the last week and 50% within the last year.

WORST ACCEPTABLE CASE (by initial release) = 50%

PLANNED LEVEL (by one year after initial release latest) = 80% or more.

PRESENT CAPABILITY (System Omega) = 0% (entire database down in these conditions)

BEST KNOWN CASE (System Alpha of Manufacturer X) claims 50% levels.

AUTHORITY: MARKETING REQUIREMENT PSD 32:3:16 28 March 1988 (JST).

The software engineer, in this case a dataware specialist engineer, will have to make specifications to meet these requirements; which might, for example, include the following:

DB.FAILSOFT.DIAG: all records will contain a system field which can mark the health status of the record, as diagnosed by the deep database diagnosis programs, any application program, or manual diagnosis.

DB.FAILSOFT.FIELD-ERR-POINTER: all records will contain a system field, which will point to a detailed list of diagnosed error logs, or suspected error logs, relating to fields in the record, or relating to fields in other records which are highly related, but under evaluation for possible errors or inconsistencies. (More specification detail needed at this engineering level.)

The softcrafters will use these specifications, and many more like them, in order to: code their programs to do the things indicated; prepare unit test cases to prove that the design solutions are in place; prepare system test cases to prove that the planned and worst case levels are met; and write systems maintenance documentation for the features, the code, the test cases and the user documentation.

■ 18.13 Cross-checking

Tagging is the natural pre-requisite to cross-checking. Inspection is among other things a cross-checking process.

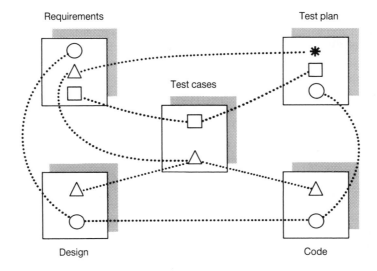

Requirements

Test plan

Test cases

Design

Code

Figure 18.4 Thorough cross-reference checking is necessary for software reliability.

My cross-referencing recommendations for serious software producers are that:

1. All program code contains cross-references to its higher level documentation, and to test cases. All test cases should cross-reference the code and higher level documentation.
2. All user documentation contains references to its test sets and to its higher level documentation (references invisible to the user).
3. Inspectors should be provided with extracted cross-referenced documentation (not merely the cross-reference tag) and test sets for thorough inspection. They should not have to dig manually through piles of documentation.

In short; do full cross-referencing of everything the human eye can see of the system, and use automated help to keep track of it.

■ 18.14 Operational aspects of high reliability

External monitoring

Reliability is not something you test into a system, nor is it something designed in once and for all. A software system is exposed to a constant series of threats to reliability. These come in the form of modifications to the system, new supporting system software versions, and new data combinations among others. The TRW Series book *Software reliability* (Thayer *et al.*, 1978) gives a quite detailed list of error classifications.

This implies plenty of extra supporting logic, and plenty of redundancy in files, tables and databases to allow for error detection and (at an even greater cost in systematic redundancy) error correction (Gilb, 1976b) and (Gilb and Weinberg, 1984). It may imply softecting a series of software interfaces – softfaces, I call them (Gilb, 1983b).

Monitoring data

The quality of data in tables and databases is in a constant state of decay (getting more out of date) and subject to all kinds of corrupting influences (people and logicware mainly). You need to design in a series of things to allow automatic monitoring of the quality of the data.

The attitude still persists that once data has passed some superficial input tests, it is 'good'. Nothing could be further from the truth. The truth is that in any database of a million records there are probably over one hundred thousand elementary data items which are incorrect, out-of date, or suspicious, according to my experience.

To achieve a highly reliable system you must design deep file and database cross-checking logicware as part of the basic architecture. In some cases only the ultimate users can complete the application related details, but producers can give them the tools and a starter system. You must have designed the files with enough systematic redundancy to make diagnosis easy. For example, you will want a record level hash total (Gilb, 1977) at the application program record level to detect accidental tampering with a record.

■ 18.15 Additional technology

Distinct software – spare parts software

In hardware everyone accepts the 'Tandem^{TM}' principle of using dual on-line hardware redundancy to ensure a high level of availability. For years airline reservation systems have duplicated all their on-line files to ensure availability of data in the case of breakdown or corruption. Every software programmer knows the ease with which they can cope with unexpected bugs in a new release of a software package by simply reverting to the last version which was satisfactory.

Yet whenever I mention the idea of distinct software (Gilb, 1977) I am immediately met with scorn and scepticism, even among well-informed colleagues. We are so keen to discuss program structures, that this most powerful of all structures for maintainability and reliability is ignored as if it were not worthy of consideration.

Part of this scepticism is due to lack of understanding of the economics of the method. Most people assume it will double their software production problems, but this is far from the truth. (See the references which show why this is not the case.)

In summary, distinct software is really the least expensive way to get really high availability, reliability and maintainability. We are talking about instant detection of random bugs, before databases are corrupted and users misinformed. We are talking about on-line spare parts for instant repair of the failing software components. We are talking about a very high level of availability using two, three or four versions of the software if necessary (Avizienis, 1984).

Humanized input code design

I still find that most software professionals have little understanding of the potential for increased reliability of the human and data parts of the software system through better design of the man-machine dialogue. In particular they have not been trained to appreciate the potential for automatic human-error detection and automatic correction of the codes and texts which humans key into a system.

I think that most systems are still designed with what I call the 1890 Hollerith Punched Card Mentality. All identifiers are unique numeric codes like those on a bank account or credit card. They are right, or they are wrong. 'Everybody knows' that computers 'need' these codes – otherwise (implied threat) – you'll get garbage. This may have been true in the 1959–68 time frame, at least from an economic point of view. But the dramatic decrease in the cost of computing hardware has made it viable to process a more complex input concept. We can analyze highly variable inputs, with as many errors (to be corrected by the computer) and abbreviations, that a human dialogue would tolerate. For example 'Las Angelos CA' should be decipherable as that big city on the West Coast by a computer with access to a database of names of towns. This can be done with a simple (20 source statements for example) general algorithm, and does not require anticipation of all possible variants.

We have argued the case for these techniques at length in Humanized input (Gilb and Weinberg, 1984) and a summary with illustrations can be found in Data engineering (Part III message design) These techniques deal with the systematic redundancy found in most natural data processing situations, before too many fancy computer codes are thrown in.

We must not stoop to the 'garbage in garbage out' excuse for poor computer output results. We must not continue to shift the blame for poor reliability to the system user when we, by our own software engineering and softecture efforts are, in reality, in control of the results.

■ References and further reading

Avizienis, Algirdas, 1984, 'Design diversity: an approach to fault tolerance of design faults,' *Proc. National Computer Conference*, AFIPS Press, **53**, pp. 163–171

Boehm, B.W. *et al.*, 1978, *Characteristics of software quality*, North-Holland, New York

Damodaran, L. *et al.*, 1980, *Designing systems for people*, National Computing Centre Publications, Manchester, UK

Gilb, T., 1976a, *Software metrics*, Winthrop, (out of print)

Gilb, T., 1976b, *Data engineering*, Studentlitteratur, Lund, Sweden, (out of print)

Gilb, T., 1977, 'Distinct software: a redundancy technology for reliable software,' in *Infotech State of the Art Report on Software Reliability*, Pergamon Infotech, Maidenhead, UK

Gilb, T., 1979, 'Structured design methods for maintainability,' in *Infotech State of the Art Report on Structured Software Development*, Pergamon Infotech, Maidenhead, UK

Gilb, T., 1981, 'System attribute specification: a cornerstone of software engineering,' *ACM Software Eng. Notes*, July, pp. 78–79

Gilb, T., 1983, 'Softfaces' report. Available from S. Finzi, 14a Junction Road, London W5 4XL

Gilb, T., 1984, 'Maintaining Software Systems' *Data processing*, **26**, (5), 19–22, June, Butterworths, UK

Gilb, T., 1985, Evolutionary delivery vs the waterfall model, *ACM Software Eng. Notes*, July

Gilb, T., and Weinberg, G.M., 1984, *Humanized input: techniques for reliable keyed input*, QED Information Sciences Inc., Wellesley, Mass.

ICL, 1985, *Introduction to quality metrics*, Issue 1, May, ICL, Putney, UK

Ireson, (ed.), 1966, *Reliability handbook*, McGraw-Hill, New York

Thayer, T.A., *et al.*, 1978, *Software reliability*, TRW series, North-Holland, New York

19

Software engineering templates

■ Introduction

These templates are intended as general guidelines for specification of system attributes. They also define the terminology for attributes used in this book, except in cases where a specific different definition is given.

You will invariably find it necessary and desirable to invent extensions to these ideas. Do so with a good conscience. A general set of templates can never be as complete and as specific as you will need them to be in order to define a particular project's needs unambiguously, and in a manner which the client understands. It is politically important that you adopt the terminology with which your clients feel most comfortable.

The templates give an initial set of frequently useful definitions and relationships. They give a stable and familiar base from which to work. I expect many readers will want to adopt the contents of this chapter as a starting point for developing an in-house terminology of attributes.

When the need for modification or extension occurs, you will have a place to do it in (an in-house version of this chapter) so that you can share the development with your colleagues.

■ 19.1 Text format templates for attribute specification

The text format is a 'language' which can be used to describe systems attributes reasonably unambiguously. This will usually be for purposes of stating requirements specifications. But it could also be used for contracts, for system analysis documentation or for describing expected attributes in a software engineering handbook.

This format has the advantage of being easy to deal with on word processors and typewriters. It also allows more detail than the tabular overview format which illustrates some of the earlier chapters (for example Chapter 9).

I find these two formats useful for different audiences. The tabular one-page format is useful for presenting ideas at meetings. The text format is necessary as a day-to-day working tool for detailed unambiguous presentation. Many readers will prefer to use a colon symbol instead of the equal sign I have used (date: 860828). Feel free to improve upon whatever is here, by experimenting, until you feel good about both the format and the wording.

GENERAL HEADING INFORMATION

date =
author =
system =
subsystem =
approved by =

ATTRIBUTE SPECIFICATION FORMAT TEMPLATE
{Tag of attribute}:

SCALE(optional qualifier) = {the scale of measure specification}
The qualifier may be any set of conditions which must hold true for this specification to apply. For example '(after March 1999, component X only)'.

DATE(optional qualifier) = {the date or event which the other specifications apply to, when no qualifier is specified} optional

TEST(optional qualifier) = {a practical test or measuring tool which must be used to determine whether we are within planned and worst limits}

WORST(optional qualifier) = {worst acceptable limit on the scale, worse than this is defined as total system failure, no matter how good other attributes are}

PLAN(optional qualifier) = {the level on the SCALE expected by the DATE}

RECORD(optional qualifier) = {engineering limit, state of the art limit, best ever, but not an expected requirement in this system}

NOW(optional qualifier) = {some presently existing system for comparison with the planned and worst case levels. Not a requirement.}

SEE(optional qualifier) = {reference to more detail or other related documents}

SOURCE(optional qualifier) = {the authority for the specification(s)}

Table 19.1 illustrates one way the text format attribute language could be applied.

Table 19.1 Format example.

Maintainability:

SCALE = minutes to do simplest repair to software using templates in Section 19.2.2

DATE(initial delivery to customers) = January next year

TEST(unit) = at least ten consecutive repair attempts to be done within worst case level for each module

TEST(system) = at least 50 random, representative system level bugs to be inserted and then repaired within planned level requirement

WORST(by initial release DATE) = 10 minutes

PLAN(by initial release DATE) = 5 minutes

PLAN(by 3 years after initial release DATE, for on-line modules only) = 2 minutes

RECORD(lab experiment TR 23.3, 1989) = 10 seconds average

NOW(old system, last year average) = 30 minutes

SEE(marketing strategy, Part 2.3.12 Jan 31st) = input to this requirement

SOURCE(marketing requirement) = MRS Jan 28th 198x, JCP

■ 19.2 Attribute structures: names and reference numbers

The second part of this chapter will define a hierarchy of system attributes which are commonly of interest in software and related systems engineering. Our purpose is to identify terms, give a rough definition, and to show relationships between the ideas. The third part will suggest some measuring scales.

Attributes are either measures of system quality, or measures of the resources needed to build and maintain a system. Attributes can vary between certain limits and the system will still be acceptable to the user.

The primary objective of software engineering is to identify the critical attributes, and those limits for each critical attribute between which the system is acceptable. These attributes apply to logicware, dataware, documentation, interface and other software sub-ideas. They also apply to the organizations and hardware environments in which the software works. This is both useful and necessary if software engineering is to be a true subset of system engineering.

To help us to do this, it is an advantage to have a fairly complete checklist of interesting attributes (see Figure 19.1). It is also useful to have a clear concept of how they are related to each other, and how they can be exploded or imploded to form other attribute concepts. The

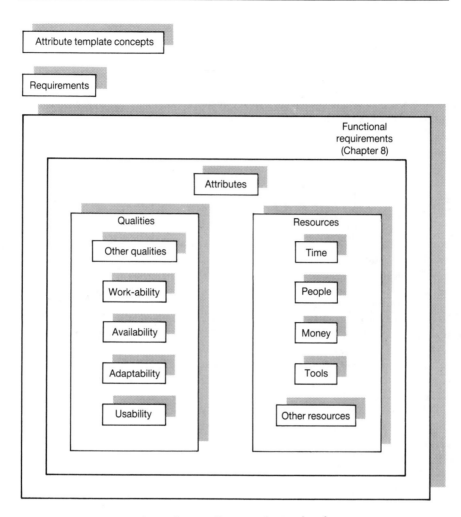

Figure 19.1 Overview of template attributes at the top level.

terms and definitions are the best I can suggest. I hope they are consistent and useful. If you prefer other terms and definitions, be sure you define your terms clearly to others.

19.2.1 Work-ability

This measures the raw ability of the system to perform work. The term 'performance' might have been used, except that performance, in the

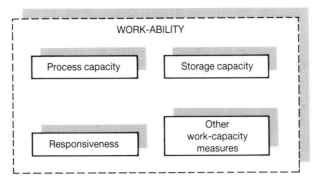

Figure 19.2 Sub-attributes of work-ability.

broadest sense of the word, includes considerations of all other attributes, such as, for example, availability and usability.

Work-ability is composed of the sub-attributes shown in Figure 19.2.

Process capacity is a measure of the ability to process units of work in units of time. For example an automated paint warehouse system was guaranteed to be able to process 210 paint-can storage pallets in and out of the system per hour.

Responsiveness is a measure of reaction to a single event. For example, 'the maximum time needed to access a single paint storage pallet at random.'

Storage capacity is the capacity of a part of the system to store units of any defined thing (pallets, bytes, lines of code, pictures, sounds, etc.).

19.2.2 Availability

Availability is the measure of how much a system is usefully (not merely technically) available to perform the work which it was designed to do.

Availability is determined by the set of ideas shown in Figure 19.3.

Reliability is the measure of the degree to which the system does what it is intended to do, as opposed to something else (like producing a wrong answer – or producing nothing). Definitions of reliability will therefore vary according to the definition of what the system is supposed to do. In general, a system which is not doing what it is supposed to be doing (an unreliable state) is 'unavailable' for its intended work tasks. See a more detailed breakdown of reliability below.

Figure 19.3 Sub-attributes of availability.

Maintainability is the measure of how quickly an unreliable system can be brought to a reliable state. In general this will need to cover not only the repair of the fault, but recovery from the effects of the fault, so that the system is ready again to do its intended work.

From a technical system design point of view, there may be little or no difference between maintainability and improvability. The difference is mainly the subjective one of deciding what is a fault needing maintenance, and what will be considered 'faulty' in the future if we do not improve it. (See the detailed breakdown which follows.)

Integrity is the measure of trustworthiness of the system. Is it in the state it is supposed to be in? Has it been altered by persons or by accident, or has it been tapped for information (which is now less secret than supposed)? Integrity is the result of the various built-in security techniques used to detect or thwart those attacks. A system which does not have its full intended integrity may be 'available' in the technical sense, but the intended results may not be available, due to reduced integrity. If you've got some garbage in there, you risk delivering that garbage, unless your design captures the garbage before it gets out.

Reliability

Reliability is a very general measure, because it can take so many different definitions, depending on what we decide to define as the 'right thing.' Reliability is simply 'doing what the system ought to', and we must have a clear definition of what the 'ought to' is, before trying to measure reliability. Software reliability, one critical part of system reliability, can fruitfully be specified and controlled for the different software sub-systems, principally:

Logicware fidelity is the measure of accuracy with which a given algorithm has been implemented for a specific software and hardware environment. Does it work as intended? For example are mathematical functions within real number tolerances? Does it work correctly to specification? Verification?

Logicware veracity is the measure of the adequacy with which the implemented algorithm relates to the real world with which it must interact. Does it do what we would want it to do, when we find out about how the 'real world' really is now? Does it solve the user's problem? Validation.

Logicware viability is the measure of how well the logicware meets design constraints in areas such as speed of execution, space requirements, security.

Dataware is the 'passive' data in the system (inputs, outputs, files and the stored programs, as opposed to the 'active' algorithm: the program being executed). A program can be viewed in both lights, since it is stored as data and may consume critical resources – or may be actively interpreted as a logical process.

Dataware fidelity (or *precision*) is the measure of the accuracy of representation of an idea within a particular software and hardware environment. Does the data representation lose any information which we would want to keep (because of abbreviation, compression, batch sums)?

Dataware veracity is the measure of the adequacy with which data represents the 'real world' to which it is supposed to refer. Does it give a true picture or a misleading one?

Dataware viability is the measure of how well the data meets design constraints in areas such as retrieval timing, storage space and security – for example.

(These concepts were developed from Dickson, *Proc. 1972 Rel. & Maint. Symp. IEEE.*)

Maintainability

Maintainability can be exploded into several typical sub-attributes, not all of which are useful in every case (Figure 19.4). This explosion is useful when the expected maintenance costs are high, and rapid and sure maintenance is important. This explosion will allow designers to focus on the several very different components of maintenance, and reduce the danger of lack of sufficient design for any one of them.

The term maintainability is conventionally reserved for the process of fault handling, rather than for improvement of a faultless system.

Problem recognition is the time needed for people or machines to recognize the existence of a fault in the system which needs repair.

Administrative delay is the time required after the problem is recognized, until someone or something (such as a 'distinct software' module) is activated to the task of correcting the fault.

Tool collection is the time needed to collect the documentation, analyze the programs, the tests sets, the result sets, and the files which

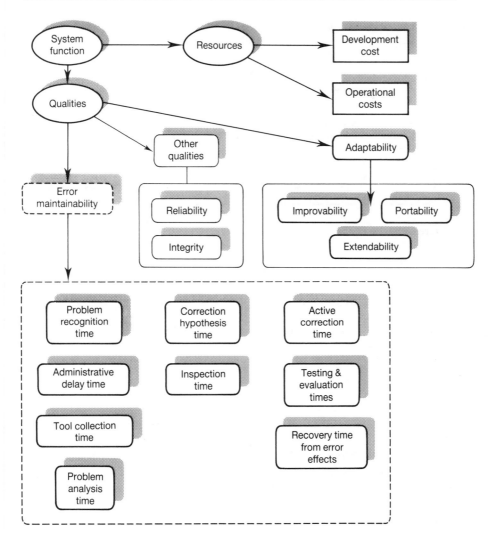

Figure 19.4 The maintenance attribute tree.

are necessary for analyzing the nature of the fault.

Problem analysis is the time needed to trace the symptoms of the fault to its source.

Correction hypothesis formation is the time needed to translate an understanding of the current cause of the fault into a suitable correction action idea.

Inspection is the time needed to inspect (using Fagan's method) the

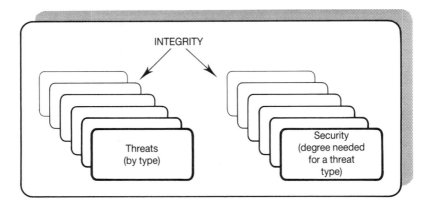

Figure 19.5 The integrity relationships.

correction hypothesis for consistency and correctness both with regard to the local change, and with regard to the total system.

Active correction is the time needed to carry out the inspected correction hypothesis correctly.

Test is the time needed to run adequate test cases to validate that the change is working as expected, and that there are no undesired side-effects as a result of it.

Test evaluation is the time needed to evaluate the results of the tests conducted.

Recovery is the time needed to recover from the fault and restore files. Note: This definition (problem recognition through to recovery) is intended to force technologists to define 'maintainability' from a user point of view, rather than a repair technicians point of view. Software engineering management should ensure that this wider view is adopted.

Integrity

The integrity of a system is a measure of its ability to survive from attacks by threats to its integrity, by means of suitable security design technology. Integrity is an objective of the system user. It is a cousin to the idea of availability. Threats are potential attacks on the system integrity (both accidental and intentional). Security techniques are devices for counteracting the attacks. See Figure 19.5.

Threat (of attack on system integrity) is measured by an estimated probability of an attack of a specific type occurring within a time frame.

A threat potential can be analyzed and estimated, however great the uncertainty. It can also be controlled by the system designer, and may well be set up as a design objective. A threat can be defined to cover any 'error' producing type of attack, from humans (intentional or not) or machines (hard or soft).

Security (the potential to counteract threats on system integrity) can be measured as the probability of counteracting attacks of a particular type.

In the most general view of the system, both maintainability, recovery and even improvability represent ideas of 'security' (of keeping the system in the state you want it to be in).

The types of attacks which must be considered by the software engineer include: attacks on logicware (corruption, stealing, disabling), attacks on dataware (corruption, stealing knowledge of, eliminating), attacks on paperware (documentation, instructions, training).

In addition, the software engineer must make sure that the related aspects of people and machines and premises are handled by the system engineering level of design. Software cannot exist or be secured in a vacuum apart from the hard factors within which it operates.

Integrity is arithmetically related to threat frequency and security effectiveness

Note the mathematical relationship between these three ideas; integrity is a function of the threat potential and the security strength. Knowing two of these factors allows you to calculate the third. But to be realistic you must work it out on a threat type by type basis. The combined set of type calculations gives you total integrity, security or threat potential for the system.

A simple formula is:

INTEGRITY = Σ [1 $-$ Threat $\times$ (1 $-$ Security)]

19.2.3 Adaptability (detail)

Adaptability (Figure 19.6) is the measure of a system's ability to change. Since any system can somehow be changed to almost any other state, given enough resources, the primary concern is with the need for resources (such as time, people, money and tools) needed to make a certain degree and type of change. So, adaptability is a measure of a system's ability to change 'efficiently.'

Improvability

Improvability is a measure of the efficiency of making minor adaptions, changes and improvements to the system. It is almost identical to the concept of maintainability of faults (Section 19.2.2), except for the fact that there is no 'fault' (yet, or at this time) with the system, only the

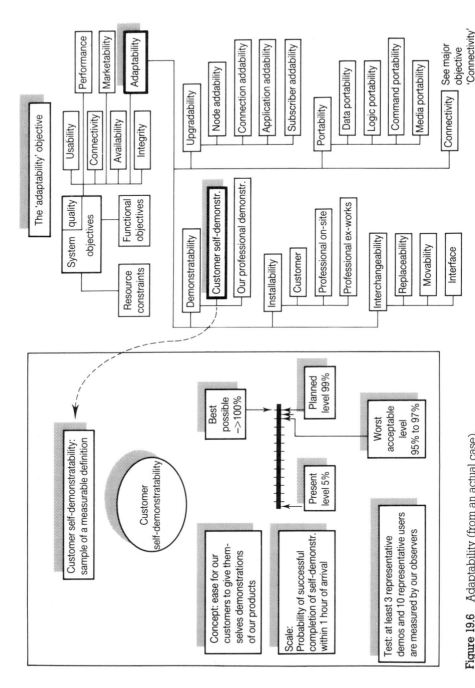

Figure 19.6 Adaptability (from an actual case).

desire to improve. The basic measure is time to change the state of the system, which depends on a clear definition of the degree of change to be effected (for example one instruction, or 2000 records, or 100 pages of documentation, or a combination of these). Improvability, like its sister maintainability, can be exploded into about ten interesting sub-measures of the change process. See Section 19.3.3 for a more detailed breakdown. The only difference is that there is a reaction to future needs rather than past faults. For this reason we refer you to the definitions given in the corresponding maintainability steps, but note that the concept of a fault or problem needing 'correction' is exchanged with the concept of a 'change need', and instead of recovery, there is no fault to recover from.

We recognize the need for changes in documentation for both keepers of the software, operations, users, and corresponding retraining.

Extendability

Extendability is a measure of the ease of adding new factors to an existing system. In order to define it you will need to consider the degree of extension (functions, lines of logic, data) the cost for the extension in resources invested, and the impact (side-effects) of the extension on any critical properties of the system, such as performance, security, reliability, running cost.

Portability

Portability is a measure of the ease of moving a system from one environment to another. To define it you must consider the size of what is being transported, the original and the target environments ('compatability'), the means of transport (hand conversion, automated conversion), the resources needed to transport the system, and the attributes of the new system compared to the old (side-effects).

19.2.4 Usability (detail)

Usability is the measure of how well people are going to be able and be motivated to use the system practically.

Entry requirement

This is the measure of the human requirements for success in learning and handling the system. This might be expressed in terms of physical

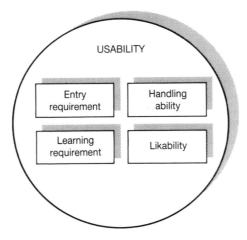

Figure 19.7   Usability.

requirements (vision, hearing and manual dexterity) and in terms of intelligence, educational, cultural or vocational requirements.

Learning requirement

This is the measure of resources, principally time, needed to attain some measurable level of ability with the system – for example passing a test. The tests could be set at several levels of proficiency – giving several learning requirements. Further, the learning requirement would be expected to vary with the entry level capability of the subject, and other factors (teacher, motivation).

Handling ability

The measure of net productivity over time, when error time is deducted. The handling ability can be specified differently for different classes of entry level people, who have undertaken defined learning processes.

Likability

The measure of how well people like to use the system. This could be measured by opinion surveys, for example. It might also be measured by turnover rates of employees. If people are negative in their attitude towards the system, many critical factors might be threatened, even if

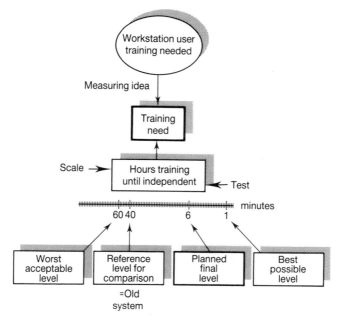

Figure 19.8 Specification of a usability objective.

productivity is high. The most dramatic examples occur when trade unions refuse to accept systems (such as newspaper type-setting done by reporters).

19.2.5 The resource attributes

Resource attributes are measures of the costs of existence (development, use and maintenance) of a system. We are primarily concerned with critically limited resources here, because they must be identified so that we can design appropriate solutions within this limit. We also need to tell the designers which resources are most scarce in this particular case. The worst case levels, and planned levels of each resource will tell the designer what to aim for. Resource requirements are a 'budget' concept. Resources belong to the category 'attribute' because they quantitatively describe dimensions of function.

Time

This measure covers two aspects of development: calendar time elapsed to build a system (when will it be delivered?), and working days needed to accomplish a task.

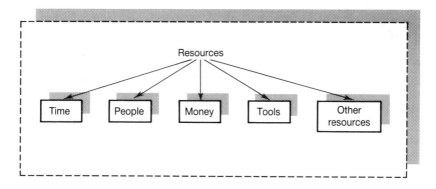

Figure 19.9 Limited resources.

Practical hint: *Don't be too concerned with defining the attribute category itself. The important thing is to get a specification somewhere of all critical attributes.*

People

This measure covers all people-related resources such as 'work years' to construct a system, and people needed to staff or operate it.

These serve as limiting objectives or 'constraints' when designing a system, and when controlling its resource consumption in operation. If a goal was set that a system would only require one human clerk operator per terminal per day, and in practice it required two (because of legal regulations concerning continuous hours sitting on a terminal) then there is some evidence of a design error – and perhaps the need for redesign of the system.

If fifteen people are needed to produce a system and only five are available, the development is resource limited.

Money

This covers all types of monetary costs of building and maintaining the system. 'Maintenance cost' would fit in here, even though maintainability is also specified as a quality. Money is a budget limit. Maintainability is a quality which has some influence on whether we stay within the budget limit.

Tools

This could also have been called 'plant.' It covers all physical resources which can somehow be limited, and can be critical to our success. It includes computer capacity (use of any sort of computer and communications hardware), office space, air conditioning capacity, and the rights to use software packages and designs.

Other resources

There are other possible resource categories. For example marketing costs has been used here. Others are goodwill, reputation, and image. These can be measured and are often paid for handsomely. Certainly they could form part of software product objectives.

■ 19.3 Measures

Icon is $-|-|-$. Keyword is SCALE = [some measures].

Here are some examples of measures for the attribute ideas. This can only be a sample checklist of possible measures, since a complete list would be tediously long. The main objective should be that you select a measure which represents what you and your clients feel are interesting, useful and practical. If in doubt, select several measuring tests for use at one time. This does little harm and may give insight or at least help settle an argument about which measure is best.

19.3.1 Work-ability measures

Process capacity

General: units per time.

Examples:

- transactions per second;
- records per minute;
- bytes per line;
- bits per node per second.

Responsiveness

General: action per time (under stated conditions).

Examples:

- time from question understood by operator until answer displayed on screen (no load);
- response time (when worst case activity load exists);
- time until beginning of execution of a logic page not in primary memory;
- time from telephone contact established with client until satisfactory delivery of answer completed (assuming no load on central processing facility or lines).

Storage capacity

General: units stored per container.

Examples:

- bytes per record;
- characters compressed per 1000 bytes of storage;
- characters per line (bold double size format);
- source instructions;
- color pictures per diskette;
- sound syllables per 1000 bytes.

19.3.2 Availability measures

General: probability that a system is operating satisfactorily at any point in time, when used under stated conditions:

- availability (general measure) = [time actually available] / [time that should have been available];
- intrinsic availability = [operate time] / [operate time + active down time]
  - or   = mean time to maintenance (MTTM) / [MTTM + mean active down time];
- [operational availability] = [operational time] / [operate time + off time − total down time]
  (total down time = active down time + down time when system was not actually needed);
- [use availability] = [operate time + off time] / [operate time + off time + total down time].

Examples:

- % time database contents actually available to requests during office day per month;

- % time correct and up-to-minute updated material available immediately to requestor;
- % time a remote and foreign node is available;
- % time a printer on same office floor as user is available to begin printing within one minute;
- % time closest physical terminal is available for use (not down or used by another);
- time which the up-to-last-night maintenance changes to logic-ware are available from local storage, offline to main processor center.

Reliability (scales): mean time between failures (MTBF). No examples.

Maintainability (scales)

General: The most conventional measure of maintainability 'mean time to repair' (MTTR) applies to software also.

It can also be expressed as: the probability that when maintenance action is initiated under stated conditions, a failed system will be restored to operable condition within a specified time.

An even richer concept of maintainability is given by the explosion which divides the maintenance process into the main phases between existence of a fault, and complete elimination of the fault and its effects (in Section 19.2.2).

Examples:

- time (minutes, usually) needed to repair nine of ten simple (artificial but typical) bugs;
- average time (minutes) needed to repair a destroyed byte in a file;
- minutes needed to identify the cause of an artificially inserted 'test' bug (this is only part of maintenance, but it is critical, and is a cheaper test);
- hours needed, on average, to complete all ten maintenance phases for a set of at least ten real faults in the system;
- time in minutes needed to restore the database to a correct state after being hit by 100 artificial errors in random records and fields;
- seconds needed to find and execute an alternative distinct software module without the fault found in the normal module ('spare parts software repair technique').

Integrity measures

General: Integrity is the measure of 'wholeness' of the system, of freedom from any sorts of attacks from intentional sources (saboteurs,

Subject: Software quality ('Maintainability')

Attribute specification

Definition Name :Quality	Scale	Test	Worst limit	Plan	Best yet (Record)	Now (Our old system)	Reference
.0 Problem recognition	time	1st occur: to find	24 hr	60 min	1 min	hours to weeks	user view !
.1 Administrative delay	time	assign fix: to begin	1 week	60 min	5 min	days to months	for high priority bugs
.2 Tool collection	time	maint. log of Act.PR	1 hr	10 min	2 min	30 to 100 mins	all doc. & tests
.3 Problem analysis	90% found time	maint. log of Act = AN	50 min	5 – >9 min	30 sec	hours to days	artificial bug test
.4 Correction hypothesis	time	maint. log of Act = CO	1 hr	5 ? min	<1 min	no data	
.5 Correct it activity	time	maint. log of Act = SP	3 hr	30 min	<1 min ?	no data	
.6 Change inspection	time	maint. log of Act = IN	same week	same day	same hour	over 1 wk	high priority only
.7 System test	time	maint. log of Act = ST	8 hr	within 24 hr	<30 min	hours	dedicated test hardware
.8 Recovery	time	oper. log of Recov.	24 hr	2 hr	<1 min	over 24 hr	worst possible destruction
.9							

Figure 19.10 Maintainability measures. The numbers are indicative only. They are not general recommendations.

thieves) or non-malicious sources (failing hardware, accidental physical file destruction by the operator and software errors).

A 100% integrity implies that no attacks have succeeded.

Examples:

- the degree to which all software (data and programs) is both untouched by any sort of corruption, removal, change or addition and is not penetrated by unauthorized people, for any purpose, such as for getting 'know-how';
- the time needed to recover from a double bomb attack at two different program and data storage sites, if carried out by knowledgeable saboteurs;
- the percentage of a database which is probably 'clean' based on sampling deep diagnosis (auditing in depth) of at least 1000 records. See Jim Grimes' article in *EDPACS Journal*, 1/77 on deep Bell Laboratories database diagnosis.

19.3.3 Adaptability measures

General: The ability of a system to be changed without uncontrolled side-effects.

Comment: Changing a system is not the issue by itself. We must consider the costs (time, people, money) of making the change, and the potential effects on quality attributes, such as performance, maintenance cost, reliability, security and other critical attributes.

Examples:
Up to 10% of lines of code shall be changed yearly without having more than 5% negative impact on any controlled and measured attribute, such as work capacity, reliability or maintainability.

Improvability measures

General: Time needed to complete minor changes.

Comment: The time might be expressed 'per line of code or unit of data.' The measure could be further defined as applying to the ten-step process above. (Changes need recognition time to re-documentation and training.) If you want to get very serious about this measure, you should specify separate time measures for each of the ten sub-processes.

Examples:

- minutes needed to effect the complete ten-step improvability process, for a test set of ten changes, of one to five lines each.
- minutes from problem analysis through test evaluation for sample changes requiring at least ten lines of code change.

Extendability measures

General: The ease of adding a certain degree of new function to an existing system without degrading critical attributes.

Examples:

- ability to add 10% additional logicware, while retaining all other controlled and critical attributes within 5% of former values;
- number of additions which can be added to old system without any change to that system or its documentation, except the actual addition (the ability to 'plug in' additions);
- ability to add up to 200% new data to the database yearly, without more than proportional degradation in performance, and no degradation in reliability, availability, security or any other critical attribute below planned levels.

Portability measures

General: The effort needed to move the system from its home environment to a specific or general-type target environment using method.

The effort should be expressed as percentage of the effort needed to construct an identical system from scratch in the target environment (complimentary %). For example if conversion is only 1% of total rebuilding effort, then there is 99% (100–1%) portability. It is also vital that the measure be made with regard to possible change in other critical attributes, normally that these attributes are not degraded critically.

Examples:

- the COBOL programs and all associated command languages, files and documentation, shall be at least 98% portable to any standard (define more specifically) COBOL environment which we choose to use within the next ten years, without performance, reliability or maintainability degradation.
- the files and their associated database handling/inquiry software

must be at least 99% automatically portable to any hardware or software environment supported by (XXX), without any significant (5%) degradation of other attributes, within three months notice. The penalty for non-delivery is the cost of completing the conversion to this standard at a price related to the 1% change cost.

19.3.4 Usability measures

General: The degree to which the system can be used productively by the intended group of people.

Examples:

- time needed to get a new person, of a given educational standard, up to minimum net productivity levels;
- on the job training necessary to qualify as an operator;
- minutes needed alone with system, for self-instruction, to result in a useful result for a novice user.

Entry requirement measure

General: The qualification level required before a person can begin to learn to use the system.

Examples:

- ability to read English or Spanish (for a New York cash dispenser);
- typist experience at n words per minute, and terminal hardware course completed satisfactorily (for learning a word processing package);
- completed secondary education with at least two foreign languages.

Learning requirement measure

General: The time needed to learn to use a system until a measure of proficiency is proven or demonstrated.

Examples:

- hours classroom training on average before able to pass operator's test;
- minutes in shop before prospective software buyer can take over further learning alone, without aid of shop assistant;

- days of on-the-job experience and training with instructor before qualified to operate the system alone for any test.

Handling ability measure

General: Net productivity measured by some tasks, after training successfully completed, with proper entry requirement, perhaps after a period of practical experience.

Examples:

- correct pages of text per hour from nine machine-written and hand-edited manuscripts as input;
- electricity customer calls per day expedited at our on-line workstation;
- airline tickets per hour handled, for which data is captured correctly, immediately after people pass the competence test;
- keystrokes per product, ordered on the telephone, average for an expert clerk.

Likability measure

General: The degree to which actual users (sometimes prospective users) of the system have a positive attitude towards it.

Examples:

- percentage of users with more than six weeks experience after completed training, who will say in an anonymous opinion survey that they strongly prefer this system to the old one;
- percentage of trade union members who will vote for adoption of the new system;
- percentage of people in shop who try the system for more than 15 minutes, who purchase it then or later as a direct result of comparison with competitive systems;
- percentage of people who have experience with the system and at least one main competitor who will declare that it is clearly the best overall system for their purposes.

■ 19.4 Tests: measuring tools and methods

This section is an aid to finding a specific method for measuring attributes. It is not intended to be thorough, but to indicate methods for central concepts and to refer to literature which does go deeper.

Most tests are indirect measures of the 'real thing' we are after. This involves a practical compromise between the cost of making a measurement, and the quality of measurement we get.

For each measuring concept there are certain to be a number of different ways to measure it in practice. The costs of a measurement must be included in the cost of building and maintaining a system. The system designer must select a test which is consistent with the restrictions on system resources, but which gives sufficient control over the planned system qualities.

It is not the intention here to provide a complete handbook or catalogue of all possible tests for software engineering. We intend to give a selection of typical tests and some of the more interesting test ideas. We expect that these will serve as initial help for the beginner, who may be wondering if there is any test at all which will serve his purposes. We expect the more advanced software engineer will prefer to tailor the tests to the particular environment and tools at hand, perhaps only using these ideas as basic guidelines, or as a source of stimulating ideas.

The tests will be organized so that they correspond to the previously defined measures, and they will be defined by the following terms:

Synonyms: other terms or names which might be used for this test
Method: a description of the procedure for conducting the test
Dangers: precautions for obtaining meaningful results
Resources: the costs of performing the tests
Quality: the accuracy, reliability, multiple usefulness of a test
Alternatives: the reference to other possible ways of getting the measure
References: to deeper literature regarding this test
Example: a sample of how a real specification for a test might look.

19.4.1 Process capacity test

Synonyms: performance, work capacity.

Method: chosen units of useful work are measured per unit of time. This might involve manual logging of work activity, or computer logging. In general, computer aided counting of activities and time is preferable, because of the larger, more frequent samples and because of the possibility of continuing the measurement during normal operation.

Dangers: measures might not be taken while the system (both computer and people involved) are under maximum stress or activity. The people involved might be too 'expert' compared with the average. The files might be unrealistically small test files.

19.4.2 Responsiveness test

Synonyms: response time, waiting time.

Method: a time is measured between two events in an 'ask–answer' process. A key feature of this measure is selection of appropriate points to measure. A narrow measure of computer response time is perhaps less interesting than the more complete and realistic process, and which includes the time needed to formulate the request to the computer, and the time needed to understand and begin to act on the response given by the computer. Here is a list of possible points for a typical inquiry process:

1. Time to receive or read the element that triggers the inquiry.
2. Time to translate that need into a question or inquiry language.
3. Time to give that inquiry to the computer.
4. Warm-up time or initialization procedures (if needed), such as getting diskettes into drives, getting handbooks.
5. Waiting time for processing and response by the computer.
6. Time needed to understand the response so that necessary action can be initiated.

From a practical point of view, the human processes surrounding the inquiry may be more important than the simple machine response time. From a software engineering point of view, a great deal can be designed in order to improve these human phases (see Gilb and Weinberg, *Humanized input*).

Dangers: Such measures are usually quite sensitive to the other loads on the system and to the state of the file structure. If there is a very light load on the system, the machine response time may be artificially fast. If the file has had many changes without a reorganization, the response might be artificially slow.

References: Gilb, T. and Weinberg, G.M., 1984, *Humanized input*, QED Information Sciences Inc., Wellesley, Mass.

Example: 'The response time average shall be calculated on the basis of not less than 100 inquiries, or not less than 10 representative operators.

It shall be measured in seconds from the point at which the customer has explained the problem, until the point at which our operator can begin to give a correct answer. The computer system should be under a normal daily load during this measurement, even if a simulated load must be used.'

19.4.3 Storage capacity test

Method: Normally, **manufacturers'** ratings are used as a departure point. These, however, rarely give an accurate picture of useful storage, since there are a number of 'overhead' factors which steal useful space. The testing of storage capacity is therefore primarily a matter of finding out what these overhead uses are.

Dangers: Overheads are not necessarily constant. In particular, software supplied by others may in later versions consume more of the available space than you initially measured. You would be wise to expect this to happen, and to try to protect yourself against unreasonable use of this space by others (for example by using contract clauses giving you free extra hardware as compensation).

Example: 'The secondary disk storage on-line capacity for application data shall be at least 100 million bytes useful space when all necessary software and application programs are included. The test is the system's own "space available" measure.'

Alternatives: The inspection method has been used by IBM to measure violations of planned program storage space during design and coding stages. This gives early warning protection against unwanted growth in logic or data storage.

19.4.4 Availability test

Synonyms: up-time, useful time, effectiveness, dependability.

Methods: The availability of large computer systems includes the hardware, software, and human support aspects. It is often clearly defined in the contract for the system, and a certain per cent availability is a pre-requisite for accepting the system for payment. The tests are conducted over a 30-day period, with a possibility of repeat tests if necessary to validate a suspected lack of availability. The tests are conducted in a real environment, if possible during the period of the day when the system should be available. Logs are kept, signed by both parties, of breakdown and recovery times and causes.

Dangers: Bear in mind that single components of a system may have a much higher availability than the total system of which they are a part. It is therefore important to define clearly which system components are to be a part of the measure.

Resources: Availability tests of the kind conducted over 30 days for large systems are costly.

Alternatives: You can approach this measurement via the directly related reliability and maintainability measures.

References: Bernacchi and Larsen, 1972, *Data processing contract and the law*, Chapter XIII, Maintenance, Little Brown, Boston.
Rau, John G., 1970, *Optimization and probability in systems engineering* Chapter 7, System Availability and Dependability, Van Nostrand Reinhold, USA.
Musa, J. *et al.*, 1986, *Software reliability*, McGraw-Hill, New York.

Example: 'The availability shall be measured by means of a sample of at least ten representative nodes in the network (average availability of them) by notes in the log beside the node, supported by automatic system node statistics. In addition to node and system readiness availability, a statistic shall be kept of the number of times a user wanted to use the node, but it was unavailable to them (they waited or went elsewhere) at the time they wanted it.'

19.4.5. Reliability tests

Synonyms: correctness, down-time, functional test.

Method: In general, some sort of input (not necessarily 'correct' or 'rational') is given to the system, and the resulting output is evaluated against some 'correct answer.'

For reliability of files and databases, the recommended method is the use of a deep (extensive) computerized audit program to sample records and fields.

Resources: In logicware, the number of test cases needed for 'complete' testing is very large (a 21 statement program can have 93 billion unique test paths, and every unique test path can have millions of possible data combinations). Testing cannot be used to prove the absence of errors, but if a test case gives incorrect results, it may be used to demonstrate the presence of an error (E. Dijkstra, paraphrased). High cost of testing can be reduced by various techniques: logical structuring of the algoirthm to reduce the number of unique test paths, use of test case generators, use of automatic test path analysis.

Alternatives: The use of distinct software (see references at end of Chapter 18). Distinct software uses one or more extra versions of the algorithm to produce independently arrived-at outputs for comparison. Reliability is measured either in operation or by test cases, using this comparison procedure. The software modules are constructed by different means (people, algorithms, languages) to increase the probability of different faults. One immediate advantage of the method is that it gives the possibility of continuous, operational protection for live systems, and that a 'spare module' is then usually available to provide a 'correct' result when the error is discovered.

The inspection method is the best early measure of software reliability (see Chapters 12 and 21).

References: Hetzel, W.C., 1973, *Program test methods*, Prentice-Hall, New Jersey.
Thayer, T.A. *et al.*, 1978, *Software reliability*, TRW Series, North-Holland, New York.
Musa, J. *et al.*, 1986, *Software reliability*, McGraw-Hill, New York.

Example: 'The reliability of the system shall be cumulatively measured at all times in actual operation by means of a triple distinct software system, and a supervisor which logs all discrepancies in detail and creates a measure of the reliability of the software.' or more conventionally: 'a random sample of 1000 test cases shall be used to measure logicware reliability.' Or for dataware reliability: 'the results of a 1000 record sample of deep database diagnosis shall be used.'

19.4.6 Maintainability tests

Synonyms: bug repair effectiveness, error correction, MTTR (mean time to repair).

Method: The time needed to correct errors is measured by means of logs or daily work repairs. In many cases the tests are conducted with artificially inserted errors.

Alternatives: The distinct software method can be applied to correction of random bugs, most straightforwardly by means of three distinctly different programs (but functionally identical in outputs for same input). The supervisor module uses a two of three voting decision for correction, but logs the status and outputs of all cases. The supervisor can then also measure the time needed to correct the bug by using the outputs from the 'correct' modules. It can also measure cases where it has not been able to resolve the answer of correctness. The timing of these can still be measured by computer if a human operator is asked to make a choice of answers.

References: Parikh, G. and Zvengintzov, N. (eds.), (1983), *Tutorial on software maintenance*, IEEE Computer Society Order No. 453 (includes Gilb on maintenance design with DBO).
Thayer, T.A. *et al.*, 1978 *Software reliability* TRW series 2, North-Holland, New York (a rich variety of measuring ideas related to maintenance of large real examples).
Parikh (ed.), 1980, *Techniques of program and system maintenance*, Ethnotech, Lincoln and Little Brown (includes several articles by Gilb on measurement and distinct software).
Glass, R.L. and Noiseux, R.A., 1981, *Software maintenance guidebook*, Prentice-Hall, (not quantitatively orientated).
Gilb, T., 1976, *Software metrics*, Studentlitteratur, Lund, Sweden, (artificial bugs and distinct software) (out of print).

Example: 'The maintainability test will be conducted by insertion of random, artificial, representative bugs in logic, data and documentation (ten each area). Maintainability will be calculated by the average time needed for qualified, equipped maintenance people (at least three, working with all bugs each) to find and correctly change errors and validate by a simple reliability test.'

19.4.7 Integrity test

Synonyms: security (not equal, but common usage), survival test.

Method: Threats of different types are simulated to measure the ability of installed security techniques to counteract them. There is no such thing as integrity 'in general.' You have to identify specific threat types and test a series of them.

Examples: 'A qualified employee is secretly enlisted (with security persons approval and protection) to try and penetrate the system with various types of corruption, destruction and fact-stealing. The degree to which such penetrations are detected and thwarted is measured against the list of actual attempts.'

'Students are given the challenge of penetrating the system from the outside (they are not qualified employees or security cleared) in various ways.'

'Simulate loss of a main database and primary back-up file. Measure the time needed to get a database system updated, verified and on the air.'

'Ask your cleverest programmer to modify a program in some way to give him some benefit (payment) without knowledge of any except security people. Measure the time before these mechanisms are discovered, and whether they were discovered before or during activation.'

19.4.8 Improvability tests

Synonyms: maintainability, repair, fixing, enhancement.

Method: Basically the same as maintainability, except the artificial bugs are not used. They are replaced by a specification of a change which is desired in the results produced by the system. The time needed to complete a defined series of change tasks correctly is the basic test measure.

Danger: Special attention must be paid to the possible introduction of unintended side-effects, such as wrong outputs in other parts of the system, or performance degradation.

References: See references to **Maintainability**.

Example: 'For ten simple modifications specified, measure the time needed on average for an average programmer to write down a correct and complete change (including updates to files, documentation and test cases).'

19.4.9 Usability test

Synonyms: User friendliness, productivity, ease of use.

Method: The time needed for people of given qualification to learn to use a particular system well enough to produce results at a certain rate or to pass a test of proficiency – is measured.

Dangers: Under strong motivation (for example fear of losing a job) employees may be able to attain high levels of performance with systems of very poor design. For this reason we have introduced the concept of 'likability'.

References: Shneiderman, B., 1980, *Software psychology*, Little Brown, (Winthrop Edition) and Shneiderman, B., *Designing the user interface*, 1987, Addison-Wesley.
Behavior and Information Technology (periodical) published by Taylor and Francis (London) is particularly good at human factors measures in its various articles.

Example: 'A group of ten qualified beginners, actual new employees, shall pass a 30-question test on using the system, by means of actually doing things on the system successfully, unaided by other people, within a two-hour test time limit.' Usability is measured as the number of minutes on the job required by nine out of ten people to pass the test.

20

Principles for motivating your colleagues to use quality metrics

■ Introduction

Chapter 20 suggests ways to motivate people to use measurable quality requirements even when they resist the idea.

■ 20.1 Appeal to their need for clarity

Do the 'ambiguity test.' Each key team member tries to write metric goals.

Those professionals in your team who are serious about their work need to both express their own ideas clearly, and to understand precisely what their colleagues and clients want. If you feel they are expressing themselves unclearly, you can say 'Do you want to communicate your ideas more precisely to the development team? Or are you happy to let them choose an interpretation of what you have intended?'

Alternatively if the problems come, for instance, from the client's stated objectives, you can say; 'Your managers (or client or marketing department) are not expressing themselves well enough for us to be sure about what they really want. Let us not take a chance on using our own interpretation of these unclear objectives. Let us force them to take a clear position on what they want before we take a chance and make fools of ourselves by cost estimating or constructing something different from what they will claim they intended.'

In order to make this absolutely clear to any doubters among your colleagues, use the ambiguity test. It can be carried out on one objective or on a whole set of them. One sample unclear objective will make the point quickly. Take as many people who are involved and knowledgable about the project as you can, and get them to individually attempt to translate the objective ('better usability') into a metric using the method described in this book; scale = ?, test = ?, worst = ?, plan (field trial) = ?, plan (full customer release) = ?, plan (with high quality end of the market) = ? Ask the participants to clarify the question marks in writing as best they can. If they feel uncertain, encourage them to show the range of uncertainty or to note alternative interpretations. If any two individuals have even remotely similar interpretations of an unclear objective when they do the ambiguity test, it is an exception which can be used to demonstrate the rule. By letting your group examine the various interpretations all together, you can be sure that they will all recognize the need to agree on a single common metric interpretation of what is to be accomplished – and when.

■ 20.2 'The boss will have it no other way'

Encourage managers to accept nothing less than a clear metrics statement.

The position of the leaders, both those with formal authority and those whose opinion is respected by their peers, is important.

The President of one client company of mine, who had himself been shown that his own previously 'woolly' pronouncements could be stated unambiguously, declared that the entire company should in future state all objectives quantitatively. (He was running a 23 000 person international computer company.) He made it quite clear to all his direct subordinates that they need never again submit any plan without the key objectives being stated numerically. This meant not only the financial objectives, but also the quality and benefit objectives, the (hitherto) 'intangibles.'

The Quality Director of the company was really concerned about how to translate his own long-range corporate quality plans and proposals into such metrics. But he recognized that it could and should be done, and he knew the President was not going to accept anything less.

The President hoped that by setting the example himself (corporate non-financial goals all quantified) and by making sure that people on the next level down from him also did so, that the gospel would be spread through the layers of the organization.

In fact it wasn't that simple. The message seemed to get stuck somewhere in middle management. This was largely short-circuited by spreading the message directly to product development people via handbooks, brochures and courses, towards which the Quality Director took an initiative.

■ 20.3 'The team will have it no other way'

Encourage all team members to insist on their right to clear objectives.

Make sure the development team are concerned with their team performance. Point out that their mutual success will be determined by being able to focus their efforts on a common and unambiguous set of goals. Point out that lack of clear goals will lead to totally unnecessary discussion about approaches to solving the team's common problems. Invariably when people are having a heated argument about technological alternatives, they are not arguing from the same unambiguous set of objectives. When faced with such arguments, introduce a discussion about unambiguous goals. Invariably one of the arguers turns to the other and says something like 'Oh! Well, if those are the objectives, then I would have to agree with you.' This allows face saving, and both parties can be said to be 'right' (for their interpretation of the objectives), while both were 'wrong' for not clarifying their assumptions about objectives before picking a fight. In software, the classical argument is about which programming languages are 'best.' This is always an argument based on many dimensions of quality and cost, and it is highly dependent on the exact levels of those attributes which are required. All programming languages are probably 'best' for some particular set of objectives, some time.

You might like to use the opportunity presented by a team conflict regarding the best technology or organizational approach to introduce the quality and resource metrics objectives as 'the great peacemaker.' The lesson, once observed by individuals on the team, will not be forgotten for the rest of their professional careers. Use the impact estimation table (Chapter 11) as a formal device for helping participants to see the impacts of their technological ideas on the metric objectives. See particularly Section 11.14, solution comparison and analysis.

Team members have a right to know where the team is going. Otherwise they cannot be an effective part of that team. Tell them that they have that right, but that they will frequently have to remind others of it, and that they will frequently have to create a discussion about the unambiguous interpretation of the team-and-product objectives.

■ 20.4 Group consensus

Metrics are the only reasonable way to let everyone know what the common objective is. Give everyone a shot at influencing the goals. Give everyone the latest updated and agreed goals.

In many present-day cultures and working environments the opinions of the team members are considered more decisive than that of the boss. This may be for several reasons. Sometimes people are more motivated to perform well if they are allowed to influence their working situation. Sometimes the fact that group decisions are made, rather than managerial ones, is a part of the national or the corporate culture.

In such cultures, goal metrics allow successful communication among the team members, and form the basis for suggesting changes to team goals. Metrics are, because of their lack of ambiguity, less subject to manipulation-after-the-fact. They are a tool which deserve, and usually get, more support from the ordinary team member than a set of words from a manager, who perhaps cannot be relied upon to support the very objectives which his team members thought he asked for.

■ 20.5 Show them that early metrics are not a formal commitment

Show them how to write a suitable caveat, so that they can get started without being afraid of being committed to initial guesstimates. If they think early metrics are a commitment 'forever,' they may get nowhere.

Many people, under pressure, have been burned by their failure to deliver impossible measurable 'commitments,' which were made inadvertently without realizing that others considered them to be firm commitments. Such people can be expected to resist attribute metrics because of negative experience. They know that many of the software attributes, which we shall now try to put a number on, are uncertain in final outcome. It is perfectly reasonable that they should not be willing to let their name be associated with commitments which they do not feel they can maintain, and which can result in unreasonable expectations from others.

The more software attributes we try to control by quantification, the more difficult this problem will become. After all, when quantified goals were only budgets or deadlines, there were so many opportunities to 'cheat' by reducing the non-quantified quality areas in order to be able to deliver within the measurable resource constraints.

At some point in the development of an improved software engineering culture, everybody will know that the numbers arrived at early are not a commitment – they are a way of exploring the possibilities. However, until that culture is established – and it could take years – you will have to make the situation quite clear, usually in writing. But, you must also make it clear by your actions. Don't pressure people on these numbers. Protect them when they get caught in the use of them by others and get put under unreasonable pressure. The job of a manager is often to protect his people from such outside pressures so they can get on with producing.

Practical hint: *You might have to use written caveats. The simplest one is to practice giving estimates with explicit uncertainty factors like: 60 ± 20% or 60–80% or 60??. However entire pages may need a 'rubber stamp' like 'Exploratory Uncommitted Estimates Only.'*

> **Practical hint (cont.):**
> *Or you might include in such documents the following:*
> *'Warning: the numbers in this document do not represent*
> *predictions or promises. They are used to improve communica-*
> *tion about possibilities in a complex system. Unless otherwise*
> *explicitly indicated, you can expect realities to be very different*
> *from these numbers. Final numbers may depend on changed*
> *priorities, new technological decisions and implementation*
> *experiences.'*

■ 20.6 Do the first draft for them

Let them see the power of the language. Be prepared to lead by making a concrete suggestion.

The mere fact that you are reading this text means that you probably know more about the subject than many or all of your colleagues. Unless you are lucky enough to be part of an unusually experienced and mature working environment, you cannot expect people to find well-thought-out quantified software quality objectives for themselves until they have seen practical and convincing examples. You must expect to have to lead by demonstrating that this can be done. This applies even if you are a junior member of the team. Naturally you will have to be diplomatic about it. Don't start off with an attitude of 'You people are sloppy and stupid because you can make ludicrously ambiguous project goals'. You will get better response from showing a particularly modest attitude such as: 'Please forgive me, since I am new and inexperienced. But, I'm not exactly sure what you intended us to achieve by your maintainability requirement. I think you are right that it is critical and deserves attention. Here is a rough draft giving my personal (but not necessarily correct) interpretation. I need guidance from you as to exactly what is wanted, so I can help contribute to it effectively.'

Do a draft. Say it's crude. Get others to help you with your struggle to find out what they want. Let them 'own' the solution too.

■ 20.7 Demonstrate the wide range of interpretations the present goal statements allow

Write down a list of the many possibly intended interpretations of the vaguer goal statements. For example 'faster response time': faster than what? By how much? When should this be delivered (field trial, in three years, when a customer contract for it exists)? Is 'response time' the time between people having a problem to be solved, and when it is solved (including deciding what to command the computer, keying or pointing the commands, correcting errors, and interpreting the responses until the ultimate useful action is initiated)? Asking searching questions like this – when you know that everyone else has made an assumption that this is the 'machine response time' – can frequently be the useful beginning of determining which system quality objectives you really have and intend to work towards.

It is not merely a matter of putting a number to an idea that is important. You also need to know which are the most important ideas to put numbers on. At the extreme, it is more important to have a rough notion of the degree to which you want to achieve 'the right quality concept' than it is to have an exact notion about what you want from a trivial quality concept.

■ 20.8 Connecting software requirement metrics to management and customer requirements

Software metrics must be connected or directly traceable to the needs of the funding parties for your development. In fact, all metric statements need to have a 'SOURCE = authority for this objective' parameter to connect the metric explicitly to some real management or marketing need. Technological work has a source of funding. We must not bite the hand that feeds us.

We are more likely to succeed in our customer's eyes when we aim directly at the targets which they have set. We are more likely to be able to communicate whatever we are doing to them if we write down the background requirement or reasons clearly. For example the customer might have indicated 'better performance,' and you might have a technical requirement for 'ten times improved recovery speed of the database.'

> RECOVERY: SCALE = minutes to recover from database break-down
> NOW = 100, PLAN = 10, WORST = 20
> SOURCE = customer 'better performance' requirement

In addition to being able to answer the question of what you are doing to meet their requirement, even though the recovery strategy is not immediately obvious as a performance increaser, you can better question whether this planned recovery level adequately solves the problem. For example if recovery is only needed once a month, then this is hardly enough alone to improve performance of the system, and we have to look for additional strategies.

Point out that with measurable requirements, outside management and customers can be told to stay away from the development effort and not meddle with it. You can demand to be judged on your results in terms of the agreed planned objectives. Otherwise, with unclear goals, it is tempting for outsiders to 'suggest' things you should do to get to the objectives they have in mind but which nobody has forced them to articulate with metrics yet. There is a real danger here that the customer or marketing people's power will be inadvertently misused to build them the solutions they specify, rather than a system with their real objectives.

■ 20.9 Show them how to connect metrics to design

Software quality metrics alone can seem rather abstract initially to most people who have to learn to deal with them. You are largely dealing with people for whom the computer program is software. Performance and space in storage are the measurable realities. Measurable concepts of security, maintainability, portability and usability are but abstract 'motherhood' notions for them. You will have to progress quickly into the actual uses of the metrics to turn them into meaningful realities.

> **Practical hint:** *My favorite initial 'teaching' trick is immediately to connect the proposed technical solutions to the quality metrics using the impact estimation table (Chapter 11). This is not a solid reality, of course. But it does force people to think about the meaning of both their objectives and the technological solutions they are considering.*

Fagan's inspection method (see Chapters 12 and 21) provides early measures of software product qualities in several dimensions of quality and cost. It does so even more if you both collect and analyze data by category of error, as IBM does (i.e. by classes of defect such as those corresponding to the most critical qualities; for example usability, performance, compatability). Inspection can be used thus to keep interest alive in the quality requirements specification, even before the real product is available.

There are, however, few equals to the evolutionary delivery method (see Chapters 7, 13 and 15) for making metrics real to the people who must constantly tune them to the realities of their resources and to market needs and technological opportunities. Evolutionary delivery makes any quality or resource metric become real at very early stages of development (for example 5% or less of project budget expenditure). Real interest in these metrics is generated within the team for realistic consideration and control. Put key metrics on the wall, and chart progress towards them for each evolutionary delivery step. Use Deming's statistical quality control methods in doing so, to avoid misinterpretation of the natural variances of the results.

■ 20.10 Show them that metrics do not require exact knowledge

Stress the distance between 'worst case' and 'planned level'. Don't be afraid to note plus/minus deviation (26 ± 4). Remember that evolutionary delivery will correct you towards reality.

Using numbers does not imply exact knowledge. Many people find this point very hard to grasp. In fact it is because our knowledge of our technology is so inexact, that we need numeric tools to keep some degree of control over how we are doing in relation to what we want to be doing. To avoid numbers when knowledge is poor only exacerbates an already dangerous situation.

The distance between the worst case and planned levels (see Chapter 9, Attribute specification) is a built-in admission of the degree of uncertainty we expect to have to cope with. It says 'we would love to achieve the planned level within the resources, and together with the other planned quality levels. However, we may not be able to do this – but please don't fall below the worst case level whatever you do.' Remind colleagues of this fact in order to help them feel more comfortable when they are trying to put numbers on the planned levels and worst cases.

Frequent use of the plus/minus deviation notation and the question mark symbol makes people recognize that numbers are also a way of expressing uncertainty – and are a first step towards reduction of it. When I put 50% ± 40% on something, it is natural for somebody to ask a question about why that uncertainty factor is so high. The answer may lead to questions like, 'Well, is there another design solution specification which we can afford which does not contain that level of uncertainty? What if we increase the budget? Does that help us to reduce the uncertainty?'.

There is a value for increasing certainty. An explicit numeric uncertainty specification is a solid first step to recognizing exactly how much it would pay off to give you increased development resources in order to reduce the uncertainty. Even if those resources are not forthcoming, the monkey is off of your back. If the system exhibits properties within the range you have estimated, you can point out that you told them so in no uncertain terms. Management, or your customer, failed to give you resources to improve the situation. Maybe next time they will listen to your uncertainty estimates more carefully.

Remind people that initial design estimates are, in all disciplines, subject to great uncertainty. If you make use of early evolutionary delivery step measures and feedback, you will have plenty of time to correct your estimates, or your technology, before you cross the official finishing line.

A great deal of the hesitancy surrounding the use of requirements metrics stems from the danger of commitment they represent in the old monolithic (pre-evolutionary) project environment. People are simply not used to the idea that you don't have to be exactly right at the beginning to succeed.

■ 20.11 Show them that metrics are not set in stone

We must be prepared to trade off some of our wishes against higher priorities. Realities of early evolutionary measures of product and market will force us to recognize the need for change and to modify requirements.

Writing a number down on a piece of paper or in a word processor has the outward appearance of unchangeable permanence. Who knows if we will have a chance to comment on the number, in the light of future experience, before some fool makes a noise reminding us of our youthful sins of early estimation?

People naturally fear commitment to a permanent unchangeable estimate, when they know that the final reality is bound to be somewhat different, and when they know that it is not in their hands alone. To promote the use of the metrics tool, you will have to deal with this fear.

> **Practical hint:** *Make it clear that the estimates of requirements or impacts are not tied to the individual who first mentions the estimate. The team must accept the responsibility for the number. Hidden anonymously among peers ('they didn't know any better either!'), timid but creative individuals might just venture a valuable initial opinion.*
>
> *One technique to dramatize that the numbers are not static is to modify them intentionally, using such simple tools as spreadsheet software, to do impact estimation or to do attribute specification. Ask a lot of 'What if?' questions, by changing the data on the spreadsheet, to get people thinking: but also to get the message across that the numbers can be changed as easily as a budget suggestion.*

> **Practical hint (cont.):**
> *Explain that the numbers are highly dependent on many factors, which are not pinned down yet (like the budget for the development, or the other quality requirements and their priority). Explain that numbers are the best available tool for rationally exploring a complex technological design.*
>
> *Explain that no early requirements, wishes or impact estimates are holy if we decide that something else has a higher priority. There is no need to feel guilty if the final numbers five years from now are different from what anyone suggests now. But, numbers, at least approximate ones, are necessary for getting us on a controlled and efficient iteration path towards our future, even if that future involves dynamically changing requirements and technologies.*

Just because we are shooting at an evasive enemy rocket, doesn't mean we should not calculate the distance between our missile and the target at frequent intervals – even though the real distance has changed almost before we have calculated it.

The only truly unforgivable sin is to avoid clear numeric thinking totally, and to thus allow our project to drift towards initially comfortable but ultimately disastrous anarchy and chaos.

■ 20.12 Conclusion

People have good reason to fear the use of software metrics. You must be sensitive and sympathetic to them. You must be prepared to remove the causes of that fear by creating an environment where it is no longer justified. There must be more reward for trying to put a number on things than penalties for not being perfectly right. This doesn't happen automatically because 'it is the rational thing to do.' You have to make it happen through a series of moves. If you fail to do so, then the penalty will be loss of control of results, and everybody will suffer that loss together.

21

The Omega project: inspection experience

■ Introduction

Chapter 21 is a guest chapter by Alan F. Brown of International Computers (ICL), Bracknell, UK.

A client of mine on inspection, Alan Brown won a corporate excellence award for his patient leadership of change to new methods. This is inspection put into practice in an industrial software engineering environment. (Michael Fagan himself was a direct inspiration to the group at the outset.)

It should be said that Alan and his group did much more during the period covered by this case study than inspection. We were concerned with everything which would improve product quality and the long-term health of the organization.

■ 21.1 Background

The Omega project involved 180 development staff with the task of porting a micro-networking operating system to new hardware. The end product contained about 1.5 million lines of code (LOC) of which about a third is new or changed. The implementation language was primarily Pascal with 5% in assember.

Reliability objectives had been set which were close to state-of-the-art achievable limits for office systems. Consequently the project looked to new quality techniques for a solution. The Fagan inspection technique was selected as:

- it was likely to have a significant impact on reliability;
- it was well documented and easily understood;
- it could be implemented almost immediately;
- it needed no capital investment;
- the necessary infrastructure (e.g. documentation standards) largely existed;
- several encouraging case histories existed.

■ 21.2 Getting started

A new quality function was formed consisting of a quality manager and five quality consultants. Their task was to provide technical and organizational support to the development teams by:

- defining the inspection procedures;
- acting as the initial moderators;

- reviewing the effectiveness of early inspections;
- helping to put inspection plans in place;
- establishing and maintaining a comprehensive inspection database.

■ 21.3 Handbook

The first edition of an inspection handbook was rapidly put together. It was based heavily on IBM material, but served as a useful starting point.

The second issue of the inspection handbook followed quickly. This included error checklists generated at brainstorming sessions. Also of particular note was that, even at this early stage, 13 inspection points were defined. Five were mandatory:

- requirements specifications, because they rarely existed in written form;
- product specifications, because they were key high level documents used as input to designs, users manuals and system test plans;
- design specifications, because current design standards and practices were known to be unsatisfactory;
- module test plans, because the authors (i.e. the implementors) had had little formal training in this area;
- code, because the project had previously made little use of static defect removal processes such as desk checking.

The inspection handbook approach allowed all information on the inspection process to be collated into one document. It had three main sections: an overview of the technique; details of the inspection process for each of the 13 document types; the standard forms used for inspection summaries and so on.

Each entry in the inspection process was a maximum of three pages long and contained 11 standard sub-sections:

- objectives of this inspection;
- procedures relevant to the production of the document;
- entry criteria, including the necessary source documents;
- participants; likely candidates for inspectors;
- overview; guidance on its necessity;
- preparation; specific roles;
- defects; definitions and classifications;
- planning rates for preparation and inspection;
- reinspection criteria;

- exit criteria;
- error checklist.

■ 21.4 Forms

Some people say that formal methods are so called because of the many forms that are required! Certainly inspections are no exception. The Omega project developed seven different forms to ensure efficient administration. For example, there was a moderator assignment form used to give the moderator the necessary background information to initiate the inspection process. There was also a moderator checklist of 14 essential activities such as agreeing meeting times and booking conference rooms. There were polite Design Change Request (DCR) forms for reporting suspected defects in source documents, and less polite DCR reminders should the actionee fail to respond to the request.

■ 21.5 Training

A lucky break for the project was that a colleague had just returned from a three day inspection course given by IBM in New York. The Omega management were quick to intercept him on his return and he was immediately involved in giving a series of inspection courses. The entire project team was fully trained within two months.

So much interest was created that there was a great demand for places on the courses from other parts of the company. These were satisfied at a premium price, such that the entire project team was trained off site without cost on the budget, confirming once again that 'quality is free' (because it pays for itself).

■ 21.6 Management approach

The management team was eager to improve the quality of its products, and was prepared to make the necessary investment in consultancy, training, and resource for inspections. Even deadlines, which had previously been sacrosanct, were rescheduled.

The development teams were concerned that a 15% burden was being placed on them; 15% is classically the proportion of time spent by project teams when undertaking a full inspection program. In theory the 15% effort is more than recouped before the end of development, but the teams were not confident of their ability to implement the technique with sufficient expertise the first time around. Also, they knew that the current state of project documentation left something to be desired, as the accent previously had been on timescales rather than quality.

Management responded by adding 15% to the deadlines up to the end of alpha (module) testing, the point where independent validation began. The product release dates, however, were maintained in the belief that substantial savings would be made during the normally protracted back-end activities of validation, systems proving and field trials. All of the development managers agreed to this plan.

■ 21.7 Full implementation

The Omega project implemented the Fagan inspection technique in full. In particular:

- The *two hour limit* for meetings and preparation was imposed.
- Inspectors were allotted specific *roles* to play.
- *Many inspection points* were defined: initially 13, later 17.
- A *design change request system* was established for resolving defects found in higher-level documents.
- An *inspection database* was designed and implemented, containing records of document sizes, defects found, time spent, etc.
- Defects were categorized as major/minor, missing/wrong/extra and by type.
- Results were frequently analyzed in order to review the cost-effectiveness of the process.

■ 21.8 Ball-park planning

Initial ball-park planning estimates unearthed severe problems in logistics. If 180 staff spend 15% of their effort on inspections, this amounts to well in excess of 30 000 hours in a year. If a third of this resource is spent on inspection meetings, and if the average meeting lasts for 90 minutes and is attended by five people, then there would be well over 1300 inspection meetings. That requires over 1300 conference room bookings. There were no conference rooms in the office area. Two were quickly built! Also, if each inspection involved an average of 50 pages of documentation per person, then the photocopying machine would be required to output over a third of a million pages per year!

■ 21.9 PIPs and DIPs

To assist projects with their inspection planning, the concept of Project Inspection Plans (PIPs) and Detailed Inspection Plans (DIPs) was developed. New forms were created for this purpose.

The PIP was an overview plan for each product development, identifying the key documents to be produced, their estimated size and what proportion was to be inspected. Its main purpose was to ensure that the 15% inspection resource for that project was spent in the most effective areas.

Each PIP was supported by several DIPs, one for each planned inspection. The DIP recorded the size of the document and of the inspection team, the planning rates and scheduled dates for formal entry and exit from inspections. Its primary purpose was to ensure that document inspections, especially lengthy program source listings, had been broken down into manageable chunks. It was also used to ensure a smooth path for inspections so that the availability of rooms and trained moderators was not a problem.

■ 21.10 Estimation procedures exposed

Development plans were the first type of document to be inspected. The first three inspections raised 26 design change requests, 23 of them against the planning standard. This illustrates very vividly the effectiveness of the process in improving, as a by-product, the quality of development standards and procedures.

One recurring defect in the plans was that the estimated amount of new and/or changed code was not stated. When the three plans were reworked, and LOC (lines of code) estimates included, the Quality Manager was surprised to find that although the developments were of a similar nature and complexity, the LOC rates for the three developments ranged from 1000 to 7000 per man year. When the planners were asked to justify their LOC rates, back came the same reply, 'Alpha testing has to be completed by 1 July!'

■ 21.11 Money matters

After two months, some 30 inspections had been undertaken but none had achieved a successful 'exit' (all completion criteria achieved). Two problems were identified: firstly, the amount of rework required to clear away every single defect found; secondly, the fact that these initial trial inspections had not been formally milestoned, so there was no weekly reminder to management that rework was outstanding.

In an attempt to overcome the problem, a £10 prize was offered, to be spent in a local hostelry, to the first inspection team to achieve an exit. There were three claimants on the day that the prize was announced. Further rewards included £10 for the first inspection in which no major defects were found, £10 for the first successful exit from a test plan inspection, and £100 for the producers of the first product for which no bugs were found during validation. The last prize remained unclaimed!

■ 21.12 Quality matters

Problems are bound to arise when implementing a new technique on such a grand scale. The quality team looked for a means of being able to respond quickly with corrective actions. They came up with the idea of publishing a weekly news-sheet, appropriately entitled Quality Matters. This was used to keep the development teams informed with detailed changes to the procedures, hints on increasing effectiveness, clarification of the 'rules', feedback from inspection progress reviews, and inspection statistics.

The approach was light-hearted, with headlines such as 'Inspection Team Wins Thirst Prize', a reference to the first winners of the £10 prize. There were short anecdotal stories, such as the one about the author of a test plan who was asked to annotate the plan and its source design document in order to clarify the relationship between the product design and each test. When the plan was returned it contained not only the annotation but two extra tests!

Another innovation by the quality team was the introduction of an 'inspected for quality' stamp. This appeared on the front page of all documents which had successfully exited from the inspection process. It was under-signed by the moderator as confirmation that a professional inspection had taken place and that all known defects had been reworked to his satisfaction.

■ 21.13 Gathering momentum

For the first ten weeks the inspection program trundled along at a fairly modest rate of 3.4 inspections per week. Developers were finding the start criteria difficult to achieve and moderators were operating by the book. Also, defects were being found at an alarming rate: 56 per inspection.

Table 21.1

Week	Weekly figures Inspections	Defects	Hours	Cumulative figures Inspections	Defects	Hours
1	3	137	73	3	137	73
2	3	121	68	6	258	141
3	6	322	195	12	580	336
4	3	276	139	15	856	475
5	4	180	105	19	1036	580
6	3	207	101	22	1243	681
7	3	192	126	25	1435	807
8	4	343	215	29	1778	1022
9	2	62	77	31	1840	1099
10	3	61	88	34	1901	1187
11	2	82	82	36	1983	1269
12	5	265	224	41	2248	1493
13	1	35	54	42	2283	1547
14	6	139	151	48	2422	1698
15	4	164	101	52	2586	1799
16	8	147	192	60	2733	1991
17	13	421	388	73	3154	2379
18	12	208	372	85	3362	2751
19	10	299	244	95	3661	2995
20	6	126	102	101	3787	3097

As the projects moved into the coding stage, the pace increased but so did the quality of work. The next ten weeks, averaged 6.7 inspections per week, but the defect finding rate halved to a more comfortable 28 per inspection.

At its peak, during weeks 17–19, the Omega project conducted 35 inspections in three weeks, finding and removing 928 defects for 1004 hours of effort.

The basic defect and resource data for the first 20 weeks are given in Table 21.1 and illustrated in Figure 21.1.

■ 21.14 The database

An essential element of any inspection system is the historical database. The Omega project developed their own computerized system with the following main features:

- recording of document details, e.g. type and size; resource usage (preparation, inspection and rework); defect classification (major/minor, missing/wrong/extra);

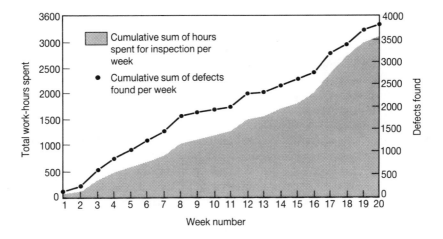

Figure 21.1 Defect and resources data from the first twenty weeks of Omega.

- simple menu driven system;
- screen images, for data entry, which are identical to the inspection summary report forms;
- analysis and report generator for producing inspection summaries, project summaries, defect analyses, personal summaries and document analyses.

The document analyses provide valuable information on the effectiveness of each type of inspection, producing vital statistics such as document quality, in terms of defects per page, return on investment, in terms of defects per hour, and inspection reading rate, in terms of pages per hour.

■ 21.15 Progress reviews: identifying problems

Public progress reviews were held periodically to discuss the problems and benefits as seen by those taking part. A summary of the feedback follows.

The problems were:

1. There were general weaknesses in some *documentation* areas, particularly requirements specifications and design specifications.
2. The company's *content standards*, for key documents in the development process, did not form a hierarchically related set. This sometimes led to confusion as to which high level

documents to use for comparison with low level ones in inspections.

3. Recurring defects were being found. For example, quality attributes were always inadequately described in product specifications. Better standards and more training were needed.

4. Clerical assistance was sought to ease the moderators' burden in arranging meetings, booking rooms and photocopying documents.

5. There was a unanimous request for better cost-benefit analysis of inspections. Staff were sceptical of figures that simply showed defects per hour or defects per page.

6. There was concern over the cost effectiveness of inspecting very high level documents such as development plans. It was not often possible to relate the defects found to the likely cause of bugs in the end product. Consequently there was less satisfaction to be gained in finding such defects. The management view was that high level inspections had been very effective in establishing better standards for such documents and for putting projects on a much firmer footing.

7. Implementing inspections on already existing products was very costly and generally unsatisfactory. For example, a 20 000 LOC compiler was being ported. This involved changing about 1000 LOC – mostly fragmented. In practice this would require inspection of the complete revised product rather than just the changed lines. However the project resources were based on a 1000 LOC project. Furthermore, the existing design documentation would have to be completely rewritten as it was an inadequate source document for code inspections.

8. There was an overload on key designers for their services in both design and specification inspections.

9. Staff were concerned that management were paying too much attention to inspections, and not enough on the other strategies which were part of the general quality improvement program.

■ 21.16 The benefits

The benefits identified included:

1. Good general education. Staff know much more about what is being developed. They are also much more aware of the need for complete and clear documentation and of the purpose of each type of document.

2. Improved document quality. As soon as inspections were

implemented, the quality of project documentation increased tremendously.

3. Good meeting practice. Inspection meetings started on time, had a clear agenda, went at an even planned pace. People came fully prepared, and actions were not only recorded, but followed up. These practices were beginning to rub off onto other types of meetings.

4. Small problems are not overlooked. There is a temptation to leave small problems until later to fix, but they have a habit of reappearing as much bigger problems.

5. The 'preparation' phase provides a guarantee. There have been no fruitless inspections, whereas the previous design reviews had often been undermined by a lack of pre-meeting preparation.

■ 21.17 An ex-employee's view

Not all staff received the technique with open arms. Firstly there were the prima donnas with large egos, who objected to the idea of peers reviewing their work. Secondly, there were the cowboys, who believed that they had the ability to produce code direct from specifications without any need for design documentation, other than the occasional cigarette packet or back of envelope.

Several cowboys were exposed when design, code and test plan inspections were declared as mandatory on all projects. It is difficult to inspect a design which doesn't exist. It is also difficult to inspect code and test plans against non-existent designs.

One designer objected so strongly that he saw no alternative but to resign from the company. Here is an extract from a farewell letter that he wrote to his Personnel Officer:

'Inspections are a total overkill of the quality problem. The excessive cost in time and demoralization far outweighs any benefits. The main preoccupation seems to be in trying to prove their (the inspection team's) worth by counting defects, most of which are of a trivial nature. Perhaps a more cost-effective approach would be to encourage adherence to the existing procedures. Quality of code should be left to each individual. My arguments against the inspection technique include:

- very time consuming: reaching epidemic proportions;
- completely disruptive: almost every day involves some aspect of inspection, often on someone else's project;
- dubious effectiveness: defects would be found anyway by comment cycles and testing, and far cheaper;

- totally negative: simply looking for defects is demoralizing;
- chronically bureaucratic: yet more 'forms' – of doubtful value;
- unpopular: anything which doesn't directly affect the production of a program is resented. Some chores, like producing support documentation, are obviously necessary. Others, like inspection, are not;
- resented: non-productive elements of the project are seen to have nothing better to do than invent procedures to impede the producers. This is particularly resented as productive manpower is scarce;
- too much is inspected: development plans, specifications, design documents, test plans. Sometimes you can't move for inspections;
- frustrating: having worked hard to meet a dead-line, some bureaucrat then blocks the handover because trivial inspection exit criteria haven't been met;
- increase in documentation: detailed design documentation has to be produced just so that it can be inspected;
- flexibility: inspections are undertaken simply because there is a milestone to be met. The participants are never asked whether they feel it would be **worthwhile**;
- logistics: many hours are lost trying to find spare conference rooms and photocopiers.'

(He forgot to add that the automatic feed of the photocopier would not accept cigarette packets.)

■ 21.18 Modifying the technique

Another group of sceptics, having moved outside the Omega project, formed a Quality Circle to discuss how the inspection process could be tailored to suit their preference for informality. They felt that the emphasis had been placed too much on the classification of errors and gathering of statistics, rather than on fixing problems. They were also concerned about the effectiveness of independent moderators who often had little background in the subject being inspected.

They developed an informal 'inspection' system, dispensing with the moderator and his statistics, and adding a 'third hour' for discussing solutions. They retained the principles of attempting to find defects early, making use of error checklists and producing inspection plans for each project. The management view was, somewhat reluctantly, that the informal system was likely to be more effective than formal inspections for this particular team, because the people involved believed in the modified process, and wanted to make it

Table 21.2 Cost-benefit analysis. (Brackets indicate that the defects were too complex to assess, and an average value has been applied.)

Doc. type	Insp. hours (Excl. rework)	Defect removal cost in hours	Likely activity to find defect	Defect removal cost in hours
Product plan	13	1	coding	70
		2	beta test	30
Product plan	29	0.3	low-level design	20
		0.5	field trial	[19]
Specification	19	4	low-level design	35
		[1.3]	?	[19]
Specification	74	0.5	beta test	10
		0.2	beta test	10
Specification	27	0.1	beta test	10
		[1.3]	?	[19]
Specification	22	0.1	alpha test	3
		[1.3]	?	[19]
Specification	28	6	beta test	60
		0.1	beta test	1
Specification	33	1	alpha test	10
		1	beta test	10
Specification	58	0.3	alpha test	4
		0.2	low-level design	2
Code listing	37	3	beta test	15
		[1.3]	?	[19]
	340	25.5		385

work. In any case, it was a big step forward from the quality control techniques in use before inspections were introduced.

■ 21.19 Cost-benefit analysis

In response to a request to analyze the 'real' benefits of the inspection program, two major defects were chosen at random from each of ten inspection reports, which were also chosen at random. The inspection teams were asked to assess when each defect would have been found, if it had not been removed by inspection, and what the likely cost would have been to fix the problem at that later point. Table 21.2 above summarizes the results, further illustrated in Figure 21.2.

The figures show that the estimated cost (385 hours), of fixing only a sample of two major defects per inspection at later stages, outweighs the total cost of the complete inspection plus specific rework (365.5 hours). At the time of this survey an average of 11 major defects were being found per inspection. Hence on major defects alone the cost savings were being estimated at over 500%.

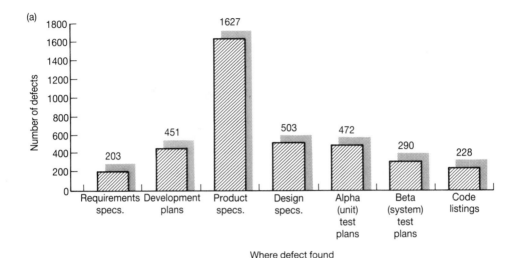

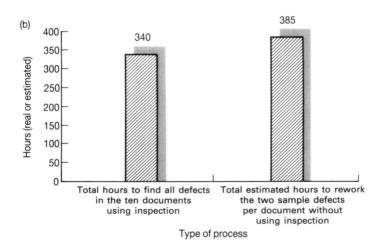

Figure 21.2 Omega analysis (a) total defects analysis (b) cost of inspection vs alternative later defect removal cost (estimated).

Table 21.3 IBM data.

	Missing	Percentage Wrong	Extra
Design	61	34	5
Code	26	62	12

■ 21.20 Missing/wrong/extra analysis

The missing/wrong/extra data collected, confirmed the theory that the majority of defects in high-level documents are of type 'missing,' whereas in low-level documents rather more are of the type 'wrong.'

Typical figures reported by IBM are given in Table 21.3 and the Omega project figures are listed in Table 21.4.

One very interesting figure from the Omega data is the 29% coding defects classified as 'extra.' This underlines the indiscipline which had prevailed prior to the introduction of inspections. Programmers, working from inadequate designs, had got used to adding their own ideas here and there!

The difference between the alpha test plan (ATP) and the beta test plan (BTP) figures is interesting. ATPs were produced by developers who, in general, had not been formally trained in the art of testing, whereas BTPs were written by professional validators. Not surprisingly there were 63% more defects in the ATPs, and 71% of the ATP defects were of type 'missing,' i.e. developers did not always know what was required in a test plan. Validators should know better and, indeed, only 51% of BTP defects were of type 'missing.' They tended to get

Table 21.4 ICL data.

	Total Defects	Missing	Percentage Wrong	Extra
Requirements	203	63	34	3
Development plans	451	61	33	6
Product specifications	1627	56	40	4
Design specifications	503	53	39	8
Alpha test plans	472	71	26	3
Beta test plans	290	51	39	10
Code listings	228	26	45	29
Total and averages	3774	56	37	7

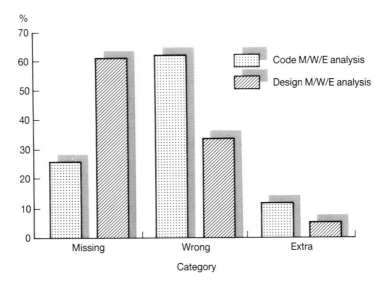

Figure 21.3 IBM figures on missing/wrong/extra analysis.

more 'wrong' entries as they were not as familiar as the developers with the product specifications. They also recorded 10% defects of type 'extra,' often due to trying to test features not supported by the increment in question.

■ 21.21 Alpha test plan defects

A closer look was taken at the types of errors being made by developers when writing ATPs. ATPs cover module tests done by coders on their own work.

Table 21.5 below shows the impact of inspections on four ATPs.

The original plans contained descriptions of 66 tests, each test consisting of one or more test cases. After inspection, only 34 of these tests remained unchanged, i.e. error free; 10 had been clarified (minor changes), 22 had been enhanced (further test cases added) and 26 totally new tests had been added. It was estimated that the resulting increase in test coverage was about 57%. The main areas affected were regression and performance testing.

For the record, the four inspections cost 43 hours and resulted in 18 hours of rework; 24 major and 48 minor defects were found and removed.

Table 21.5 Alpha test plan defects.

Type of test	Before inspection	Number of tests after inspection			
		unchanged	*clarified*	*enhanced*	*new*
Functionality	25	16	5	4	6
Error handling	32	18	3	11	3
Regression	8	0	2	6	14
Performance	1	0	0	1	3
Totals	66	34	10	22	26

■ 21.22 Comparison with desk-checking

There was a lot of resistance to introducing code inspections. Several projects had already reached the testing stage, so the potential benefit of reducing test time would be lessened. 'Can't possibly be cost effective' was a typical plea.

In certain cases, project teams were allowed to desk-check their code instead of inspecting it. A formal procedure was introduced which required the independent desk-checker to record the amount of time spent, the size of the code and the number of defects found. In this way, it was possible to compare the relative effectiveness of desk-checking and code inspection. Table 21.6 overleaf shows some interesting results.

Desk-checking revealed no major defects at all. Perhaps this is not surprising as the amount of time spent on desk-checking each line of code was up to seven times less than for inspections. However desk-checking recorded the highest figure for total defects per hour; a good example of how statistics, taken out of context, can be misleading. The rest of the data shows emphatically that desk-checking is not the technique to use for producing zero-defect software.

Also observe the different inspection results obtained by Groups A and B. Group B found far fewer defects in their code, but took far less time about it.

■ 21.23 LUERAs (likely user error reports avoided) classification

Difficulties are often experienced in inspections when trying to estimate software reliability based on defect data. There are two key problems. Firstly unless the percentage effectiveness of the inspection

Table 21.6 Desk-checking and inspection compared.

	Group A desk-checking	Group A inspection	Group B inspection
Non-commentary LOC	3240	7388	3720
Total hours excluding rework	14	236.5	67.5
Rework hours	1.5	69	17.5
LOC per hour, excl. rework	231	31	55
LOC per hour, incl. rework	209	24	44
Major defects	0	66	10
Minor defects	11	129	23
Major defects per K NLOC	0	8.9	2.7
Total defects per K NLOC	3.4	26.4	8.9
Major defects per hour	0	0.3	0.15
Total defects per hour	0.7	0.6	0.4

process is known, then it is not possible to predict with any accuracy the number of defects remaining in the document. Secondly, many of the major defects raised on high level documents and test plans cannot be equated with bugs in the end product. For example, the absence of any statement on 'user documentation' in a development plan is clearly a major defect; so is the absence of resilience tests in a test plan. But neither of these defects can be considered as likely to affect directly the software MTBF (mean time between failures) of the end product, since the defects would never be formally reported by end users as bugs.

To establish a more realistic basis for predicting software reliability, the concept of LUERAs (likely user error reports avoided) was established. Each defect, including Design Change Requests, was reviewed and identified as a LUERA, if it was likely that *at least one user would report a problem* if the defect was not corrected before release. For the Omega project, 12.7% of the total defects were classified as LUERAs. These had been found at a cost of 7 hours each.

■ 21.24 The Achilles' heel: clear requirements

Throughout the Omega Project, the lack of clear and agreed requirements was the Achilles' heel. The marketing function had refused to put pen to paper, so eventually the development unit wrote a set of requirements themselves. One motivational factor for doing this was to create a source document against which development plans and product specifications could be inspected.

The resulting 80-page requirements specification was split into

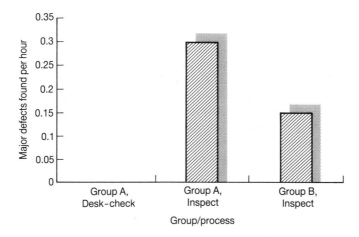

Figure 21.4 Desk-checking and inspections compared.

three logical sections, and inspected by three teams. As there was no higher level hierarchical document to inspect the requirements against, the teams carried out 'pseudo' inspections, using their experience and knowledge of the marketplace instead.

The results were astounding. Altogether 168 major defects were found at a cost of 94 hours. A further 105 hours were spent in rework.

As defect removal processes, such as inspection, are unlikely to be more than 70% effective, it was likely that at least 70 major defects remained. By now, however, most of the projects were well into the coding phase, so there seemed little point in re-inspecting the requirements.

One of the defects which was not uncovered in the high level specifications was that there was no commercial business case for the planned development! Three months later the inevitable decision was made to 'redirect' the project.

■ 21.25 Diary of key events

November 1983 Omega management attended a presentation by Michael Fagan on the inspection technique.
December 1983 decision made to implement inspections on all developments; first in-house inspection training course; first trial inspections
January 1984 inspection handbook published

February 1984	all project staff fully trained; inspection program begins
March 1984	1000th defect found; first successful inspection exit
April 1984	2000th defect found
May 1984	3000th defect found
June 1984	100th document inspected
July 1984	4000th defect found
	Project redirected

22

The production planning case

■ Introduction

The purpose of this chapter is to provide an actual case history as background to the use of the principles which are the subject of this book.

■ 22.1 Project background

The Corporation involved is a large multinational with tens of thousands of employees. It is vertically integrated, and so whatever it produces in one factory is frequently used by other factories in the group. The case study revolves around the production units, which are several factories for a major group of products midway in the vertical product integration. They were known as Midway Manufacturing Organization (MMO).

The MMO was not a profit center, and although many people felt that it should be one, this idea was strenuously resisted by top management. This was represented to us by David Vance, who was in charge of the effort to re-organize the MMO into a balanced economic unit.

The Corporation had experienced rough times in the last few years. Other multinationals were giving fierce competition, especially on the hitherto well-protected home market. There was a lack of truly innovative product ideas coming out of the labs in spite of heavy spending there. The company had recently trimmed its work force by about ten thousand employees, and the pressure was still on for people to seek early retirement.

The soon-to-retire Chairman of the Board, in his early days a strategic planner for the Corporation, was clearly shaken by his turbulent experiences at the helm of his ship. He said: 'I hadn't contemplated for one moment the possibility of having to reduce the dividend. In the last quarter of 1980 we were losing money on these exports at a rate of about $400 million per annum and it would have been a great mistake if we had over-reacted to that, because once you lose export business it's very difficult to get it back again.'

These statements reflect his dilemma.

His solution area is best expressed by his statement 'Nowadays, I see a need to be able to respond quickly and flexibly to unforeseen changes such as the 1973 quadrupling of oil prices.

■ 22.2 The production planning project

It seemed to me that few, if any, of the Chairman's problems and considerations had filtered down to the dozen people in the six month old Production Planning Project committee (PPP). However it became clear as we asked questions of David, the responsible top executive, that this project had to produce a more than $400 million cost effectiveness improvement in the MMO factories, or the Corporation would have to face elimination of the entire facility. They simply could not afford to continue paying more for these particular intermediary products than they were available for on the international market. A lot of people's jobs seemed to be involved, and the issue had political implications as well.

In spite of this the Project Group seemed to consist mainly of people oriented towards building improved computer programs for more efficient scheduling of plant work and materials. At one point I asked them to estimate how much of the needed $400 million savings they expected to generate within the required three years if they managed to make a 'dream' system work perfectly. The consensus was a maximum of *five per cent!*

Clearly the project was in deep trouble. They sensed this, and that was one reason why an outsider like myself was brought in by the Project Leader, Martin Bale.

■ 22.3 Vague goals

Before I arrived on the client site to work for four days together with the project committee, I asked Martin to send me some background data for study, including the goals of the project. The material he sent me had the vague and unclear goal specification which characterizes too much management thinking:

- 'Faster planning,' but nothing about how much faster, than what, and which kinds of planning.
- 'Better plant utilization,' but nothing about the present utilization or how much was expected in the future, or what time frame was required for results. Nor was there any specific information about which parts of the complex concept 'plant' were to be given priority.

These were typical of the rest of the goals stated: nice vague ideas with which nobody could disagree, but which nobody could or would express precisely, so that those responsible for actually planning the change could possibly know what was expected of them.

Clearly, for example, if everything was 'bettered' by one per cent in the next three years, these goals, taken literally, would be achieved. But just as clearly, the project would fail to save this part of the company from dismemberment.

What was required in the various areas to give the $400 million savings in annual costs? You can't simply tell a computer or a systems expert 'save me millions.' They have no idea of how to do that; they do know how to spend your money and time by building 'systems' which sometimes work – and sometimes fail.

I asked Martin if he could try to work out more specific measurable goals before I came, so we would save time and be able to get on with the constructive task of solving a well-defined problem. He promised to try, and there was a one day meeting as a result, but Martin refused to show me the results, because he felt they were so poor. In the end we had to use over two days of our effective three and a half days of meetings, just to get a clear consensus of what the goals for this project really were!

■ 22.4 Establishing the real goals

I came a day earlier than anticipated to the site, since I thought it might be interesting to see their factories and computer systems in operation, and perhaps talk informally with various key people about the problems and experiences they had. The next morning, the first official day of my three-day assignment I held a morning lecture for about 50 company employees, including our project group, about Software Management Tools and Design by Objectives. This, in addition to some copied written documentation sent out in advance, was the only preparation the project group had for making use of formal tools such as attribute specification. They were, in fact, going to learn how to do it 'on the job.'

■ 22.5 The first-draft attribute specification

Early after lunch I threw the project group into the deep end, and assigned them the task of writing a formal, quantified multi-dimensional attribute specification for the project they had already been working on.

I made the point that ideally they would all come up with the same goals. If their goals differed, that implied that they were working at cross-purposes with each other, and possibly counter to the needs of the organization. There should be only one official set of goals and it should be able to be interpreted in the same way by all the people working towards it. It should also be official, and signed by a responsible executive. No such document existed yet.

After a couple of hours work it became clear that everybody had produced entirely different statements of the goals towards which they had been working. This is often a moment of truth for such a group. Obviously they had been wasting their time up to this point.

Dan Croydon, a very smart senior analyst, had made an attribute specification which was closest to what I wanted to see, so we used a copy of his version for further discussions about what the real goals were.

The discussions showed a lot of confusion among the participants about what the problem was and even what the nature of the solution was supposed to be. Some participants clearly viewed themselves as technicians, only there to make a new computerized planning system. One of these created quite a stir when he openly said he feared that his last hope of continued employment in the company was to be involved in making this computerized planning system, and if the planning led in other solution directions, he literally felt he would lose his job. There was a very high emotional content in this, and it threatened the success of the group throughout the rest of the week.

In fact several people were clearly more worried about their personal job security than the proper solution of a problem involving both them and the job security of thousands of colleagues. When matters get that twisted, then the problem must lie in the way management motivates and communicates with employees.

We had one phase of discussion, during which it turned out, by a public vote by the group, that half of the group didn't even believe that the 'Midway Manufacturing Organization' actually existed in a real and legal sense as a subsidiary of the Corporation. They claimed it was only a 'concept'. The next morning, Dan caused quite a stir by bringing in a five-page document of recent date which documented the existence of MMO and even gave some new goal statements of which nobody was aware. The paper was signed by our top man David, and nobody could get Dan to reveal how he had come by the mystery document!

Imagine! Six project committee members weren't even aware of the corporate existence of the entity they were supposed to be saving!

Using the new document as a basis we proceeded to derive goals as directly as possible, with the addition of measurability and quantification ideas. We then invited the chief responsible executive, David Vance, to attend a 'hearing' where we would try to get enough information about his intentions to make a really good and official document.

■ 22.6 The hearing

Dan Croydon led the hearing, and was joined by the rest of the group. David Vance was in the hot seat regarding clear management goal formulation, and I sat back in the room with a teacher's pride of seeing my new pupils making effective use of their new communication tool of quantified attribute specification.

David stayed on the hot seat for over two hours, and made really substantial contributions to our understanding, though in many cases he did not have ready answers and asked to be able to get back to the matter later. After he left us, the group reflected aloud that 'nobody seems to have asked him such tough questions before.'

The attribute specification was 'cleaned up' as a result of David's input, and we gave Dr Rob Voight, the same man who feared for his job, the task of getting David's official signature on the revised document.

Rob came back from a meeting with David at which David agreed that the goal specification was nearly complete and correct, but there was one major goal still missing, that neither he nor we had mentioned the previous day. That particular goal, which was something to do with the level of capital expenditure on the project, was formally identified later.

At last we were getting close to a clear official goal statement for the project! A sense of victory over our problem, and a sense of relief at getting out of the swamp of uncertainty seemed now to pervade the group. Now there was only one more detail that remained – solving the problem.

■ 22.7 The solution

The solution process could only be sketched in the day which remained, but it provided some critical insights.

The previous evening I had made extensive notes regarding five parallel evolutionary development processes which were needed if the Corporation was to reach its demanding goals in the three years allotted to us. Only one of these five parallel evolutionary processes was concerned with the better computerized production planning process which until now seemed to be the only effort being made to achieve the results required. But we had already established that this effort was at best a five per cent contribution to the solution of the total problem (as was now identified). So it was necessary to get this message over to the client – that they had to initiate several projects in order to succeed.

The other parallel processes were named 'marketing', 'quality control', 'forecasting', 'organizational tuning' and 'unidentified' (just to say we didn't pretend to have all the answers now). This started a very productive discussion, about who was responsible for these things (some said we were, some said we were only responsible for the narrower 'works production optimization' evolutionary plan).

Time being short we decided to spend the remaining hours concentrating on the production planning side in more depth, so as to illustrate the consequences of the planning method.

■ 22.8 Evolutionary planning

The evolutionary plan for production planning was developed by a top-down method of exploding high-level general ideas into more detailed ones.

After leading the initial breakdown at the top level, I was able to sit back while Martin Bale took over enthusiastically and led the group through several more levels of 'when to do what' planning.

The objective here is to spread the change activities out in time, so that you are not faced with one gigantic (or a few almost gigantic) revolutionary phases to implement in, say, three years time. Some of the changes are implemented early in the project in the real organization, like 'this quarter' and 'this year.' This is partly to be certain of achieving some results years earlier than if they are packaged together with too many distracting details. Naturally we chose the 'juicy' items first. Then we broke down each succeeding implementation phase idea into about six to ten sub-ideas, listed them on a flip chart and rated each one on a scale of zero to nine for both value and cost. Those items which had a high value to cost ratio were chosen for earliest implementation.

We got to about five levels of planning, by only detailing the first one in each sequence, and everybody thought we were detailed enough. But when our attempt to make cost and value estimates for this failed, the group realized that there was not enough definition in the idea, and so a sixth level of explosion was agreed upon.

It was mildly shocking that our smallest incremental delivery could be estimated to be about one twenty-eight-thousandth of the entire project! We decided to make a detailed estimate for this first increment of all, which was in fact a profit-margin report. Our group's programming expert, Graham, undertook to work out the details.

He presented us with an estimate of $400 for the step (and even with the ten line report generation program which would extract the report from our present databases!).

It seemed as though we could begin to change the organization in the direction pointed to, beginning that very day!

■ 22.9 The final battle

Then we found we were in trouble.

Dan, supported by some of the more thoughtful members of the group, pointed out a fundamental discrepancy between the detailed planning ideas we had, and the high-level goals of the project. We agreed, and began to analyze the causes.

It seemed we had taken a wrong turning at the high levels of evolutionary explosion. Some members asked whether this meant that our time had been wasted. Others pointed out that it was only the clarity of goals and of the structure of the planning we had used which enabled them to spot our inconsistent thinking! They were right. We had only used two hours to learn this lesson. Replanning the evolutionary plan would only 'waste' that amount of time.

We had no more time, though we got the participant's written reactions to the whole exercise, for the benefit of feedback to colleagues who did not attend. Most comments were overwhelmingly positive.

- 'We finished up with the beginning of an "evo" plan (terrible word) with quantified costs and values, allied to organizational goals'.
- '. . . an extremely powerful analytical technique (attribute specification); similarly evo is also powerful'.
- 'I like the techniques – found the (use of them) mind-boggling. Great!'

■ 22.10 Postscript

It is too early to judge the final result of this effort. But something happened to the project, the participants and the top management involved – in a constructive direction.

The Corporation, only weeks later, made experimental use of the management tools in a variety of projects, all of which have received excellent feedback.

■ 22.11 Post-postscript

The Corporation and MMO Division have survived profitably.

Index

431